Mediating Multiculturalism

Mediating Multiculturalism

Digital Storytelling and the Everyday Ethnic

Daniella Trimboli

ANTHEM PRESS

Anthem Press
An imprint of Wimbledon Publishing Company
www.anthempress.com

This edition first published in UK and USA 2022
by ANTHEM PRESS
75–76 Blackfriars Road, London SE1 8HA, UK
or PO Box 9779, London SW19 7ZG, UK
and
244 Madison Ave #116, New York, NY 10016, USA

First published in the UK and USA by Anthem Press in 2020

British Library Cataloguing-in-Publication Data
A catalogue record for this book is available from the British Library.

Library of Congress Control Number: 2020936448

ISBN-13: 978-1-83998-563-8 (Pbk)
ISBN-10: 1-83998-563-1 (Pbk)

This title is also available as an e-book.

Some parts of this work have been adapted from:

Daniella Trimboli, 'Faces Sailing By: *Junk Theory* and Racialised Bodies in the
Sutherland Shire', *Crossings: Journal of Migration and Culture*, vol. 6, no. 2 (2015): 181–91,
https://doi.org/10.1386/cjmc.6.2.181_1.

Daniella Trimboli, 'Affective Everyday Media: The Performativity of Whiteness in Australian
Digital Storytelling', *Critical Arts: South-North Cultural and Media Studies*, vol. 32, no. 3 (2018): 44–59,
https://doi.org/10.1080/02560046.2018.1488879. Copyright © 2018 Critical Arts
Projects & Unisa Press, reprinted by permission of Informa UK Limited, trading as Taylor &
Francis Group, www.tandfonline.com on behalf of Critical Arts Projects & Unisa Press.

A thorough and diligent attempt was made via ACMI to contact authors Fatma Coskun,
Kenan Besiroglu and Rita el-Khoury regarding reproduction of material, but was
unfortunately unsuccessful. The authors are encouraged to contact ACMI or
Daniella Trimboli should they have any questions or concerns.

For my brothers Matthew, Domenic and Tony

for always standing behind me when I need to step forward

CONTENTS

FIGURES

FOREWORD

Sandra Ponzanesi

To talk about multiculturalism today seems not only obsolete but also irrelevant. Yet nothing could be more untrue and problematic. Despite the decline in the popularity of the term and the somewhat shared feeling that multiculturalism has failed or is inadequate, multicultural coexistence and conviviality is more a reality now than ever before.

The necessity of continuing to address contemporary migrant flows, with the unresolved tensions about increasing diversity and intercultural conflicts, only testifies to the need to revisit multiculturalism not as a top-down policy instrument but as a part of everyday reality that is not going to wane any time soon. Doing multiculturalism as a form of participatory culture, where different voices and creative representations are given pride of place, is the focus of *Mediating Multiculturalism: Digital Storytelling and the Everyday Ethnic*, which offers a groundbreaking and innovative intervention into the notion of multiculturalism as 'mediation'. This mediation takes place not just through different media and fields of media expertise but also through the articulations of different forms of everyday cosmopolitanism, where negotiations of identities, belonging and citizenship are the focal point within a wider national and transnational understanding.

This book provides an invaluable read for anyone wanting to know more about the international dynamics of multicultural theory, policy and culture, understood through the bottom-up perspective of migrants' creative practices. Digital storytelling offers an engaging entry into the possibility for self-expression, self-representation and self-creation, mediated through the tools and practices of different media affordances and infrastructures. It is analysed as a genre that confirms or deviates from normative notions of whiteness and ethnicity, offering new creative insights into the multiplicities of everyday life for migrants and 'strangers' as subjects in Australia.

The book is particularly successful in bringing theoretical sources and creative material into dialogue to see whether the 'subaltern' subject can speak, even if this is within the narrative framework provided by institutionalised forms of digital storytelling. As this is a medium that enhances the voice of the other, it is particularly critical to dissect and analyse the genre in its potential, contradictions and reinforcing normativity. But the author takes this a step further by writing: 'This analysis leads the book to consider how digital stories can allow for extensions of performativity and affect as political forces of change: capable of disrupting and resisting norms of whiteness to create alternative realities of everyday multiculturalism detached from racialisation' (p. x). Digital storytelling is studied as enabling media practices for migrant groups, where the possibility of self-expression takes centre stage, showing how ethnicity can be produced and manipulated for positive affirmative actions and offering a useful intersection between cultural diversity and the arts. Everyday multiculturalism emerges as indicative of a broader shift in cultural studies, where the local, mundane and unofficial aspect of cultural difference is magnified: 'Paying attention to what bodies are saying, or doing, placed the emphasis of this analysis on the mundane but material effects of culturally diverse storytelling for subjects of multiculturalism' (p. x). Migrants shape a multimodal narrative of their own that allows them to combine the past and the present by using photographs, films, sounds and narration to achieve particular effects. Interestingly, this apparently empowering new tool, which allows strangers, migrants and others to find their own voice, is connected to the notion of multiculturalism and how ethnicity and integration get coded to normalise cultural diversity instead of opening up new venues for forms of belonging and participation.

The author's focus on individual and collective storytelling manages to capture a complex reality of migrants living in Australia and dealing with different degrees of rejection and integration. Some of the stories are built as a collective tool to create tolerance and acceptance among different ethnic and religious groups, reinforcing normative ideas of happiness, love and success; others are ironic and unsettling.

Theoretically sophisticated and empirically original, this book weaves together multiculturalism, performance studies, affect theories, media studies, postcolonial studies and ethnic studies in a marvellous way, producing new ground for rethinking living together with difference.

ACKNOWLEDGEMENTS

First and foremost, I acknowledge the traditional owners of the land on which I was privileged to carry out the majority of this research and writing, namely, the Wurundjeri and Boonwurrung peoples of the Kulin Nations and the Musqueam, Squamish and Tsleil-Waututh nations of the Coast Salish peoples. I pay my deepest respects to their Elders, past and present, and acknowledge that their lands remain unceded. My book deals with multiculturalism and racialisation in relation to migrant cultures located in Anglo-settler colonies, but the wounded heart of these issues is undoubtedly the initial violence of colonial invasion and its continued denial and re-perpetration. All migrants in these settings are uninvited guests on Indigenous lands.

I acknowledge Emerita Professor Sneja Gunew, a scholar whose profound intellectual legacy has inspired much of this book. Thank you for your time and care as a supervisor of this initial body of work and for your considered and astute readings and feedback. Thank you for being not simply one of the best thinkers I know but one of the best people; I feel truly fortunate to have you in my life. Thank you to the numerous people who critically engaged with this work when it was in dissertation form: Chris Healy, Rimi Khan, Greg Noble, Sandra Ponzanesi, Nikos Papastergiadis and Fazal Rizvi.

Sincere gratitude to the Alfred Deakin Institute of Citizenship and Globalisation (ADI) at Deakin University, in particular its director, Fethi Mansouri, for giving me the opportunity and support to develop this book during my postdoctoral fellowship. Special thanks to Melinda Hinkson for her assistance and advice during my fellowship. Your graciousness, insight and intuition as both an academic and a feminist ally have been very anchoring for me.

I am indebted to all of the people who created and shared their digital stories online – a brave and beautiful thing to do – and those who gave me the permissions to reproduce elements of them herein. I hope you read the analyses of the stories in the spirit in which they were undertaken: with respect and genuine hope for greater inclusivity for us all. My thanks to the artists, filmmakers, digital storytelling participants and art practitioners who offered their time and insights via interviews with me. A special thank you to the Australian Centre for the Moving Image, Big hART and Curious Works, and art practitioners Michelle Kotevski and Helen Simondson for their assistance with my project and their commitment to the production of community-based art.

Thank you to my brilliant academic friends and peers Dr Elena Benthaus, Tia di Biase, Dr Noni May, Dr Emma Maguire and Paula Muraca for always holding space for me. In fact, to all the amazing women and femme academics I am surrounded by at ADI and beyond, who make what can be a treacherous environment to work in rewarding and worthwhile.

I wish to acknowledge the organisers and participants of the Transregional Academies 'Histories of Migrant Knowledges', UC Berkeley, May–June 2019, where I workshopped the final chapter of this book. To Drs Safdar Ahmed and Michel O'Brien: collaborating with you this past year has been a breath of fresh air and allowed me to think through some of the finer points of this book.

My immense gratitude to the team of Melbourne-/Naarm-* and Vancouver-based doctors and health specialists who have helped me manage a chronic illness since 2011, especially Dr Nelum Devi-Soysa, Dr Hong Xu, Ms Esen Uygen, Dr Juan Mulder, Prof. Kate Stern, Ms Alex Caldwell and Ms Marta Karela. I could not do my work, or anything much at all, without your expertise and care.

I live so much of my life online that it would be remiss of me not to thank those of you who tune in and engage with me on social media – my 'intimate public' as Lauren Berlant would call you! I have shared with you the ups and downs of this book-writing journey, and you have provided me with solace, encouragement and a very helpful dose of humour when I needed it. I hope you know that I see you and am grateful for the online community we carve out together.

Finally, the people who make everything I do possible: my family and dear friends. I especially thank my brothers Matthew, Domenic and Tony, and their beautiful partners and equally beautiful kids, for their unconditional support. Thank you to my mum, Sheila Trimboli, and her partner, John Remfry, for being in my corner and helping me get this book over the line. Thank you to my amazing sister from another mister, Zarah Hage, for everything you have done and continue to do for me, to Robyn Clasohm and Craig Mumford, and to all the Wilson Street crew for your boundless love and friendship. It really does take a village and mine is breathtaking.

The below acknowledgement is for the women on the Trimboli side of my family, generously translated into Platioti dialect by Luci Callipari-Marcuzzo, her mother Anna Callipari and cousins Giuseppina Romeo and Pina Pangallo.

Vogdio canusciure una persona importante chi fici umbra di chista ricerca e pure tutta a mia vita: mia nonna, Caterina Trimboli, fu Caterina Virgara. Caterina partio per l'Australia cu tre di suoi fidiogli da Platì, Calabria a 1955, tre anni dopo u suoi marito, Domenico vini ca. A canusciu a chista fimmina pe paroli chi dicivinu e cuntavanu e pa fatti chi succeriru – muoriro quando mi patre ero troppo giuvane. Eo canuscia ca pechi sugno diaspiaciuta pechi tutti sacrifici chi fici, non nepe opportunità u vidi na vita lunga, u vai a scuola, o se cunta i stori chi di supia di suoi sette fidiogli. Sicuramente non eppe

*   Naarm is the word used by the Boon Wurrung people of the Kulin Nation to refer to the bays adjacent Melbourne, and thus the Indigenous term for Melbourne city, which is located on unceded land of the Kulin Nation.

l'opportunita u vai a l'universita, o passa anni cercando na cosa importante e interresante. Eo era a prima da mi famidgia, da parte di mamma e di mi patre, u finisce laurea da l'universita, pensando di dove vinimo, canusciu che non ne una cosa picciola. Eo vodgio penso che una picciola cosa represento a mia nonna Caterina, come a fimina Trimboli, e vi ringrazio a sai per l'amore e graditudine a dia e la forte e coragiusa Trimboli chi hanno venuto a presso i dia, cui suoi fidiogli (e u miei ziani), e la suoi fidiogli (e li miei cugini). Chisto libro e il vostro, come e il meo.

INTRODUCTION: MULTICULTURALISM AS A CRISIS OF CONTRADICTION

The twenty-first century has been a time of unprecedented migration and intensified global mobility, two compounding phenomena enabling cultural plurality to become a commonplace feature of contemporary societies. Jarringly, the dominant and previously most-utilised governmental framework for managing culturally diverse communities, namely, multiculturalism, has suffered a serious decline in popularity. As Andrew M. Robinson (2011, p. 29) succinctly noted on the topic of multiculturalism in 2011: 'The last decade hasn't been kind to multiculturalism.' Indeed, since the turn of the century, multiculturalism has not just been 'losing ground' (p. 11) but has frequently been posited as a past societal mode – declared 'inadequate', 'failed' or simply 'dead'. These reactions have circulated in both the domains of public rhetoric and scholarly endeavours, most frequently in locations long-attached to multiculturalism, notably Canada, Australia, the Netherlands and the United Kingdom, but also in the United States and other Western European countries (see Vertovec and Wessendorf 2010).

In this book, I argue that the continued discussion about the success or otherwise of multiculturalism registers the topic as alive as ever, albeit in a mode of crisis. It is not so much that multiculturalism has become irrelevant; rather that the framework through which its relevance has been conventionally understood is not malleable enough to capture the shifting and increasingly contradictory nature of contemporary cultural difference. Since the inception of multiculturalism in Canada in the 1970s, and its subsequent adoption in other countries such as Australia, the ways in which people move and engage with one another have become increasingly hybrid. At the same time, issues that multiculturalism promised to solve/tensions it hoped to alleviate continue to recirculate – racism, inter- and intra-community conflicts, institutionalised discrimination, to list a few. One need only glance at race riots in Cronulla, Australia, the Black Lives Matter movements in the United States and the rise of white nationalist parties in the United Kingdom and Western Europe for cursory evidence.

The sense that multiculturalism has failed has been attributed to many factors. For some, the identity focus of theoretical multiculturalism has been inadequate to address the complexity of lived cultural difference, while the political aspects (programmes and policies) have failed to service this complexity adequately. As Australia and comparable colonial nations enter an era of 'evolving hyper-diversity', whereby diversity itself is diversifying (Ang et al. 2002; Noble 2009, p. 47), these inadequacies become increasingly evident.

Certainly, the messiness of the term 'multiculturalism' has not helped matters. As Sneja Gunew (2012, p. 1450) outlines, scholarly discussions about multiculturalism often generate confusion because so many elements are designated 'multicultural'. Multiculturalism is approached as both a philosophy and a political theory, alongside the simultaneous impetus to 'unpack the term "culture" itself'. Gunew explains: 'As a political theory with policy dimensions, multiculturalism has often been described as marking a shift from previous stages where differences remained unrecognized and were simply subsumed into dominant groups and institutions [. . .] Multiculturalism as philosophy is linked with preserving universal rights for both individuals and distinctive groups, although there are often tensions between the two' (ibid.). Both the philosophical and the political domains have difficulty conceptualising multiculturalism into neat frameworks, ultimately because it is impossible to compartmentalise culture (p. 1451).

Previously (though this is far from a thorough survey), scholars have carried out meticulous analyses of multiculturalism by examining its relationship to migratory patterns (Castles 1992; Vertovec 1996), nationalism and citizenship (Castles 1992; Jakubowicz 1994, 2011; Stratton 1998, 2011; Modood 2007; Levey 2008), concepts of ethnicity and race (Gilroy 1987, 1990, 2000; Gunew and Mahyuddin 1988; Jakubowicz 1994, 1998; Hall 2000; Gunew 2004; Modood 2005) and the idea of universal recognition (Taylor 1994; Kymlicka 2007, 2012). In an Australian context, multiculturalism is often studied from a social sciences or political theory perspective and includes the work of Lois Foster and David Stockley (1984), Stephen Castles et al. (1988), Andrew Jakubowicz (1994, 1998, 2011), James Jupp (1984, 2007a), Geoffrey Brahm Levey (2008), Mark Lopez (2000) and, most recently, Andrew Jakubowicz and Christina Ho (2013). Cultural studies perspectives on Australian multiculturalism gained traction in the 1990s, especially through the work of Ien Ang (in Stratton and Ang 1994; Ang 1996, 1999) and Jon Stratton (in Stratton and Ang 1994; Stratton 1998), and it is within this cultural studies tradition that I situate this book.

Multiculturalism takes different forms in different locations, but its basic impetus and structure has been informed by human rights ideals emerging in Western, liberal democracies following the Second World War (Kymlicka 2010, pp. 35–38). This book is concerned with the role of multiculturalism in former British settler colonies, specifically Australia, but notes resonances with multicultural narratives in the United Kingdom, Canada and the United States. These geographical contexts are ripe for cross-comparison not only because of the way their respective multiculturalisms have emerged, but also because digital storytelling, the genre I use to unpack multiculturalism in this book, started in the United States and then moved quickly to Australia, Canada and the United Kingdom.

When it comes to the contemporary terrain of multiculturalism within these locations, lived, studied or otherwise, it is clear that contradiction is a prominent feature. Mobility, cultural hybridity and interconnectedness are as heightened as ever, at the same time that aggressive nationalist practices are exaggerated and borders are tightened. In Australia, the highly fragmented and diverse cultural landscape of the twenty-first century has exacerbated the instability of its multiculturalism, which continues to struggle against a prevailing Anglo-Celtic 'battler' mythology. Thus, the tension between the multifarious and mobile aspects of the Australian population and the nationalistic, security-conscious aspects has surfaced in ways that are both familiar and strange. Hybrid cultural products and encounters develop in a continuous and seemingly mundane manner. Yet, the nation is also experiencing the reprisal of white, racist resistance in the form of independent political parties and vocal community groups.[1] This paradoxical condition has wedged itself within practical and theoretical work on multiculturalism, stalling its critical development and leading to what scholars have termed the 'crisis' of multiculturalism.[2] The task for contemporary studies in multiculturalism must therefore be to unpack the paradoxical conjuncture of cultural plurality and formulate ways to navigate its contradictions.

The everyday turn

In the past decade, there have been two approaches employed to address the so-called crisis. The first retains the importance of multiculturalism by inflating and promoting its positive attributes. The second, which can broadly be described as critical multiculturalism, problematises the field by retexturing its meaning and attempting to reconnect its political/theoretical domain with its everyday manifestations. In some instances, the second approach renounces the concept of multiculturalism altogether, echoing the public sentiment by positioning it as a past phenomenon. Vijay Mishra's monograph *What Was Multiculturalism?* (2012) is a notable example. In this book, I argue that multiculturalism remains a highly productive force worthy of attention, while also acknowledging that methodologies for governing, theorising and living cultural diversity need to move beyond what have become, by way of some understandings of multiculturalism, routine, even empty tropes and gestures. In the spirit of Vijay Mishra, and in much the same manner that Stuart Hall (2003) has utilised the word 'creolisation', I am less concerned with the term this new kind of critique assumes than I am with the particular kind of work the critique does and enables. Like Mishra (2012, p. 18), I am interested in tracing the various assemblages that have created this particular historical moment of multiculturalism.

The starting point of this retracing is the 'everyday', a node common to the two main approaches. The turn to the everyday mirrors trends in cultural studies and artistic domains, which have both consulted on-the-ground experiences in an attempt to redefine cultural difference. I take particular interest in the burgeoning field of everyday multiculturalism, which explores cultural difference from a grass-roots or 'street'

---

1. For example, Reclaim Australia is a coalition of people who, according to the official website, have formed because they have 'had enough of minorities not fitting in and trying to change our Australian cultural identity' (2015, online, 10 April). The organisation petitions for such things as the banning of Muslim headdress and halal certification and promotes Australian unity in the form of such things as 'pride in the Australian flag and Anthem at all levels of schooling'. Other similar groups include: Rise Up Australia, the Australian Defence League, the United Patriots Front, True Blue Crew and Antipodean Resistance. The anti-migrant and anti-multiculturalism principles of these groups are mirrored to varying extents in official political parties such as Aussie Battler Party, One Nation, Family First and Australian Conservatives.
2. See Ien Ang and Jon Stratton (1998), Greg Noble (2005, p. 108; 2009) and Paul Gilroy (2006, p. 65).

perspective. The field aims to address a perceived gap between the ways in which multiculturalism is understood at a governmental and theoretical level and how it is experienced in day-to-day life.

The use of the everyday has a distinct philosophical history in Marxist scholarship, notably through the work of Henri Lefebvre (1991 [1947]), who argued that socialism should be less about productive revolution and more about revolution in the realm of everyday life (cited in Goonewardena 2008, p. 24). Although Lefebvre repeatedly emphasised contradiction and entanglement in his conceptualisation of the everyday, it carried an idealist tendency, in which the everyday meant, or at least came perilously close to mean, an authentic, utopic space free from structural powers. There is no doubt that the use of the everyday in everyday multiculturalism and digital storytelling is influenced by the Lefebvrian tradition and its idealist tendency in particular; however, I do not attempt to follow this influence as a line of inquiry in this book (I will leave that to the Lefebvrian scholars!). My intention is, rather, to demonstrate how 'everyday practices' of cultural difference and related digital media are often taken to mean authentic and autonomous from the State, when in actuality they can represent and reinforce State-based norms of race. If there are crossovers to the Lefebvrian conceptualisation of everyday life in my analysis, it is with Lefebvre's argument that the everyday is always on its way, but never articulated (see Blanchot and Hanson 1987). To me, this element of Lefebvre's everyday represents the most compelling, and resonates with how I use affect theory in my analysis herein.

While I recognise that the interdisciplinary analyses of everyday multiculturalism have enabled the tensions and nuances of cultural difference to be explored in interesting ways, I argue for a critical readjustment to the way the field is contextualised. In particular, I wish to move away from the idea of everyday multiculturalism as that which 'fills in' a gap, or that which 'just is' in everyday life. Multicultural life and the plethora of terms associated with it – cultural diversity, cultural difference, ethnicity and so on – are terms that act in highly political ways and create material consequences. Rather than attempting to locate an 'authentic' space of everyday cultural exchange, I seek to examine how these so-called everyday exchanges are entangled with State discourses and materialise racialised corporealities. I argue that only by discerning how 'everyday' multicultural bodies are produced and implicated (favourably or otherwise) in relation to the nation can multiculturalism studies, and related policies and programmes, begin to move beyond the racialised binaries it is plagued by.

Multiculturalism media: Artistic practice and digital storytelling

Research for this book began in the arts realm, an area that has been intrinsic to the fashioning of multiculturalism but largely overlooked by everyday multiculturalism. This oversight can perhaps be attributed to ongoing tendencies to separate art from the everyday – in its most restrictive definition, art is a sanctioned space reserved for certain types and classes of people. Yet, the arts provide fertile soil for formulations and discussions of cultural diversity. Indeed, the arts have historically played an influential role in the conceptualisation of multiculturalism in Australia and similar colonial nations, propagating cultural exchange and translation.[3] It is not surprising, then, that the 'crisis of multiculturalism' is somewhat paralleled within the Australian arts industry, along with the Western arts realm more broadly, when it comes to questions of cultural diversity.

Signalling this predicament was the UK report *Beyond Cultural Diversity: The Case for Creativity: A 'Third Text' Report*. Edited by Richard Appignanesi (2010a), the report expresses a growing disharmony between the arts and the notion of diversity. In the Western arts industry, the quest to recognise difference began during the 1960s/1970s, a period labelled the 'first-wave' of institutional critique.[4] The second-wave of institutional critique emerged during the 1980s/1990s, a time when postmodern thought was gaining momentum. These two waves of critique drew on difference in a politically active way, provoking questions about ethnic subjects and the nations they were located within (Papastergiadis 2005, 2012a). Appignanesi (2010b, p. 5) argues that in this decade, artists, critics and scholars are on the crest of a third-wave of critique, attempting to deal with the ways in which difference has come to mean something simultaneously empty and forceful. Appignanesi summarises: 'Let us be clear. Cultural diversity is a meaningless tautological expression. It tells us nothing but that cultures differ. Something other is hidden behind this mere description. The empty formulation disguises a prescriptive conduct' (ibid.). In an attempt to deal with the oxymoronic nature of diversity in the arts industries, many artistic projects have become invested in the domain of the everyday, in the hope that it will reveal more articulate and authentic cultural experiences. It has long been recognised that community-arts organisations tend to employ an 'everyday' focus (see Hawkins 1993; Grostal and Harrison 1994); however, recent examination of professional/contemporary visual art projects can also be seen to be walking the line between everyday life and contemporary art. Complementary to this trend in twenty-first century art practices is the incorporation of new media forms. With the increased capacity and accessibility of media technologies, together with what Ien Ang et al. (2011, p. 4) describe as a move away from the gallery or museum as the 'place' of art, the digital and the everyday have intertwined to become a prominent feature of contemporary art practice (see also Papastergiadis and Trimboli 2019).

Digital storytelling in particular stands out as a popular way of artistically exploring cultural diversity, especially in the past decade. It began in the United States in the 1990s, as part of movements to make new media more accessible and democratic. Joe Lambert pioneered the digital storytelling genre as a form of media-making that would allow ordinary people to tell and share their stories. The genre's claim to ordinary and authentic experiences has seen it become popular for artists and arts organisations wishing to engage with difference – where the need to create genuine connection is deemed crucial (Burgess 2006, p. 9).

Digital storytelling has a number of definitions, but all generally refer to 'combining the art of telling stories with a variety of digital multimedia' and almost all digital stories combine a mixture of digital graphics, photographs, text, audio narration, video and

3. See, for example, Gunew and Rizvi (1994); Papastergiadis et al. (2015).
4. Richard Appignanesi (2010b, p. 7).

music to present a particular idea or theme (Robin 2006, p. 1; Lovvorn 2011, p. 98). Usually, the films are three- to five-minutes long, based on individual experiences and narrated in the first person, and they almost always involve the use of personal photographs or home-movie footage. Digital storytelling thus places an emphasis on the implied freedom and subjective neutrality often carried by discourses of creativity or artistic expression more generally. There is a common assumption that there is less external manipulation of digital stories, that they are more transparent than other forms of screen media. As such, the genre tends to be considered a truer or 'more real' representation of daily life. In these ways, a number of parallels can be drawn between the impetus of digital storytelling and everyday multiculturalism alike.

It is not surprising, then, to see the proliferation of digital storytelling in community-based arts projects that seek to equitably represent 'culturally diverse' community stories and, likewise, to note the frequent use of cultural difference as a theme explored in digital storytelling, usually via narratives of migration and ethnic identity. At least half of the Australian digital stories housed at the Australian Centre for the Moving Image (ACMI) are on these themes. Similarly, a significant portion of stories housed at StoryCenter (formerly the Center for Digital Storytelling) in the United States is dedicated to these themes. Indeed, the StoryCenter's current website forefronts its imbrication in questions of ethnic and racial identity by stating on its 'About' page: 'StoryCenter is committed to challenging white supremacy and supporting social justice, in every aspect of our work.'

Digital storytelling and whiteness

I deliberately target digital storytelling in this book because it palpably illustrates how the notion of the everyday can get deployed for less-than-everyday means in work pertaining to cultural difference – a problem I see in the scholarship of everyday multiculturalism. Digital storytelling practitioners commend the ordinariness of the genre because it allows representations of the minutia of everyday life, for example, family interactions, to surface. This element, together with the relative accessibility of the genre, allows it to *present itself* as part of everyday life, further assisted by the fact that the genre often *takes place* in spaces considered to be a part of everyday life, for example, the classroom. More recently, digital media scholars such as Alicia Blum-Ross (2015) and Lauren S. Berliner (2018) have done important work on the notion of digital participation, illustrating how the democratic claims of community digital projects are not so much the site of individual agency as they are the site of institutional aims (see also Literat et al. 2018). My intention in this book is similar; however, I home in on the relationship digital storytelling has with everyday multiculturalism and cultural difference in particular.

I therefore take StoryCenter's claim that it challenges white supremacy to task by asking: how does the mode of digital storytelling construct, mobilise and/or limit the 'ethnically diverse' or non-white person? Specifically, what are the ways in which digital storytelling projects engage with concepts of cultural diversity and everyday multiculturalism to create material and affective possibilities for the racialised subject? Do digital storytelling projects generate new subjectivities or do they reproduce traditional stereotypes? After all, the stories in the thematic collections I analyse often formulate a response to the following implied questions: who is the 'ethnically diverse person' and what are their 'real' daily experiences? In addressing these questions, I embark on a deconstruction of the ethnic/racialised body as it comes to be constituted through digital storytelling.

As such, the book positions digital storytelling as an iterative performance that is produced and directed in certain ways and, as Belinda Smaill (2010, p. 138) writes in relation to the documentary form, 'establishes the presence of the performing subject by directing our attention to that subject'. This presence is bound up with certain fantasies of the self and the Other in Western multicultural nations and ultimately impacts the ways in which the various bodies involved in the performance are articulated. Taking further cues from Sneja Gunew (2004, 2017) and Elizabeth Povinelli (2002), I consider how, via the practice of digital storytelling, multicultural subjects become embedded in relations of power that both constrain and mobilise performances according to particular notions of whiteness. Further, I analyse how performative slippages may present themselves in digital storytelling to reveal alternative aspects of lived cultural difference and subsequently destabilise the normative discourse of whiteness in Australia and similar multicultural locations.

This line of questioning adopts the approach to whiteness and critical multiculturalism introduced by anthropologist Ghassan Hage in the book *White Nation* (1998). Here, Hage argues that although the 'celebrate diversity' banner waved by Australia appears to embrace cultural pluralism, in fact, it re-establishes a white national fantasy. Following Hage, I consider how digital storytelling projects interact with the broader notion of multiculturalism and examine whether such projects work to destabilise or reinstate the forceful fiction of whiteness. I target the ways in which the focus on cultural difference in digital storytelling projects can subtly reinstate the rigid boundaries of racial homogeneity that the projects attempt to deconstruct.

The book thus analyses the 'how' and 'what' aspects of digital storytelling projects, rather than categories of aesthetic or new media quality. The analysis is always focused on what the genre does – how it constructs and impacts ethnicity and race. I use a Foucauldian framework that concerns itself not with where power originates, or why it operates, but how it is always productively exercised. (In short: what do these digital storytelling projects in Australia *do*?) The examination of 'doing' could just as importantly be carried out via a lens of gender, sexuality, queerness or class; and I remain alert to the ways in which manifold norms are bound up in any digital storytelling project and analysis. However, I have chosen to concentrate on the normative discourse of whiteness, in particular, the ways in which ethnicity and race become 'essentially' linked in the digital storytelling process.

A note here on my use of 'whiteness', a term as slippery as it is powerful. It is crucial, first, to recognise how whiteness travels globally, but also lands in particular places in particular ways. Sneja Gunew does an excellent job in her book *Post-multicultural Writers as Neo-cosmopolitanism Mediators* (2017) to map the chameleon-like way that whiteness, especially in the Australian context, links itself to Europeanness and, even more specifically, to Anglo-Celticness. This linking is clearly evidenced in the Australian context, where Southern and Eastern Europeans were for a long time relegated as 'black' (Gunew 1994), but it is also seen, as Gunew (2017, pp. 25–27) traces, in North America and in Anglophone postcolonial theory more broadly. Toula Nicolacopoulos and George Vassilacopoulos (2010, p. 32) describe the construction of Australian whiteness as a particular (and absurd) 'ontological condition' that simultaneously positions 'Indigenous peoples as non-Australian, and designated migrant groups as [. . .] "perpetual foreigners within the Australian state"', extending that 'dominant white Australia seems to render indispensable a perpetual position and re-positioning of the foreigner-within as white-non-white or as white-but-not-white enough. This repositioning is an effect of the impact that the ongoing violent dispossession of the Indigenous peoples has on the nature of white Australian ways of being'. In the Australian context, Southern Europeans become 'sufficiently *like*, while remaining suitably *unlike*, the dominant white Australian subject position' (Nicolacopoulos and Vassilacopoulos 2010, p. 45; emphasis in the original), where the point of comparison for 'likeness' is Britishness. Although it is crucial to recognise the situatedness of whiteness, this ontological structure chimes with that seen in other former Anglo-settler colonies; for example, Himani Bannerji (2000, p. 108) illustrates that hegemonic whiteness is similarly encoded in North America through a national narrative premised on 'European/English' settler colonialism, which functions as 'the ideology of a nation-state'. 'Whiteness/Europeanness' serves as a 'key bonding element' that allows other European bodies, despite their distance from idealised Anglo-Englishness, to 'form a part of their community of "whiteness" as distinct from nonwhite "others"', though a distance from full inclusion always remains (ibid.). Likewise, in the United Kingdom, 'Englishness is predicated on whiteness' (Nayak 2017, p. 295).

In what follows, I explore how some subjects of digital storytelling projects come to be seen as migrants or ethnics, distinct from Anglo-Celtic Australians, even though the latter are, of course, also migrants and ethnics. Indeed, many of these non-Anglo-Celtics self-identify as ethnic or migrants[5] – an identification that in and of itself points to the entrenched discursive force linking Anglo-Celtic with white, non-ethnic and, significantly, *at home*. It is because of this self-identification with the term 'migrant' that I use the term 'migrant digital storytelling' to describe digital stories authored by non-Anglo-Celtic Australians, while recognising the problems this undoubtedly entails.

What work is done in the name of the everyday? Foregrounding the background as methodology

The field of everyday multiculturalism is a worthy attempt to deal with the paradoxical dynamics of mobility in the twenty-first century. Recognising a despondency in multiculturalism rhetoric, everyday multiculturalism scholars attempt to exemplify its dynamic texture and value. However, by focusing on the everyday, these studies tend to overlook the

---

5. Colour Code (2018) focus groups with non-white Australians found that the preferred term for their demographic was 'migrant', even though, as co-founder Roj Amedi (2018, personal communication, 27 November) notes, 'migrant' can also include other European migrants who are not necessarily part of Colour Code's community, that is, European migrants who formerly were considered non-white but have since been accepted as honorary white Australians.

entangled context or 'background' of the crisis they attempt to understand, and which of course extends beyond ordinary or everyday encounters. Similarly, by proclaiming 'ordinariness' in the telling of cultural difference, digital storytelling runs the risk of reinstating the fictive but forceful boundaries of racialisation even as it attempts to deconstruct them. After all, cultural difference that operates in and through State formulations can quickly fall into long-standing hierarchies of racialised subjects. Without proper attention to this entangled context, multiculturalism studies not only struggles to deal with the paradoxical element of multiculturalism but can perpetuate it into a binary lock-hold. As such, paradox becomes not only intrinsic to multiculturalism studies but symptomatic of it, foreclosing the capacity to productively deconstruct racialised discourses. Given the oft-repeated belief that 'history is repeating itself' when it comes to issues of race and social justice – and the growing global relevance of 'the migrant' – it is timely to take stock of the scholarly terrain of digital storytelling and consider how capable the medium is of breaking long-standing racialised structures. What can digital storytelling teach us about the status and future of multiculturalism in contemporary societies? Can digital storytelling remediate multiculturalism in new, progressive ways?

In this book, I attempt instead to use the paradox productively. I consider what digital storytelling can reveal about everyday multiculturalism as well as what everyday multiculturalism (and related studies) *conceals* about the lived experiences of cultural difference. Is the everyday really a sanctioned, authentic space where cultural difference exists beyond the State? What comes to *matter* when multiculturalism is studied as an everyday phenomenon? Finally, I ask: how can the contradictions embedded in multicultural life be used to *re-matter* the bodies it addresses?

These questions underlie the analyses presented throughout in an attempt to ensure the background or context of everyday multiculturalism is foregrounded. This foregrounding has led the research to unfold in a particular manner, and the structure of the book attempts to do justice to the sequence of this unfolding. The book is divided into three thematic sections, each of which works to consolidate both the theoretical and empirical arms of the research.

In Part One, 'Convergences', the key phenomena being studied – multiculturalism, digital storytelling and the everyday – are chartered within a historical context. A theoretical framework emerges which enables the analyses thereafter. This framework involves three theoretical tools – Michel Foucault's apparatus of security, Judith Butler's theory of performativity and aspects of affect theory. A combination of these theories is useful for addressing the complexities of cultural difference in neocolonial contexts such as Australia, helping to illustrate how the formation of multicultural subjects is bound up with formations of a white nation. The use of the theories set up a tiered system that allows the analysis of subject formation to move from a macro perspective (in the form of apparatus of security) to a micro perspective (through the application of affect). In other words, the structure allows for an analysis of how multicultural subjects are constructed in relation to the macro, or public discourses of multiculturalism, as well as the more nuanced and seemingly private or micro interactions that occur at the level of the body. It must be noted that this process is defined as highly interrelated, so that the subject's encounters at a micro level are always implicated in the relationships of power at a macro level. This three-tiered optic is utilised in the hope of ensuring this study does not collapse into another attempt to 'fill the gap' between everyday and institutionalised encounters and formations of multiculturalism. Instead, it works to consider what sets of relations exist within this so-called gap and how these relations can be channelled for different material effects in a highly mobile world.

Part Two, 'Multicultural Bodies', begins to flesh out digital stories using the theoretical framework mapped out in the previous section. The analysis defines two kinds of digital stories – individual and collaborative. Individual digital stories are produced in a workshop environment by a single author and are the product of the most conventional method of digital storytelling creation. Collaborative digital stories are co-authored in community-based arts settings, often across longer periods of time. Across the five chapters of this section, individual digital stories typical of the genre are compared with a collaborative digital story to elucidate the similarities and differences of each. The analysis utilises the theory of performativity to study how digital stories pertaining to ethnic diversity manifest according to norms of whiteness, comparing the narrative structure, aesthetic techniques and audio components of the case studies. The comparison allows for new insights about how everyday multiculturalism normatively structures both the individual body and the body of the nation. I situate materiality at the forefront of the case study analysis, because, as Burgess (2006, p. 211) argues, digital storytelling is 'a means of "becoming real" to others, on the basis of shared experience and affective resonances. Many of the stories are, quite literally, *touching*' (original italics). Exploring the ways in which materiality is endlessly reconstituted through the mode of digital storytelling can reveal both limits and possibilities for the everyday 'multicultural Australian' in this country.

These case studies are revisited in the third and final section, 'Future Digital Multiculturalisms', but this time in conversation with some new case studies that are atypical of the digital storytelling genre. Doing so reveals instances in which digital storytelling produces counter-normative moments. This section extrapolates on these instances to propose a new form of digital work that would enable a critical conceptualisation of everyday multiculturalism. The final chapter proposes the use of a troubling performativity, via the notion of diasporic intimacy, as a way to unhinge multiculturalism studies from the contradictory bind faced in contemporary multiculturalism and in work on race/culture more broadly. At the very least, it seeks to use the paradox as a performative hinge through which new and de-racialised forms of cultural meaning can be evinced.

Part One

CONVERGENCES

This section comprises three chapters which establish the foundations and parameters of the cultural phenomena I am exploring in this book: multiculturalism, digital storytelling and the everyday. A historical analysis of multiculturalism as a liberalist, State-led initiative is provided, with a focus on the Australian context since the 1990s. The section works to illustrate how shifts in multiculturalism are often reflected in shifts in artistic pursuits and how notions of 'the everyday' and 'cultural diversity' become entangled in both domains in the twenty-first century. I undertake a broad analysis of everyday multiculturalism scholarship and its relationship to questions of whiteness and materiality, as well as an overview of the history of digital storytelling and its technical and methodological components. Chapter 2 provides definitions for the two types of digital stories used in this book: individual digital stories (those stories produced in a workshop environment but by a single author), and collaborative digital stories (digital stories co-authored in community-based-arts settings). Finally, the section introduces a new theoretical framework for analysing digital stories and everyday digital media as it pertains to cultural difference, merging a three-tiered optic:

1. Michel Foucault's apparatus of security (State level of analysis)
2. Judith Butler's theory of performativity ('everyday' level of analysis)
3. Affective economies (the body/author-viewer level of analysis)

Chapter One

DIFFERENCE RETURNS TO THE EVERYDAY: MULTICULTURALISM, THE ARTS AND 'RACE'

Multiculturalism is both too much and too little. For some it discourages integration, and for the 'unintegrated' it precludes it.

– Pardy and Lee (2011, p. 309)

The diversity worker has a job precisely because diversity and equality are not already given. When your task is to remove the necessity of your existence, then your existence is necessary for the task.

– Ahmed (2012a, p. 8)

Since the 1970s, multiculturalism has been the framework adopted by Western liberal governments to recognise and service the needs of different migrant and cultural groups. Duncan Ivison's (2010) survey of multiculturalism suggests there are three different multicultural logics: protective or communitarian multiculturalism, where recognition of ethnocultural groups is paramount; liberal multiculturalism, the most popular form in which the pursuit of universalism rather than protectionism is the core goal; and, finally, imperial multiculturalism, a critique of the former two, which places power at the centre of its analyses and seeks to unpack the conditions of the other logics. In this book, I am ultimately concerned with all three logics, arguing that they all emerge, in some form, from the second – liberal multiculturalism – and it is this logic that infiltrates the multicultural narratives of former Anglo-settler colonies of Australia, Canada, the United Kingdom and the United States. As Levey (2010, p. 19) describes, liberal multiculturalism emerged not only *in* liberal democracies but *from* liberal democracies and is therefore underpinned by the broader goal of enacting Western liberalist principles. How this structure manifests in each place is, of course, highly context specific, so that 'although we can pick out certain broad elements that most forms of (liberal) multiculturalism share, there will also always be important differences' (Ivison 2010, p. 2). For this reason, I focus on Australian multiculturalism, but frequently zoom out to broadly contextualise its relationship to multiculturalism in comparable nation-states.

Vertovec and Wessendorf (2010, p. 3) outline that multiculturalism has typically involved policies and practices that affect the domains of public recognition, education, social services, public materials, law, religion, food, and media and broadcasting.

Changes to these domains have worked to minimise discrimination, promote equal opportunity, increase participation and representation, deliver better access to services and foster cross-cultural understanding and acceptance (p. 4). Like many other surveys of multiculturalism, 'the arts' is not listed as a separate domain of impact. Interestingly, surveys of multiculturalism rarely mention the role of the arts, even though the latter has most certainly influenced the former. Indeed, the relationship between multiculturalism and the arts has been vital in the development of ideas pertaining to cultural difference, and the main phases of multiculturalism have tended to be mirrored in, if not intrinsic to, changing modes of artistic practice. In this chapter, I trace the shifting stages of Australian multiculturalism and consider how these shifts are implicated in changing understandings and modes of artistic practice.

Although initiated with positive intentions, multiculturalism has suffered increasing criticism. These criticisms have always been present, as Will Kymlicka's (2012) survey of multicultural policies in Western democracies emphasises, but they have become louder in the past 20 years. Multiculturalism has not just been losing ground (Robinson 2011, p. 11) but has frequently been posited as a past societal mode, declared inadequate, failed or simply dead. These reactions have circulated in both public rhetoric and scholarly endeavours, but little attention has been paid to the relationship between the shifts in multiculturalism and artistic discourses respectively.

Multiculturalism and the arts

While there are certainly detailed differences and complexities in the historical development of multiculturalism, its trajectory can be broadly characterised into three main phases or models: minority rights-based, cultural pluralist and universalist/cosmopolitan (Nicolacopoulos and Vassilacopoulos 2011). Unsurprisingly, the characteristics of these phases are reflected in the position and role of cultural difference in the Western arts industry, as mapped out by Anthony Appignanesi in the report delivered in the United Kingdom in 2010 on arts and cultural diversity.

In a comprehensive study of Australian multiculturalism titled *From White Australia to Woomera*, James Jupp (2007a, p. 82) explains that the formation of Australian multiculturalism was instigated by the large and vocal contingents of Eastern- and Southern-European immigrants. The post-war migration schemes had greatly diversified the cultural constitution of Australia, shoring up questions of cultural access, maintenance and equity, questions answered mostly by the State governments at this time. In the 1970s, the Australian government took its cue from Canada, a fellow member of the Commonwealth that was also experiencing pressure from minority cultures. Minority Canadian cultures were arguing that its Federal government needed to better cater to the specific needs of ethnic communities and better acknowledge the plurality of the nation as a whole. The 1970 Canadian Royal Commission on Bilingualism and Biculturalism analysed Anglophone and Francophone heritage in Canada, but *also* gave considerable attention to Canadians whose heritage was neither British nor French. It was this study that led to the conception of multiculturalism, a management strategy soon adopted by Australia (p. 80).

Under the guidance of Gough Whitlam's Labor Party, the government acknowledged that new migrants had different needs and required greater attention in immigration policy. The beginning of formalised Australian multiculturalism in the 1970s was thus based on a 'minority rights model' which recognised that socio-economic inequalities existed centred on ethnic difference (Nicolacopoulos and Vassilacopoulos 2011, p. 145). This formally shifted the view of cultural difference as something needing to be assimilated into white Australia, as had previously been the dominant management strategy. The Federal government began to be advised on strategies of cultural adaptation, and in 1973 the Minister for Immigration Al Grassby referred to Australia as 'multicultural' for the first time (Koleth 2010, p. 4).

This move to multiculturalism is reflective of the shift in European art institutions in the late 1960s and early 1970s to the inclusion of African and Asian artists, albeit a relatively minimal shift within what remained a stringent white-colonial framework of art history (Appignanesi 2010a). Such a shift was instigated by what Appignanesi (2010b, p. 7) terms the 'first wave' of institutional critique in the arts. This wave was greatly influenced by the work of London-based Rasheed Araeen, who pioneered minimalism in the 1960s. Araeen went on to found *Third Text*, a journal dedicated to representing ethnic artists and politicising the need to rewrite colonial art history to include cultural difference (p. 10).[1] These critical movements were slighter in Australia; non-Anglo Australian artists remained largely invisible during this period, and screens, galleries and radio stations remained mostly white (Ang et al. 2008, p. 8). The Australia Council was formed in 1973 to oversee the implementation of arts policies and express an 'Australian identity', but the presence of migrant communities within this expression was missing (Blonski 1992, p. 3).

A positive move occurred in 1975 when Grassby initiated SBS – the world's first station to develop multicultural public service broadcasting (Ang et al. 2008, p. 4). SBS was designed to provide important government information to migrants in their own languages (pp. 9–10). Nevertheless, the artistic work of migrant communities remained cut-off from institutionalised art practice and policy. By the end of the 1970s, the Australia Council was under attack for the lack of support it offered ethnic artists (Blonski 1992, pp. 2–3). These artists were 'challenging the notion of a universal aesthetic and demanding a renegotiation of what constituted "Australian" art, "ethnic art" or indeed, the very use of the designation "ethnic"' (p. 3). The council thus began to adjust and the 1980s saw what Ang et al. (2008, p. 19) describe as an ethno-multiculturalism in the arts: a focus on 'catering to the special needs and interests of migrants and ethnic communities'.

This ethno-multicultural mode of arts management and practice was mirrored in national policy at large, as Australia moved into a model of multiculturalism that Nicolacopoulos and Vassilacopoulos (2011, p. 150) term the 'cultural pluralist model'. The Fraser Liberal government of 1975–82 continued the work started by Labor in the early 1970s and in 1977 institutionalised multiculturalism as an *official* national

---

1. Richard Appignanesi, editor of this *Diversity* report, later edited *Third Text* for a decade, from 2004 to 2014.

policy. It commissioned two reports in 1977 – the Australian Ethnic Affairs Council's (AEAC) *Australia as a Multicultural Society* and the *Galbally Report*. Based on the reports' recommendations, the Fraser government extended the notion of multiculturalism from a minority-needs basis to a more overt recognition that cultural diversity was both implicit in and valuable to Australian culture. The AEAC report concluded rather ambitiously that 'Australia should be working towards [...] not a oneness, but a unity, not a similarity, but a composite, not a melting pot but a voluntary bond of dissimilar people sharing a common political and institutional structure' (1977, cited in Jupp 2007a, p. 83). This period thus saw greater institutional recognition of ethnic rights and representation, so that cultural diversity was not simply acknowledged as existing in Australia, but as being valuable and in need of integration into systems and organisations (Nicolacopoulos and Vassilacopoulos 2011, p. 150).

Working towards such an ambition was, however, slow going, with relatively few programmes implemented to specifically address the report's principles of plural composition (Jupp 2007a; Nicolacopoulos and Vassilacopoulos 2011, pp. 150–51). In the first instance, funding was siphoned off to ethnic advisory organisations who could help provide resources and assistance to specific ethnic groups. Ultimately, the management of multiculturalism continued to be structured by a centralised white Anglo-Celtic value system. Ethnic boards were appointed but always reported to the white managerial centre, rather than being actively involved within it (Jupp 2007a, p. 43; Nicolacopoulos and Vassilacopoulos 2011, pp. 150–51). Moreover, it was argued that this model of multiculturalism neither practically managed the various differences it aimed to consolidate nor allowed for an accommodation of those differences that people wanted to maintain as distinct. Indeed, arguments abounded about the entrenched racism of the policy, with some claiming that multiculturalism was a neocolonialist system, the contemporary version of Australia's assimilation or White Australia Policy (Armitage 1995; Ashcroft et al. 1998, p. 163). Multiculturalism was seen to welcome difference so long as such difference was prepared to change, or 'melt in' to, the dominant, white culture. In other words, if said difference was prepared to be *less different*.

These debates were on the priority list of Paul Keating's agenda when he was elected as the new Labor prime minister in 1990. This election foresaw a new era in Australian politics and a new deployment of 'cultural diversity' (Ang 2001, p. 153). Renewed policies and initiatives were established that encouraged the celebration of difference as opposed to the maintenance of a unified identity.

Once again, the use of cultural difference in this manner was evidenced clearly in the arts, a long-time contributor to renegotiations of race, ethnicity and the white-European canon of modernity. The Australia Council Multicultural Advisory Committee – initiated and chaired by cultural theorist Sneja Gunew – attempted to move away from an arts movement that had remained in the 1989 *Arts for a Multicultural Australia Policy* about 'social harmony' and 'unity' towards an openness to diversity and fragmentation (Blonski 1992, p. 10). Such work greatly contributed to research and policy directives that critically engaged multiculturalism and the arts. At the end of the 1980s, the notion that Australians should celebrate cultural diversity and work from models of pluralism rather than commonality became popular and prevailed into the 1990s (Ang et al. 2008,

p. 20). This period is thus described by Ien Ang et al. as one of 'cosmopolitan multiculturalism' – a time which encouraged Australians of all backgrounds to embrace a 'global cultural diversity' (ibid.).

Nicolacopoulos and Vassilacopoulos (2011, p. 151) define this third model of Australian multiculturalism as the 'universal rights model', in which the historic linking of ethnicity with citizenship becomes systemically abandoned. The Labor Party's *National Agenda* of the 1980s reframed ethnicity as one of several *choices* for Australian citizens, thereby generalising service delivery to all citizens, regardless of their ethnicity. Simultaneously, ethnic community organisations and boards were co-opted into amorphous State services, leading to their depoliticisation (Jupp 2002 and Castels 2000, cited in Nicolacopoulos and Vassilacopoulos 2011, p. 151). A range of arts programmes and initiatives were (and continue to be) implemented under the banner of cultural diversity. At a governmental level, however, the cosmopolitan period of multiculturalism was short-lived.

The election of the conservative Howard Liberal government in 1996 foresaw a renewed assimilationist discourse and an overall retraction of multiculturalism from the national narrative. For Prime Minister John Howard, multiculturalism was less important than 'One Australia'. This conception of Australia acknowledged that Australians came from various parts of the world, but required a fervent loyalty to Australian 'institutions [...] values and [...] traditions', in a way that transcended 'loyalty to any other set of values' (Howard 1999, cited in Jupp 2007a, p. 106). Multicultural policies established during this period focused on security, border control and 'appropriate levels' of immigration; proposals based on diverse rights and pluralist values were often not endorsed (Koleth 2010, p. 13).

The common public sentiment of this time was that Australia had been *too* lax and *too* embracing and was now 'paying the price' in the form of a loss of Australian values. Indeed, for those Australians Hage (1998, p. 189) labels as 'Hansonites' – supporters of Pauline Hanson's One Nation Party[2] – there wasn't so much a fear that Australians were losing control of their nation to 'foreigners' as there was a fear that they *had already lost* control. This concern was exacerbated in the early years of the twenty-first century. During this time, terrorist attacks in the United States, London, Bali and Spain and an increase in asylum-seeker arrivals and crimes by so-called ethnic gangs provided props for validating the government's position, namely, to proceed with caution with regard to Australia's ethnic constitution (see Poynting et al. 2004). These mainstream reactions were mirrored in the United Kingdom and other Western European countries

---

2. Pauline Hanson began her political career as a councillor for local government in Queensland, Australia. In the mid-1990s she was elected into Federal parliament as an Independent. In 1997 she founded One Nation, a populist, right-wing political party with an anti-Indigenous rights and anti-multiculturalism platform. The party disbanded a few years later but Hanson's political aspirations and involvement have continued into the present moment. Hanson reformed One Nation in November 2014. The Australian public has also welcomed Hanson as a pseudo-celebrity over the years, exemplified by her participation in the popular competition television series *Dancing with the Stars* (2004) and *The Celebrity Apprentice Australia* (2011).

(see Vertovec and Wessendorf 2010; Nayak 2017), evincing a type of 'emotional geopol-itics' (Pain 2009, cited in Nayak 2017, p. 297) that defied national borders.

The return of Labor to power in 2007 brought about the possibility of change in this area. However, under the leadership of Kevin Rudd (2007–10), Julia Gillard (2010–13) and Rudd once more (June 2013–September 2013), multiculturalism was politic-ally managed in more or less the same way as the previous Liberal government. The Gillard Labor government reinstated multiculturalism in its immigration policy port-folio in 2011 and expressed a much greater affiliation with 'multicultural Australia' than Howard. But while this government's approach to multiculturalism softened in some ways, it remained aggressive in many others and tended to mirror the discursive tone of Howard. In particular, it echoed Howard's suspicion of non-white Australians, and his nationalistic emphasis on a united, patriotic nation, as symbolised by the name change of the Department of Immigration and Multicultural Affairs to the Department of Immigration and Citizenship.[3] Gillard also readopted many of the policies installed by the former government to manage asylum seekers and refugees.

The hostility of this anti-asylum-seeker discourse intensified following the successful leadership challenge by Kevin Rudd in the weeks before the 2013 Federal election. Moving to the opposition's agenda of tighter border control and heightened nation-alism, Rudd introduced the most severe asylum-seeker and refugee policies ever seen in Australia. These policies included navy interception of all boats, offshore processing and no chance of Australian settlement for any refugee arriving by boat. Shortly after, in September 2013, the Abbott Liberal party was elected to govern. It claimed that Labor had failed to keep Australia's borders secure and, as such, began implementing severe policies that narrowed the scope of multiculturalism further still. A colonial narrative is evident in Abbott's pre-election speech, which asked the Australian public to decide who was 'more fair dinkum', and declared:

> The functions of government are to deliver a stronger economy, to provide national security, and to build a stronger and more cohesive society [. . .] One thing that's been most dismaying about the current government is their attempts to turn Australian against Australian [. . .] it's extraordinary that a government which has failed to stop people coming illegally to Australia by boat has tried consistently to demonise people coming to Australia legally and working and paying taxes from day one. You'll never find this kind of divisiveness from me. I am proud of Australia as an immigrant society, I am proud of the fact that people from all over the world have come here *not to change us but to join us* [. . .] [it] will increase under a Coalition govern-ment. (Abbott 2013; italics added)

Unsurprisingly, policies towards immigration and cultural diversity subsequently became more severe than critics of other conservative Australian governments could have

---

3. The removal of the word 'multicultural' from Federal management suggested a lessening of its importance. It was also indicative of a relinking of ethnic difference to a managerial model of Australian citizenship, where citizenship is earned via active participation in white Australian activities and narratives (see Stratton 2011).

anticipated (Grewcock 2014). Implicit in the border security rhetoric is a debasement of multiculturalism, which has only been further reaffirmed in the successive re-election of the Liberal government in the Federal elections of 2016 and 2019.

Cultural diversity and its critics: Two key approaches to the crisis of multiculturalism in the twenty-first century

Given the many forms of government changes and multicultural resistance and criticism, it is not surprising that multiculturalism is currently experiencing an existential crisis in Australia. This is evident beyond Australia, particularly in Anglo-settler colonies, but also in other parts of Europe, as Vertovec and Wessendorf (2010) meticulously demonstrate. Changes to the way identity was understood theoretically towards the end of the twentieth century made way for a reimagining of multiculturalism and ethnic rights, but whether this has helped or hindered the so-called multiculturalism crisis is debatable. In particular, the interpretation and deployment of identity categories such as 'ethnicity' became much more fragmented in the 1990s. Influenced by postmodern philosophers like Michel Foucault, Jean Baudrillard and Jacques Derrida, cultural critiques began to move from investigations of identity to an elevation of difference (Ang and St Louis 2005, p. 292). Attending to 'ethnic needs' at large was increasingly considered inadequate for negotiating the differences between ethnic communities in Western countries, its inadequacy exacerbated by the increasing mobility of people and information across the globe. These theoretical debates translated to new approaches to studies of multiculturalism.

The first approach to multiculturalism studies in the twenty-first century retains the celebratory component of liberal multiculturalism though the terminology shifts somewhat from notions of equality and ethnic needs to one of cultural diversity. The celebratory approach is common in education literature and is associated in many ways with Charles Taylor's (1994) liberal multiculturalism and politics of recognition. Initially, the acknowledgement of diversity was an exciting shift in art and cultural politics, welcomed by those who felt rigid identity categories failed to acknowledge the variances and tensions within and across identities. However, the meaning and use of cultural diversity has more recently come under scrutiny. While there are useful dimensions to this approach, I argue that its vehement promotion of cultural difference can enable racialisation to continue, albeit in discreet ways. I thus join a range of cultural studies academics, cultural theorists, artists and art critics who see themselves at a critical cross-road, or on the crest of a third wave of critique regarding cultural diversity (Ang 2003; Cooper 2004; Ang and St Louis 2005; Beng-Huat 2005; Lowe 2005; Ang et al. 2008; Appignanesi 2010a; Fisher 2010; Ahmed 2012a,b; Idriss 2016).

The term 'cultural diversity' carries with it a range of definitions and interpretations, although it has, across these variances, some similarities. First, as Jean Fisher (2010, p. 61) notes, the term is always related to notions of social justice, acting as a site of debate in nations which have a legacy of 'injustice, inequality and discrimination against minority groups'. This dynamic is certainly the case in Australia and the greater West, where the effects of imperialism and colonialism are redistributed through its institutions and systems of knowledge. Second, it carries with it a relation to agency, or the degree to which individuals are 'free' to act as 'political and legal subjects' in any given society (ibid.). Finally, the term 'almost always implies a majority monoculture against which all else is "diverse", predicated on an hypostatisation of cultural and ethnic (or other) differences' (ibid.). This latter point is crucial because while diversity certainly has and can refer to a range of identity markers, its development in the West has been in reference to racial or ethnic markers of difference. It has, in this context, emerged in societies defined as being ethnically plural, or 'multicultural', in constituency. Fisher's discussion is in relation to the UK context; however, it translates usefully to Australia. Ang and St Louis (2005, p. 296) explain how ethnic, linguistic and cultural differences become officially sanctioned by the Australian State through multiculturalism: 'The celebration of cultural diversity [. . .] is an article of faith in self-identified multicultural societies.'

To substantiate this concern, it is useful to explore how cultural diversity is represented in the arts environment, a significant contributor to the formation of multiculturalism in Australia and beyond. According to Aaron Seeto (2011, p. 28), cultural difference in Australian contemporary art has tended to be either overly determined or entirely absent. In many cases, cultural difference continues to be unrepresented, or if it is present, misrepresented, taken up according to certain rules, which are governed by the normativity of whiteness. This point is confirmed by the major report by Diversity Arts Australia (2019, p. 4) into cultural diversity, which concluded that 'there is a significant under-representation of CALD [Culturally and Linguistically Diverse] people in leadership and decision-making roles in every area of the creative sector'. So, even though Australia is a diverse nation, and culturally diverse artists are high in number, the core of the arts industry is Anglo-Celtic.

Many art critics agree that this issue has emerged because the application of 'cultural diversity' in Western society has been of a reactionary nature, that is, a mere 'tool' or 'sector' of politics aimed to address the changing ethnic constituency of Western countries (Appignanesi 2010b, p. 5; Araeen 2010a, p. 44; Fisher 2010, p. 62). This reactionary application has meant, as Seeto (2011, p. 28) argues, that cultural diversity in Australian curatorship has taken up the somewhat empty multiculturalism rhetoric of needing to '"build bridges", cross cultures and engage new audiences'. Ultimately, such rhetoric serves the dominant culture, which demands that the relevance of culturally diverse art be repeatedly elucidated.

Fisher (2010, p. 63) explains that this has the potential to place the artist in 'a straight-jacket of conformity that, on one hand, risks crippling artistic creativity, and on the other, confines them to a limited range of "thematic" shows and critical discourses'. Araeen takes up a similar argument with regard to liberal multiculturalism in Australia (2003) and the Western context at large (2010a). Although he acknowledges the success of younger generation artists as a result of multiculturalism, Araeen believes it has meant their work has come to represent a 'cultural specificity': 'only meant for those who are considered "others"'. Consequently, this allows for 'the colonialist separation between people based on racial or cultural difference' to be 'openly institutionalised and maintained'[4] (Araeen

---

4. The threat to creativity is clear. If artists gain entry into the contemporary art circuit because of their ethnic/racial labels – seen as 'culturally relevant' in this present context of 'culturally

2010a, p. 43). Thus, although 'cultural diversity' provides a space for ethnic Australians to explore and express their differences in a contemporary setting, it continues to ignore that 'culture within itself is already an assemblage of differences, diverse tendencies and unresolved tensions' (Appignanesi 2010a, p. 5).

The creation of the culturally diverse space also risks preventing genuine movement towards an integrated and inclusive arts and cultural ecology. While the multicultural subject is now present in the arts, it may remain transparent, that is, it might be 'seen' but not necessarily engaged with (Mercer 1999; Papastergiadis 2005). Such an argument is depicted by the continued failure of ethnic artists, including those of Asian, African-Caribbean and African origins, to be recognised as contributors to the history of European art itself (Hall 2002a, p. 80; Araeen 2010a, p. 53). Such an issue illustrates the persistent racism of the European arts industry, as well as the duplicitous work done by the discourse of cultural diversity. By focusing on the celebration of diversity/difference in art, the discourse diverts attention away from the continued racialisation of its history and systems, inexorably ignoring the influence of ethnic artists (Appignanesi 2010a, p. 10). According to this logic, critics like Appignanesi and Araeen feel that the turn to cultural diversity in artistic practice and curatorship has been deceptive.

The issues raised by the critique of ethnic diversity in Western art circuits can be translated to the cultural diversity turn in Australian multiculturalism. First, it presents the issue in which recognition based on racial/ethnic difference designates a particular, bordered space of the multicultural person and positions this person outside the white, monocultural centre. Cultural diversity has, overall, been charged with a social engineering task, designed to 'solve' the 'problem' of ethnic difference in Australia. The idea that cultural difference causes trouble consequently shadows all aspects of cultural diversity policies and initiatives. The concern here is that cultural diversity in contemporary Australia (along with the notions of 'celebration of difference' and 'ethnicity as choice') is deployed in a way that inevitably perpetuates racist realities for Australians. In the discourse on cultural diversity the culturally diverse person becomes diverse in accordance with ethnic or racialised categories. The critical dialogue and interaction designed to be opened up by cultural diversity subsequently becomes focused on the multicultural person as distinct from the white Australian. Graeme Turner's (2008; p. 573) analysis of Australian inner-city suburbs supports this, arguing that 'the accoutrements of cosmopolitanism are ever more self-consciously displayed, [and] cultural diversity has now become a local service, rather than an organic attribute of the local community'.

---

diverse arts' – how do those artists detach from this category? This is an issue many contemporary Australian artists face, as illustrated by my interview with Paula do Prado following her feature in 'Sensorial Loop: Tamworth's Textile Triennial' (2011) and her solo exhibition *Mellorado* (2012a). As do Prado emerges in contemporary art circuits and collectors become increasingly interested in her work, she becomes exponentially aware of (and anxious about) the expectations pertaining to the 'culturally-diverse aesthetic' of her work (2012b, interview, 22 March).

Multicultural studies that do not address this problem risk reinforcing the binary that they intend to critique.

Critical multiculturalism studies address the binary tension more thoroughly and form what this research has identified as the second key approach to studies of cultural difference in Australia. Critical approaches to multiculturalism have been present since the 1970s; however, as mentioned earlier, the 1990s saw the emergence of new critical analyses of cultural difference that were indicative of new postmodern cultural theories. Pioneers of this work in Australia include Gunew (1997), Hage (1998), Papastergiadis (1995, 1997, 1999, 2000) and Ang (2001).

Recently, this foundational critical work has been added to by scholars interested in the ecologies of twenty-first century migrant communities. Unlike migrant communities of the post-war period, which involved larger, diasporic migration, new communities of Australian migrants develop from a fragmented mix of people. The communities exhibit highly diverse demographics, including varying economic and cultural capital and fluctuating attachments to notions of home (Ang 2011; Noble 2011; Yue and Wyatt 2014, p. 224). Some scholars argue that the complexity of contemporary migration has triggered different formations of racism and have thus set about mapping 'neo-racism' or the 'post-racial' (Yue and Wyatt 2014, pp. 224–25). This work draws on the scholarship of Étienne Balibar and Immanuel Wallerstein (1991) on 'neo-racism', which posits that debates about multiculturalism and immigration are impacted by a new form of racism that is formed on the basis of cultural rather than biological differences. Yue and Wyatt (2014, p. 225) argue that new racism surfaced in Australia in the 1970s, following the arrival of multiculturalism, and has been in a constant state of change ever since. Significantly, they claim that 'the old racism that deemed non-Anglo and Celtic others biologically inferior is replaced by the cultural racism of new racism' (ibid.). Ethnic minorities are increasingly seen to have cultural differences completely incompatible with the dominant Anglo community and thus pose a threat to the nation (Corlett 2002, cited in ibid.).

In some ways, this argument is not dissimilar to that put forward by Hage (2014a) in his depictions of two main forms of racism: existential racism and numerological racism. Hage (1998) argues that most of the racism experienced in post–Second World War Australia is based on the perceived scale of 'the Other'. In other words, this racism arises when the presence of the Other seems large enough to engulf white Australia. Existential racism, on the other hand, is a racism of disgust and more like the biological forms of racism categorised as 'past' forms of racism by neo-race and post-racial scholars. Existential racism is the type of racism Jean-Paul Sartre (1948) describes in his analysis of anti-Semitism, in which a person is repulsed simply by being in proximity to a person from another race. Hage (2014a) argues that Sartre's conception of racism was most evident during Australian colonisation, as demonstrated in nineteenth-century representations of Indigenous Australians and Chinese migrants. I argue, rather, that numerological racism has always crossed over with existential or biological racism. Chinese migrants who arrived during the gold rush became abject subjects according to a biological racism which deemed 'Oriental' skin to inherently carry malice. But, the intensity of this abjection was also related to the perceived *scale* of the 'malice', that is, the numbers of Chinese migrants arriving were seen to be so high that domestic miners would be undercut or pushed out of the labour market.[5]

Today, it can appear as if numerological racism is prominent because of the regular condemnations of cultural or religious practices, but the sense of entitlement that drives these racist attacks inevitably leads us back to a perceived biological or existential superiority. While the trigger for racism is perhaps a numerological presence, the foundation of the racism remains the assumptions associated with racialised bodies. As will be demonstrated in Chapters 4–6, it rarely takes long for racialised tropes associated with biology and the physicality of the body to surface. This is perhaps why Hage (2014a, p. 233) sees existential racism as being once again on the rise in Australia, particularly towards recently arrived African and Indian migrants; that is, because existential racism has never *not been* present, it is just more adept at camouflaging itself in narratives of cultural diversity. Christine Kim (2014, p. 316) supports this argument, suggesting that race and racism continue to operate largely through a visual register, emanating an 'eerie familiarity' with older narratives and ultimately encouraging us to 'conceptualise race as a biological phenomenon clearly inscribed onto the body'. As such, liberal contemporary societies such as Australia are able to purport that racism is now 'a matter of either personal prejudice or part of a historical moment that we have now transcended'. She extends:

> As a means of sketching out a cultural narrative about the overcoming of race in the past century, the move from the hypervisible to the invisible simultaneously expresses the dangers of race (to mark indelibly as well as to be circumvented by those that 'pass') as well as operates as the cultural grammar that structures many of the racial discourses in the contemporary moment. In the framework of liberal multiculturalism, the individual becomes the mechanism for overcoming racism with the common-sense belief that if one is colour-blind and incapable of seeing race, he or she cannot be guilty of racism. And yet, even if we want to believe this claim that many are now incapable of 'seeing' race, how do we understand their inability to sense race at work in the current moment? And to anticipate the latter part of my argument, how are they also able to ignore the pungent stink of racism? (p. 318)

Kim's conceptualisation of race in the twenty-first century is an effective interpretation of Balibar's (1991, p. 21) concept, which argues that it is at 'first sight' that neo-racism

---

5. Australian diggers turned against Chinese workers on the Bendigo goldfields as early as 1854, even though at this point the Australians outnumbered the Chinese fifteen thousand to two thousand; similar incidents were experienced in New South Wales, for example, at Rocky River in 1856, where a group of white miners attacked a newly arrived group of Chinese (Price 1974, pp. 68–69). Anti-Chinese sentiment intensified as more Chinese migrants arrived, a reaction parallel to the growing fear of a mass takeover by the 'vast numbers' of the Chinese (*Hansard* 1881, in Huttenback 1972–73, p. 282). Supporting the miners during this period were circulating newspapers such as *Empire*, which warned of the threat posed by 'that swarming hive of the human race' (Price 1974, p. 79). In 1855, the Victorian governor and Legislative Council accepted the royal commissioners' recommendation for an entry tax into the goldfields, designed to 'check and diminish' the Chinese influx (*Report of Commissioners on the Gold Fields* [1854–55], cited in Price 1974, p. 69).

appears to be removed from old or biological racism. At *first sight* it can seem as if contemporary racism emerges only when an ethnic Other's cultural or religious practices are deemed intolerable. After all, if ethnic Australians adopt Anglo-Celtic Australian values, they can be awarded what Stratton (2009, p. 16) refers to as 'honorary whiteness', or become, in Rosanna Gonsalves's (2011, in Khorana 2014, p. 258) term, 'de-wogged'. But, being able to bypass explicit racism via 'symbolic whiteness' (Khorana 2014, p. 260) does not demonstrate the eradication of historical forms of racism. Being an honorary white is not the same as being a 'real' white – at any moment the acclaim can be, and often is, stripped from the ethnic Australian whose body inevitably renders them inauthentic (see Stratton 1998; Ahmed 2000, p. 97; Ford 2009, pp. 171–73). Ultimately, these new critiques of multiculturalism that argue cultural racism has replaced historical forms of racism are problematic and as such this book does not adopt their methodologies.

Everyday multiculturalism

Perhaps more useful for mapping today's migrant communities is the emergent field of everyday multiculturalism, a contemporary form of critical multiculturalism that responds to the renewed demystification with multiculturalism that has surfaced in the past decade. Although the field is gaining traction across the world, it is primarily located in Western contexts, in which a perceived gap exists between how multiculturalism is managed and conceptualised and how it is actually experienced in daily life. Australian scholars, most notably, Melissa Butcher, Anita Harris, Greg Noble, Scott Poynting and Amanda Wise, are pioneering everyday multiculturalism, giving the trajectory of the field a particularly Australian orientation. However, the framework of everyday multiculturalism is being rapidly adopted in the transpacific and beyond, applied to a range of ethnographies where interculturalism, cultural diversity and social cohesion are explored. A quick glance at the preeminent book *Everyday Multiculturalism* by Wise and Velayutham (2009b) attests to this global adaptation: contributing authors draw on case studies from Brooklyn, London, Sydney/Eora,[6] Singapore, Malaysia and Southern Italy, among others.[7]

The field is interested in exploring how practices of everyday life shape and reshape identities, and how this relates to the broader terrain of multiculturalism (Wise and Velayutham 2009a, p. 3). The article titled 'Pedestrian Crossings: Young People and Everyday Multiculturalism' in the 2010 special edition of the *Journal of Intercultural Studies* succinctly summarises the field as having a focus on '(1) everyday practices of intercultural encounter and exchange (the "doing" of multiculturalism); and (2) sites and spaces where tensions and possibilities around multicultural community and nation

---

6. There are a range of Indigenous place names for parts of Sydney, for example 'central' Sydney is located on the unceded land of the Gadigal people of the Eora Nation. However, the greater city of Sydney occupies other areas, all of which fall within Eora territory; therefore, Eora is used henceforth.
7. More recent examples of everyday multiculturalism in other geographical locations include Pratsinakis et al.'s (2017) work in Greece, Back and Sinha's (2016) work in the United Kingdom, Wong's (2016) Singapore study and Shan and Walter's (2015) Canada-based research.

building occur (the places where multiculturalism is done)' (Butcher and Harris 2010, p. 450). The need to specifically examine the everyday practices and sites of multiculturalism is linked to a feeling of disconnection between official discourse and on-the-ground experience.[8] Jon Stratton (2011) illustrates how the dominant culture interprets this feeling of disconnection as a residue of migrant culture, feeling that Australian life has been undermined or overrun by non-Anglo-Celtic Australians. This sense of disconnection is also evident in the fact that racism is perpetually experienced in present-day Australia, despite Australian multiculturalism being celebrated as a national accomplishment. Recent empirical research on young people and everyday multiculturalism demonstrates this polarity. The research shows that incidents of racialised tension put a daily stress on ethnic youth, either because of mistranslations of language, fear of being harassed for dressing or looking a particular way and/or the social expulsion of ethnic youth from public areas (see Butcher and Harris 2010; Frisina 2010; Harris 2010; Noble and Poynting 2010; Rathzel 2010).

Countless studies have pointed to this gap and ultimately raise the question: are we doing multiculturalism in our day-to-day lives in a way that is removed from both the political and theoretical ideal of multiculturalism? Indeed, even though the above examples suggest that the disconnection manifests in negative fashions, Anita Harris (2010) illustrates that this is not always the case. There also appears to be some detachment between the governmental idea of multiculturalism as a *united* Australian identity and the *positive* interactions that occur on the street in spite of diverse and fragmented identity alliances. As Harris explains, young people create 'spatial communities' which often go beyond 'expected ethnic and gender belongings' (p. 582). They do so because of 'everyday debates, disagreements and encounters' (ibid.). These tensions emerge over cultural differences, but they ultimately create 'the foundation for productive and ongoing dialogue and engagement with others as equals' (ibid.). In other words, Australian youths demonstrate positive intercultural exchange not only in spite of difference but because of it. The sense of equality and conviviality that can emerge is not, therefore, based on the managerial claim of a 'unified' Australian identity or way of life.

The perceived need for a new field of study is compounded by a perception that a similar gap exists in multiculturalism literature. As Noble (2009, p. 46) claims, theoretical discussions of multiculturalism tend to focus on identity categories that are inadequate to discuss the complexity of ethnicity, and the politics of multiculturalism also struggle to service this complexity. Noble goes on to suggest that this problem is created because intercultural encounters are not recognised as such; they are 'just done' (ibid.). Many scholars are attempting to bridge the so-called gap by researching the diversity of multicultural experiences of daily life (see, e.g., Phillips 2001; Gow 2005; Ford 2009; Wise 2009, 2016; Wise and Velayutham 2009a,b, 2019; Butcher and Harris 2010; Frisina 2010; Harris 2010; Rathzel 2010; Ho 2011; Hewitt 2016; Radford 2016; Knijnik 2018).

---

8. A feeling indicative of the distrust that has been expressed towards globalisation and technological revolution, in particular towards rapid digitalisation, increased mobility and the fragmentation of networks.

Although everyday multiculturalism is a relatively new field of study, the attempt to critically examine on-the-ground aspects of multiculturalism certainly is not. Everyday multiculturalism has been used under different guises for over two decades in academic scholarship (Wise and Velayutham 2009a, p. 3). The work of Ang, Essed, Hage and Stratton has explored the dynamic between ordinary citizens and multiculturalism discourse in various ways for several years. For example, Stratton (1999, 2011) explores the dynamic between citizens and multiculturalism, and Philomena Essed's (1991) notion of 'everyday racism' has also been highly influential. Hage's *White Nation* (1998) took up a critical analysis of the wider discourses at play in constructing the fantasy of multiculturalism, arguing that although the lives of migrants in Australia may have driven the policy formations of multiculturalism, their lives remain mis- or under-represented. It is also clear that although aspects of theory and policy have not always addressed the on-the-ground tensions at play, subset policies, programmes and organisations have been consistently aware of these issues and attempted to engage them in various ways. In their study of Australia's multicultural and multilingual broadcasting service SBS,[9] Ang et al. (2008, p. 50) note that the broadcaster's latest platform fed into the popular theory of multiculturalism for everyday life, 'warts and all'. SBS's corporate plan for 2004–2006 aimed at 'a more mundane and everyday multicultural spirit' (ibid.).

The current work of everyday multiculturalism builds on these foundational studies of everyday cultural life. The first attempt to map the small but growing field was made by Amanda Wise and Selvaraj Velayutham (2009b) in the edited book *Everyday Multiculturalism*. The collection includes essays from sociology, cultural studies, literary studies and political science. Common to all approaches is the underlying use of everyday multiculturalism as a way to problematise multiculturalism as both a policy-driven concept and a lived experience. Wise and Velayutham (2009a, pp. 2–3) identify 11 sub-themes of this problematisation as follows: (1) habitus and cultural capital; (2) embodiment, reciprocity, gift exchange and social exchange; (3) affect and the senses; (4) humour; (5) everyday exchanges and transformation; (6) hybridities and the notion of being 'together in difference'; (7) everyday racism and tensions; (8) notions of civility and incivility; (9) networks; (10) material culture and modes of consumption; and (11) power and interplaying discourses. These sub-themes are certainly not mutually exclusive, and several overlaps exist between each one. Sites of study typically include spaces deemed reflective of everyday life, for example, housing and neighbourhood planning projects, food rituals, ethnic precincts, education, crime and youth participation in public space and life. This research frequently adopts a constructivist approach and almost always incorporates the use of empirical data.

---

9. SBS (Special Broadcasting Service) began with radio but has since extended to television and online formats.

Reframing everyday multiculturalism

In this book, I adopt the second approach to multiculturalism studies, one that is critical and focused on the complicated manifestations of cultural difference in Australian life and comparable nations. My approach is interested in the texture of everyday multicultural life; however, I seek to qualify my 'everyday multiculturalism' approach in a few particular ways. Specifically, I retain a focus on the phenomenological underpinnings of racialisation and the embeddedness of this in multicultural life; I also stress the interconnectedness of State and everyday manifestations of multiculturalism more explicitly. As such, my approach to everyday multiculturalism always views the multicultural person and the multicultural nation as entangled.

Although the work on new racisms offers a range of sound insights, it risks discounting the impact that 'old' racialised concepts continue to have on the 'new' ethnic body. The appeal of moving beyond biological racism is understandable; after all, science, the discursive regime initially used to 'prove' the concept of racial inferiority and superiority, has long since reassessed and disproved this claim (Olson 2004, p. xvii). Furthermore, the shifts from race to ethnicity, and then from ethnicity to cultural diversity, have been taken up relatively quickly and seamlessly in the public imagination of Australia, leaving 'race' a less common and certainly less contemporary word. As Stratton (1998, p. 104) argues, multiculturalism tends to be blurred with non-racialism, so that 'the very statement that Australia is now a "multicultural nation" is often implicitly put forward as evidence that the notion of a "white Australia" is no longer current in the national imaginary, as if the adoption of multiculturalism were by definition an act of anti-racism'. Reflecting this perceived shift, anti-racist and critical race work is frequently carried out at sites deemed to be 'cultural', such as language, public engagement or artistic practice, and this further reinstates the belatedness of 'race'. However, I argue that since racist violence continues in Australia in both physical and conceptual ways, multiculturalism studies cannot yet take the leap away from historical formations of race. In doing so, I adopt Hall's (2000) and Gunew's (2004) trepidation about the cultural turn in ethnic and race studies. Both argue that the old mindset of racialised hierarchies continues to haunt the discourse of multiculturalism and its spin-off terms.[10]

A study conducted by the Human Rights and Equal Opportunities Commission (HREOC) in 2003 helps to explain such trepidation. The study, reported in Tabar et al.'s book *On Being Lebanese in Australia: Identity, Racism and the Ethnic Field* (2010), illustrates the way historical formations of race continue to vilify Australian bodies in the twenty-first century. It included the results of 186 surveys of Arab and Muslim Australians[11] in New

---

10. See also Ang and Stratton (1998) regarding the lack of language to describe a racism based on 'race' in Australia.
11. It should be stressed that terms such as 'Arab' and 'Muslim Australians', and other related terms used in this book, for example, 'Lebanese Australian', are slippery and used interchangeably at times. The identity politics and cultural embeddedness of these terms should not be overlooked.

South Wales, which asked whether participants had experienced racist abuse or violence since 11 September 2011. If yes, the details of these incidents, including the participants' reactions and whether or not the incidents were reported, were also requested. Following the survey, 34 respondents participated in face-to-face interviews in which the details of the abuse were extrapolated. The participants covered a range of ages, socio-economic demographics and religious denominations (p. 150). Two-thirds of the survey sample reported having increased experiences of racism, and 93 per cent felt there had been an increase in racist attacks against their ethnic or religious community at large. The cited incidents included: 'minor incidents of social incivility, discrimination at work and in other institutions, media stereotyping, verbal abuse and harassment, threats of violence and sexual assault, stalking, actual physical assault (such as veil-tearing and stabbing), [and] property damage' (ibid.).

Significantly, 70 per cent of participants who had experienced racism listed the perpetrators as white, Anglo-Australian citizens, for example, 'Australian', 'Aussies', 'Anglo', 'Anglo-Saxon' and 'English' (p. 151). When identifying what they felt to be the main reasons for the attacks, the participants frequently cited a mixture of racial, ethnic and religious factors, including language, phenotype, and cultural presentation and dress. Ultimately, these reasons were 'collapsed into a general sense of difference that is implicitly an expression of difference to an unstated white, Anglo-Australian-ness' (ibid.). As Tabar et al. argue, these reasons point to embodied forms of cultural capital that mark these Australians as belonging to a non-white community, visually distinguishable from Anglo-Australians (ibid.). Thus, while racism is certainly associated with cultural or religious practices, it continues to be translated through an embodied or biological prism which marks non-white bodies as less human.

These findings are reaffirmed in many other studies, even though the materiality of whiteness is not necessarily their focus. For example, Noble's (2005) work on comfort illustrates the visceral impact of Australian racism; Harris's (2010) and Noble and Poynting's (2010) studies, respectively, show ways in which the non-white body is racialised and physically surveyed in public life, so too Maree Pardy's (2011) analysis of the Muslim woman in public space as a figure of cultural difference. The book thus sets itself the task of examining how the work of biological racialisation continues in contemporary Australia, albeit under new practices and guises.

One of these guises may well be the renewed emphasis on cultural diversity. In many ways, the term 'cultural diversity' has replaced multiculturalism as the new buzzword for contemporary Australian cultural life, in such a way that multiculturalism has become a more assumed or background component of the nation. However, despite this apparent shift, this book argues that little has changed in the way Australia organises race since the initial inception of multiculturalism in the 1970s. Many critics believe that the prime ministership of John Howard led to the devolution of multiculturalism, but as Nicolacopoulos and Vassilacopoulos (2011, pp. 148–49) argue, Howard's policies merely exposed the racialised power imbalances embedded within multiculturalism that had until then remained mostly hidden. This book extends their contention into the twenty-first century of multiculturalism politics, arguing that underlying the deployment of cultural diversity there remains a highly restrictive and familiar structure of normative

whiteness. Two elements of this structure remain steadfast. First, the assertion of central white Australian values over the values of 'ethnic others', as the master of cultural
diversity's success. Second, and not unrelated to the first, there is the ability to gloss over
everyday incidents of racism that occur in Australia daily.

The current structure of managerial multiculturalism thus repeats several issues
raised in the 1990s by Hage, and taken up again by Povinelli in *The Cunning of Recognition*
(2002). Povinelli's book critiques Australian multiculturalism, arguing that by operating via the framework of liberalism it concedes the perpetual disavowal of cultural
difference. Although her critique of liberal multiculturalism is in relation to the way it
'emerges in Indigenous societies and subjects', it provides a useful tool for questioning
the inconspicuous deployment of race in contemporary forms of cultural diversity and
multiculturalism. Povinelli notes that those fighting the cause of liberal multiculturalism
are genuinely interested in the 'good' of the ethnic subject, in a similar way that support
for multicultural programmes are most often propelled by genuinely good intentions.
However, her critique draws our attention to the way limits of tolerance are implicated
in the pursuit of this 'good', a point that Hage (1998) also takes up persuasively. Povinelli
(2002, p. 52) writes: 'The nation truly celebrates this actually good, whole, intact, and
somewhat terrifying *something* lying just beyond the torn flesh of present social life. And
it is toward this good object that they stretch their hands [...] What is the object of
their devotion?' (emphasis in the original).[12] In the following chapters, the book illustrates
that the 'object of their devotion' is a material body, in particular, the nation's ability to
demarcate and vivify the white body as distinct from the non-white body. This claim
extends both Povinelli's and Hage's arguments that the object of devotion is the maintenance of dominant whiteness.

In his seminal project on Australian multiculturalism, Hage (1998) argues that the
needs-based model of multiculturalism was replaced by a white middle-class cosmopolitanism that positioned cultural diversity as a commodity for elitist consumption. As such,
he claims that 'tolerant Australians' fighting for 'good multiculturalism' may have the best
intentions, but in fact there is no such thing as tolerant and intolerant practices: both perpetuate the same racist underpinnings (p. 93). 'Those who execute [tolerant practices],
"good" as they are, share and inhabit along with White "evil" nationalists the same
imaginary position of power within a nation imagined as "theirs" [...] They enact the
same White nation fantasy' (p. 79). In this sense, those fighting the cause of liberal multiculturalism cannot be easily distinguished from those that Hage terms 'Hansonites', or
other white Australians with overtly racist attitudes. Hage recognises that Pauline Hanson
and many of her supporters *really* believe they are not racist. Combining an approach of
ethical reflexivity and a critique of inconspicuous deployments, Hage not only considers
how nationalist practices embed these ideas but, importantly, how they incorporate the

---

12. There is something significant in this outstretched hand, and it is comparable to the discussion
    of the hand reaching to tear off the burqa that Hage (1998) undertakes in his chapter in *Arab-
    Australians Today* (2002a). The outstretched hand is taken up again in Chapters Six and Seven
    as a metaphor for the corporeal performativity of race.

ideas of those he finds *less* racist. Namely, what are the conditions that constitute these supposed 'more or less' levels of racism? Similarly, Povinelli (2002, p. 52) suggests that instead of writing Hanson off as racist because her ideas seem repellent, we should, in fact, ponder them seriously.[13] Both Hage and Povinelli are here pointing to the importance of what Gunew (2004) calls the 'shifty work' of multiculturalism, and our need to be persistently critical of it.

It is important, therefore, to carefully analyse the work that gets done in the name of multiculturalism and/or its counterpart cultural diversity. This is especially the case as multiculturalism and its related domains retain their status in the imagined community of contemporary Australia. A recent study conducted by Nikos Papastergiadis et al. (2015) at the University of Melbourne found that new migrants to Melbourne/Naarm and greater Victoria continue to use the language of multiculturalism, explicating a keen desire to become an active part of Australia's multicultural society. The research indicates that the personal identities of many new migrants are intrinsically linked to the institutional construction of multiculturalism; how these migrants construct an understanding of their Australian subjectivity moves in and around this discourse. This relationship occurs in spite of multiculturalism's critics and its waning popularity as a keystone governmental policy. Maree Pardy's and Julian C. H. Lee's (2011, p. 300) empirical research further supports this point, noting that Australian immigrants and refugees frequently 'claim multiculturalism as their space'. Multiculturalism is viewed as the space in which they can attain belonging and identification with the nation, a type of guarantee for their future Australianness (pp. 300–301). I thus maintain the use of the term 'multiculturalism', positioning it as a prevalent contemporary phenomenon that cannot be overlooked.

The personal-public relationship involved in forming a multicultural subjectivity gives rise to another key aspect of my approach to the study of everyday multiculturalism, namely, the framing of everyday multiculturalism as interrelated to systematic or governmental realms. Some everyday multiculturalism scholars have a tendency to position everyday cultural encounters as removed from institutionalised frameworks of cultural difference. Paul O'Connor (2010, p. 526), for example, views everyday multiculturalism as 'miles ahead' of policy initiatives. This structure also arises in some discussions about the role of community-based or culturally diverse art as a cultural process emancipated from governmentality.[14] In his analysis of cultural diversity in Britain, Araeen (2010a,b) argues that the 'diversity of cultures' and 'diversity within' art should be seen as two

---

13. See also Ang (2001, p. 158):

    What if we were to do the unthinkable and agree with Hanson that there is something fishy about the nation's enjoyment of ancient Aboriginal traditions? About the national celebration of a social law preceding the messiness of national history? About the tacit silences surrounding the content of Aboriginal traditions?

14. Rimi Khan (2011, 2015) critically problematises this association. See also Hawkins (1993) and Andreas Huyssen (2007).

separate things, calling for a separation between art and other elements associated with cultural diversity, such as traditions and heritage. While Araeen feels diversity is a 'fundamental' rather than an 'add-on', he holds the idea of the 'free-thinker' close to his chest – believing that art has to be completely separated from culture and its institutions and policies to allow for truly creative and progressive works (Araeen 2010b, p. 18).

Cultural difference and multicultural interactions certainly occur beyond policy; however, this book argues that the distinction between these two realms cannot and should not be made so clearly. Trying to separate the culturally diverse artist or multicultural subject from institutions and/or policy overlooks the set of relations that pre-exist and exceed beyond the artist or multicultural person. Certainly, the checklist approach to cultural diversity creates a series of presuppositions for art practice and its outputs, but gaining an exterior of culture and its critique is, by definition, an impossible task. We can only come to know 'ourselves', after all, by giving the 'I' over to a set of terms which exist before and beyond us (Butler 1997a, pp. 196–97). A separation of any sort is, as Butler (2009, p. 44) writes, a 'function of the relation, a brokering of difference, a negotiation in which I am bound to you in my separateness'. Furthermore, arguing that we need to separate things into distinct fields to find 'true creativity', or, as O'Connor (2010) argues, to analyse the 'real' realms of multiculturalism, fails to critically consider the productive work that occurs within the institutions of both art and multiculturalism. As Butler (2009, p. 149) outlines, institutions and the State are able to establish 'ontological givens' through certain operations of power, which are 'precisely notions of subject, culture, identity, and religion', and the versions of these often remain 'uncontested'. The State and the institutions of multiculturalism should not be at the centre of analysis since power operates in ways and means that 'precede and exceed' (p. 146) it; but it is still an element that contributes to the assemblage of the ethnic subject and the wider terrain of cultural diversity. The everyday experiences of racism are not excluded to the realm of the individual or the personal – racist attacks are always validated by the dominant sociality to some degree, 'either by other citizens or by various institutions, and especially those of the state' (Tabar et al. 2010, p. 156).

Christopher Bowen's (2011) speech, *The Genius of Australian Multiculturalism*, helps to illustrate the public-private entanglements within the discourse of multiculturalism and ultimately the multicultural body that I examine in this book. As the minister for immigration and citizenship under the former Gillard Labor government, Bowen addressed parliament to officially reinstate Australia as a multicultural nation. The speech is noticeably sanguine, exaggerating the successes of Australian multiculturalism and ignoring its problems and ultimately giving it no new vision or reassessment. Echoing John Howard's 1999 agenda of 'One Australia', Bowen proclaims that the success of Australian multiculturalism is attributable to the way it allows other cultures to enjoy their own cultural values, but always ensures 'respect for traditional Australian values' is retained at its core. According to Bowen, this has allowed Australia to escape the perils that other multicultural nations, such as Canada, Germany and France, have experienced. Bowen suggests that the complex debate over language in Canada, the 'parallel lives' produced in Germany and the race riots in France have been the results of a lack of encouragement for integration and/or an ill-defined multicultural policy. This latter comparison with

France is particularly disturbing since it was only recently that violent race riots occurred in the Southern-Sydney suburb of Cronulla.[15] As I will argue in Chapter Five, racism was an underlying factor in the Cronulla riots, made explicit by the specific uses of the white male body during the public stand-off. By making a point of the tensions in other countries, but denying those present in Australia, Bowen perpetuates Australia's long-standing denial of racism and its failure to acknowledge the history and contributions of non-white Australians to the country.

A comparison can be made to Hage's (2002b, p. 9) argument regarding the lack of ethical consideration for Arab-Australians during the Gulf War. Hage describes how media reports of the war made no gesture towards the Arab-Australian community, an absence he attributes to the fact that the ethnic community was not 'considered worthy of a pause' (ibid.). The failure on the part of Bowen to include a pause for the on-the-ground tensions of multiculturalism indicates a repeated performance of an entrenched racism. Namely, he gives the nation a multicultural imaginary while simultaneously denying the everyday reality of the multicultural subjects that the imaginary claims to include. This denial or absence of a pause directly impacts the way ethnic bodies perceive themselves, and ultimately the choices they make from day to day. The empirical research carried out for the aforementioned HREOC (2003) project found, for example, that one of the significant reasons victims of racism do not report racist incidents is due to a belief that racism is accepted by the majority of Australians and the country's core institutions (Tabar et al. 2010, p. 159). When retelling their experiences of racism, many participants mentioned the lack of intervention and care from onlookers or witnesses. This apathy was felt even though the attacks often took place in public areas, such as roads, transportation, shopping centres or at work (ibid.).

The lack of intervention by individuals and representatives of institutions (police officers, politicians) fulfil 'the collective nature of mechanisms of conversion' or the active process through which bodies are marked as human or otherwise (ibid.). Immediately after the Cronulla riots the prime minister of the time, John Howard, denied they were a result of racism – a denial Bowen reaffirms years later in his 2011 multiculturalism speech.

Conclusion

There has been a shifting ecology of liberal multiculturalism in the twenty-first century, including the eruption of the term 'cultural diversity' in multicultural discourses. A range of moving factors has culminated in multiculturalism entering a mode of crisis in the

---

15. Although a Southern-Sydney suburb, Cronulla is imbricated with West Sydney, an area known for its pronounced multicultural constituency. 'Mark', a young man involved in the Cronulla riots, explains this spatial-social connection:

    You've got the surrounding suburbs like Bankstown, Hurstville, Lakemba, they're all west and they're also connected by the train line that goes into Cronulla. Also, that's their local beach as well. And pretty much out there it's a lot of Middle Eastern culture. There's definitely – there's a lot of Middle Eastern people out there [. . .] from Lebanon, wherever. (*Four Corners* 2006)

twenty-first century, leading to two main approaches to its study. The first approach has been to emphasise the positive aspects of multiculturalism, often with a focus on the richness that cultural diversity adds to society. The second approach is more critical, working to illustrate the complexities and issues of multiculturalism as a societal phenomenon. Often, this latter approach moves discussions of cultural difference beyond the framework of multiculturalism altogether, either in the form of a complete renunciation or as a subtle but evident departure.

There are clearly micro and macro/private and public levels to the normalisation of racism – on the ground in which the racist altercations or tensions take place, and within the broader systems of power and sociality that support (sometimes simply by overlooking) these incidences. Tabar et al. (2010, p. 159) emphasise the importance of this relationship, 'crucial not just because of the ways in which it structures the fields of significant social power [. . .] but because it also shapes the forms of conversion in everyday life'. Perhaps the most problematic aspect of arguments like that posited by O'Connor and Araeen is their failure to consider the productive work that occurs *between* the 'on-the-ground' cultural differences and the institutions that drive it.

The study of multiculturalism is not ready to be abandoned, but it does need to be reconceptualised in broader terms. A brief overview of governmental and theoretical forms of multiculturalism indicates that questions of white managerialism continue to plague both the conceptualisations and material implications of multicultural life. Materiality must be fore-fronted in analyses of cultural difference if they are to tackle the stubborn residue of biological racism within multiculturalism discourse. Multiculturalism studies should analyse the multitude of forces and relations that constitute the present moment of culturally diverse life, but always with the understanding that this analysis might look different from another angle.

A multiculturalism that is critical and attuned to the complicated cross-overs of private and public discourses must be utilised in order to adequately navigate the conjuncture of cultural difference in the twenty-first century. The following chapter turns its attention to digital storytelling, a genre in which the nation and the ordinary multicultural body overlap.

Chapter Two

DIGITAL STORYTELLING AND DIVERSITY WORK

Story has many jobs, as a learning modality through memory, as a way to address our connection to the changing world around us, as a form of reflection against the flood of ubiquitous access to infinite information, as the vehicle to encourage our social agency, and finally, as a process by which we best make sense of our lives and our identity [. . .] Story is essentially an exercise in controlled ambiguity. And given the co-construction of meaning between us as storytellers, and those who are willing to listen to our words, this is story's greatest gift [. . .] We can feel whole about impermanence. *We can bear to be ourselves.*

– Lambert (2013, p. 14, italics added), creator of the digital storytelling model

Digital storytelling has become the new ten pin bowling [of community arts]!

– Horsley (2014)

Digital storytelling is commonly understood as a narrative-based medium that blends still photography, home video, sound and voice narration into a hyper-short 'film', edited to emotively tell an individual, first-person story. While the term is widening over time and some scholars, such as Carolyn Handler Miller (2004), use digital storytelling to include such things as mobile technologies, gaming and device apps, I am particularly interested here in forms of digital storytelling with a more direct relationship to the genre emerging from the Californian-based StoryCenter (formerly Center for Digital Storytelling or the CDS). Other forms of new media storytelling can be found in various locations,[1] but the StoryCenter is responsible for defining digital storytelling as a specific genre that has proliferated globally.

While the StoryCenter began working on a model for digital storytelling in the 1990s, it was not until after the turn of the century that it began to take off as a screen genre. It then spread quickly to Australia and the United Kingdom and has since been adopted in other parts of the world, including Western Europe and South Africa. A genre can be understood as a set of texts that share characteristics in content and form. The content and production processes of the StoryCenter digital storytelling model, as well as the high level of users who have adopted it, allow the model to be understood as a *genre* of new media (Kaaire 2012). Birgit H. Kaaire describes the genre of digital storytelling

---

1. These range from social networking sites such as Facebook and Instagram to v-blogs and online broadcasting communities such as Video Blogger and YouNow.

as 'surprisingly stable', noting that the core StoryCenter model remains intact in most digital story projects (and even those that rework the model do not stray too far from its basic principles and characteristics) (p. 20). This can be attributed to the way the model has been taught and retaught in facilitated environments according to the initial framework developed by the StoryCenter (ibid.).

Digital storytelling projects have certainly bourgeoned in Australia, beginning with the Australian Centre for the Moving Image (ACMI). It has trained not only the public but also other trainers, who have gone on to train communities, organisations and – inevitably – more trainers. This method of facilitated training has significantly lessened the demand on ACMI to teach people how to use the model. Increasing numbers of organisations have adopted the model and today use it in a purely in-house fashion (Simondson 2012a).

Jean Burgess (2006, p. 207) terms the crossover between traditional communicative practices and new consumer/media practices as 'vernacular creativity'. Burgess's use of vernacular creativity is important because it resists the temptation to discuss digital storytelling in binary terms, that is, between the notion of digital storytelling as 'authentic, folk culture' and digital storytelling as 'mass media' (p. 206). Instead, 'vernacular creativity [...] includes, as *part* of the contemporary vernacular the experience of commercial popular culture' (p. 207; emphasis in the original). Situating the genre as the product of shifting popular cultures is relatively unique, as much of the digital storytelling literature equates digital storytelling with a pre-existing form of 'age-old storytelling', which acts to legitimise the authenticity of the voice (see Skouge and Rao 2009; Rodríguez 2010; Higgins 2011; Dunford and Jenkins 2017). The link between digital storytelling and folk culture is often made as a means to add weight to the overarching argument that digital storytelling is a 'truly' democratising medium. Or, in other words, to argue that voice is more naturally enabled in digital storytelling than in other media forms because it relies on a commonplace or universal form of sharing. In this way, it sets up a binary between digital storytelling and mass media culture.

This chapter provides a historical overview of the philosophical underpinnings of digital storytelling, beginning with the StoryCenter, and the methods used to produce both individual and collaborative digital stories. It then identifies the main theoretical approaches to studying digital storytelling, as well as the common benefits and issues associated with the genre. I use this work to consider the similarities and/or differences in how everyday multiculturalism has developed as a *field of inquiry* compared to how digital storytelling has developed as an *arts media practice*. In other words: how does the discourse of everyday multiculturalism reflect (or otherwise) the themes, goals and methodological considerations of digital storytelling? What aspects of everyday multiculturalism does the digital storytelling medium replicate or differ from?

History and development of digital storytelling

During the mid-1990s, Joe Lambert developed a model for new media storytelling that would enable ordinary people to share their personal stories by harnessing new internet and computer software technologies.[2] During this era, now referred to as 'the dot.com bubble', internet technologies grew rapidly. This period saw the swift development of web browsers, such as the World Wide Web, and the provision of new online sites and software from dot.coms (web companies). People's capacity to connect with others and share information in the virtual domain increased dramatically (Castells 2001). This time was, in a way, a bridging period whereby previously favoured formats for recording and sharing personal stories began to edge into the online world. For example, people (mostly in developed, Western countries)[3] began to send emails to each other instead of hand-writing and posting letters, and online word blogs began to replace the traditional diary or travel journal, acting as digital sites where people could journalise their experiences. Many people also became interested in developing sites dedicated to tracing and sharing family trees, slowly eroding the popularity of the conventional printed family tree document. Nonetheless, while web publishing tools were increasingly opening up for non-technical users, as Helen Simondson (2012a) of ACMI explains, most people did not have the skills to adequately use them.

The particular setting of technological growth and everyday documentation interests allowed Lambert to create a successful storytelling platform. Ordinary people were attracted to his model, which blended familiar forms of personal documentation (such as the home video) with new online forms (such as the video blog) in a user-friendly format. The success of digital storytelling can also be attributed in part to the renewed popularity of the memoir in both literature and online narrative that took place in Western cultures in the late twentieth and early twenty-first centuries. The popularity of these genres was, as Nancy K. Miller and Jason Tougaw (2002, p. 2) describe, indicative of an overall move to document, study and *share* trauma narratives and cultures: 'We've become accustomed in American culture to stories of pain, even addicted to them; and as readers (or viewers), we follow, fascinated (though as many profess disgust), the vogue of violent emotion and shocking events.' Narratives of extreme experiences soon folded into narratives of 'everyday trauma' or the mundane traumas of daily life that had previously been overlooked. Formerly private testimonies of trauma and everyday life consequently edged further into the public realm (see Cvetkovich 2003, 2007). The public was drawn in by the 'emotional appeal of the true story', leading to what Miller and Tougaw (2002, p. 2) describe as the 'triumph of the memoir'.

Digital storytelling complemented the renewed interest in everyday stories, appealing to the ordinary person's 'desire to document life experience, ideas, or feelings through the use of story and digital media for digital storytelling' (CDS 2012). Digital storytelling attempted to democratise media and public stories, rooting itself in movements pioneered

---

2. Lambert, originally from Texas, pursued theatre before venturing into new media and digital storytelling. He directed the People's Theatre Coalition in San Francisco, a networking and advocacy hub for local theatres, before forming *Life On the Water*, an experimental theatre organisation that supported community-based artists (Lambert 2013, p. 29).

3. In accordance with the development of technologies that was concentrated in the developed, Western world. It is important to remember, of course, that access inequalities are also still rife within this context.

by folk cultures and the activist traditions of the 1960s (Lambert 2009, p. 26). Lambert saw these traditions as 'inherently sympathetic to human experience [. . .] [seeking] ways to capture their own and other's sense of the extraordinary in the ordinary comings and goings of life' (pp. 26–27).[4] By explicitly targeting the emotions of these ordinary experiences, digital storytelling was able to gain the attention of the public, hoping, as most memoirs did at the time, to produce new relationships and form empathetic communities of daily life. As Miller and Tougaw (2002, p. 2) describe, the drive for personal testimony was related to the desire to create 'an identity-bound shared experience', or, at least, 'one that is shareable through identification'.

The basic paradigmatic principles underpinning the particularities of the digital storytelling form and process reflect Lambert's goals of democratising media and empowering everyday stories. These principles are outlined by Lambert as follows: (1) everyone has many powerful stories to tell; (2) listening is hard; (3) people see, hear and perceive the world in different ways; (4) creative activity is human activity; (5) technology is a powerful instrument of creativity; and (6) sharing stories can lead to positive change (CDS 2012). Although Lambert suggests that people experience the world in different ways, it is clear that he believes storytelling allows these differences to be reconciled or, at the very least, provides a space for positive communal action and relationship building. These principles suggest that some elements of telling and receiving stories are common for all people; that while there might be different ways to experience the world, the ways we use stories to share these experiences is universal.

Guided by this humanistic philosophy, Lambert seized on new media developments and expanded the field of everyday memoir production in a way he deemed universally translatable. He believed that in order to create a space for this type of human translation, the medium would require certain attributes. In the latest edition of his book *Digital Storytelling: Capturing Lives, Creating Community* (2013), Lambert suggests that digital stories need to be personal stories that the author is deeply attached to and that can be told in the first person. These first-person stories should reflect an actual experience – a moment or series of moments – which become scenes that convey the emotions experienced and work to draw the viewer into the story. Importantly, this narrative occurs as a voice-over in the author's own voice. Additionally, the stories should seem 'self revelatory', as if the author is sharing an insight that they themselves have just discovered, 'giving the story a sense of immediacy and discovery' (p. 37).

There is an emphasis on the position that creative activity is *human* activity. For this reason, pre-existing visual archives, such as family albums and home videos, are used to inspire people's stories and the narrative is told in the author's own voice – delivering what George H. Mead (1934, cited in Kaaire 2012, p. 19) describes as 'me' or 'I' stories. While stories can and should use moving images where effective, Lambert (2013, p. 38) argues that the use of still images in small numbers remains popular due to its ability to

---

4. The use of the word 'sympathetic' as opposed to 'empathetic' is significant and reminiscent of elitist forms of cosmopolitanism that circulate in some cultural theory. The use of sympathy, as it relates to shame and good feeling, is addressed in Chapter Seven.

'create a relaxed visual pace against the narration'. From an audio perspective, music and sound effects are used to assist the translation of meaning and enhance the impact of the story upon the viewer. Kaaire (2012, p. 19) explains that basic production software (formerly various Adobe programmes) is used to add a soundtrack, image pan (movement of pictures across the horizon) and zoom effects.

The emphasis in digital stories is on a minimalist production and stylisation: 'The stories may use feature sets available in digital video editors, but they are taught as minimally, and so used as minimally, as possible. The emphasis is a raw, more direct feel, with pans and zooms to provide emphasis, dissolves to soften cuts, and once in a while the use of compositing or other special effects' (Lambert 2013, p. 38). Another aspect of this minimalistic approach is the length of the digital story – ideally it is two- to three-minutes long and normally never longer than five minutes. Lambert notes that brevity was initially necessary because the digital stories had to be workshopped, but now it has become 'the nature of the artifact' – suiting the internet-based distribution and also setting the beginning storyteller an achievable goal (ibid.).

Finally, Lambert claims that 'intention' is an important aspect of the digital story. The StoryCenter model puts process before product, that is, it 'privileges self-expression and self-awareness over concerns of publication and audience' (ibid.). This priority is important to flag at this moment for, as will be discussed in due course, it seems to be the case that the relationship between product and process is not as clear-cut as purported here, and the existing tension between the two has never been resolved by the StoryCenter or other practitioners of the genre. Lambert argues that while the product may go on to have a significant impact or reach a larger audience, the intention of the model is to honour the individual's storytelling process, allowing the author control over the story and its distribution. The desire to ensure the storyteller has this kind of agency 'informs all choices about participation, [and] ethics-in-process' (ibid.).

The proliferation of the digital storytelling genre is tied to its step-by-step methodology, termed 'The Seven Steps of Digital Storytelling'. This methodology is relatively easy both for facilitators to teach and for participants to follow. Lambert claims that he never intended these steps to act as a 'must do' guideline (p. 54). Practitioners have tended to follow the steps strictly, especially in the early years of the genre. The methodological process is unique to the digital storytelling genre; indeed, the methodology is what *makes* it a genre: 'digital storytelling is presented not only as a genre but also as a method' (Kaaire 2012, p. 22).

The methodological steps are: (1) owning your insights; (2) owning your emotions; (3) finding the moment; (4) seeing your story; (5) hearing your story; (6) assembling your story; and (7) sharing your story (Lambert 2009, pp. 29–47).

Step 1 is to establish the type of story to be told in the digital story. According to Lambert, a good digital story will also serve as a medium through which the storyteller can or does move through a process of self-discovery.

Step 2 tracks what emotions appear as the author shares and prepares their script, so as to identify which narrative aspects convey the emotions most effectively for the digital output. Essentially, the author is urged to ask: which emotion(s) will be easiest to trigger in the viewer, and most effective in translating the meaning of the story? It is suggested that by remaining aware of your emotions the story will emit genuineness, demonstrating to the viewer that 'you believe in your story'; that you are really '"in" [your] story' (p. 58). I pick up this point in Part Two of this book, closely examining how affective elements of digital stories are implicated in the performativity of whiteness and/or ethnicity.

Step 3 of the methodology is designed to help the author identify a moment of change that will act as the pinnacle point of the story and the moment around which to build the story's scenes.

In Step 4, visual presentation and imagery become relevant. Lambert describes images as the 'metaphorical river of meaning', which can be used in a number of ways to ensure the reader 'jumps in' to the river to gain an understanding of the story and the storyteller (p. 60).

In Step 5, Lambert encourages authors to think about how others will hear their narrative. He inspires them to tell the story in simple language, with as few words as possible, and ideally in a way that they would recreate the story to a group of friends – 'off the cusp'. Authors spend time looking over their scripts to ensure the words in the narrative are used carefully and help to convey the appropriate feeling and idea.[5] This step in the methodology is also where the author identifies what sound effects and music might complement the story and how these elements can be adjusted to change the pace and mood of a given moment.

In Step 6, the author takes all of the aforementioned considerations and collections and assembles the digital story. The moment of change identified earlier is now placed within the timeline of the story and scenes are created by organising the images and sounds. The author's narration is recorded and layered with sound effects.

Finally, in Step 7, the author presents the digital story with the rest of the workshop group. This finishing step is considered crucial for providing the participant with feedback and a sense of achievement. Lambert's methodology was designed to function as a type of journey, and often workshop participants become invested in each other's stories – eager to see how they 'ended'. The seventh step is thus viewed as the pinnacle moment of transformation, where the destination of the story is realised for the author.

The subjects performing the digital stories are disciplined according to these methodological steps, which aim to ensure the finished product is persuasive and engaging. The stories are created with a specific audience in mind, for example, a family, community or organisation, and usually entail some level of distribution via the internet (Meadows 2003, cited in Kaaire 2012, p. 17). It is, in Kaaire's words, 'akin to radio – with pictures' (p. 19), made up mostly of still pictures and thus not identifiable as a movie as such. There is an understanding that in order to grab the viewer's full attention, certain techniques are required, and these ultimately rest on appealing to certain human or 'universal' instincts and inclinations. This is thus a performance directed in certain ways, and

---

5. This technique seems to contradict the way the story scripts are carefully crafted during the workshops – after all, people do not closely edit their day-to-day monologues before speaking them. Lambert wants the highly polished and edited stories to sound *as if* they were casual, unedited stories.

it also, as Smaill (2010, p. 138) writes regarding documentary, 'establishes the presence of the performing subject by directing our attention to that subject'. The constructed presence of the viewer is bound up with certain fantasies of the self and the Other and, as will be illustrated later, affects the ways in which the bodies involved in the digital performance are articulated.

Currently, two main types of digital stories can be identified in Australia: individual digital stories and collaborative digital stories. Individual stories refer to the conventional definition, as listed earlier. I am also interested here in what I term 'collaborative digital stories': digital stories that are created by a community or group of people over a relatively long period of time. Projects that incorporate collaborative digital stories do not rigidly administer the Seven Steps of Digital Storytelling, though they still utilise several aspects of this framework. These stories tend to be much longer and combine the artistic outputs created in a variety of workshops.

Theorising digital storytelling as participatory culture

The majority of literature on digital storytelling is published from 2005 onwards and offers a positive assessment of the genre. Common arguments are that the genre allows for equitable knowledge sharing, 'gives voice' to ordinary people and boosts participants' confidence by transferring a range of visual literacy and life skills. However, despite the overall positive reviews, some authors contest the efficacy of the genre, especially when practiced according to the StoryCenter model. These tensions are indicative of the broader critical gaps and become particularly relevant because of the way in which certain participants are articulated as ethnic Others in migrant digital storytelling projects.

The most common argument is that the genre can open up a space for equitable knowledge sharing or to 'give voice' to ordinary people. Illustrations of this argument are seen in the names of the digital storytelling projects often discussed. For example, *London's Voices* (Thumin 2009, cited in Copeland and Miskelly 2010, p. 194), *A Centre of Voices from Ohio 2003* (Klaebe 2006, p. 25), *Silence Speaks* (Reed and Hill 2010) and *The Pacific Voices Program* (Skouge and Rao 2009). Definitions of voice are rarely provided, but it can, generally, be read as referring to the capacity to share personal stories with others. The ability to share personal stories is intrinsic to the digital storytelling genre. The autobiographical outcomes are shared with others in both private circles (family and friends) and public arenas (community groups, organisations, online).

The opportunity for digital storytelling to provide 'voice' is also attributed to the Story Circle, Step 1 of the digital storytelling methodology, in which all project participants gather together and share script ideas. The Story Circle is viewed as a safe space where storytelling participants can share something personal. The participants subsequently gain suggestions from others in the Circle about how to develop their respective narratives in a compelling way. Many scholars suggest that this interaction gives participants validation: the authors are assured that their stories have meaning and value, and this ultimately contributes to a stronger sense of self or identity. Thus, the digital storytelling model involves speaking in one's *literal* voice for the audio narrative, but this speaking is also representative of a metaphorical 'speaking up' by one's subjectivity, whereby participants in digital storytelling programmes can be heard by others and recognised as a valid subject. Indeed, some scholars repeat Lambert's (2006) suggestion that sharing in the Story Circle acts as a kind of therapeutic telling (e.g. Raimist et al. 2010; Reed and Hill 2010, p. 270; Higgins 2011, p. 8).

The provision of voice has much to do with the technological nature of the digital storytelling model, which was specifically designed to be accessible and relatively easy for lay people to master. Lambert developed the model in such a way that people with minimal technological skills could grasp basic image editing and sound layering and create an effective, moving image mini-film. This accessibility is increased by the relatively easy availability of the software used for digital storytelling, described by John Higgins (2011) as 'prosumer'. Some researchers argue that by allowing people to build their digital story using personal artefacts, such as personal photos, arduous research work and content construction is cut down, making the creative process less daunting (Alexandra 2008; Simondson 2012a,b). This aspect of the digital storytelling method is also not too far removed from memory practices of the ordinary person, as it utilises similar techniques to the compiling of a family album or framed photo collages. Those new to digital storytelling can find this familiarity useful for creating stories. It follows then that the genre is frequently described as a 'scrapbook studio' process (Kaaire 2012, pp. 19–20).

The argument that digital storytelling gives voice to marginalised peoples in a mostly uniform manner, regardless of the group in question, is evinced across scholarly fields. The reference to the provision of voice in education literature, for example, frequently parallels how cultural studies and community development literature discuss voice. Scholars such as Monica Nilsson (2010) work within an education framework to examine the importance of digital storytelling for marginalised students in education classrooms. Nilsson (2010) illustrates how digital storytelling appealed to nine-year-old Simon, who, diagnosed with Tourette's syndrome, was often highly agitated and uninterested in classroom activities. Simon enthusiastically engaged with digital storytelling, finding it easier to construct self-narratives with the use of images, sounds and music. According to Nilsson, Simon was motivated by the autobiographical aspect of digital storytelling and felt 'heard' when he shared and explained his digital narratives with teachers and peers.

The creative and multimodal aspect of digital storytelling is also welcomed by Althea Scott Nixon (2009) who argues that it expands the category of 'literacy' in a way that allows students more opportunities to learn in 'their own way'. They might, for example, struggle to write a narrative in words, but find effective ways to do so visually (see also Jamissen and Skou 2010). This argument is mirrored in the cultural studies work by Helen Klaebe et al. (2007) who argue that digital storytelling provides ways to engage community members in public storytelling, allowing authentic, agentive selves to be included in public history projects (see also Bromley 2010). The anthropological work of Peter Anton Zoettl (2013) further touches on the ways in which the multimodality aspects of participatory video can bring to the surface new awareness of cultural contexts and encourage confidence in identity formation.

While the ability of digital storytelling to give voice is considered relevant for *all* ordinary people, the literature commonly celebrates its ability to give voice to those people deemed marginalised or silenced in public discourse.[6] Marginalised groups of people discussed in the literature include: migrant groups (see, e.g., Scott Nixon 2009; Wexlar et al. 2011); youth, especially those considered 'at risk' (see Podkalicka and Campbell 2010); members of the LGBTQI+ community (see Borghuis et al. 2010); AIDS sufferers and others with disabilities (see Skouge and Rao 2009; Reed and Hill 2010); religious or ethnic minorities (see Lee-Shoy and Dreher 2009; Reed and Hill 2010); aged members of the society (see Davis 2011); and those in low socio-economic sites or suburbs (Podkalicka and Campbell 2010; Davis 2011).

Many scholars working in education pedagogy or youth development agree that ethnically diverse young people can benefit from sharing stories via digital storytelling. Bernard R. Robin (2006) flags the link between digital storytelling and ethnicity and race specifically when discussing the genre's educational uses in the multicultural classroom. He argues that digital stories that focus on personal narratives provide students with an opportunity to learn about people from different backgrounds, gaining 'an appreciation of the types of hardships faced by fellow classmates' (p. 2). He also suggests that sharing autobiographical experiences through new media shortens the distance between local-born and foreign-born students, encouraging empathy and connection. In turn, digital storytelling is seen to assist teachers in facilitating discussions about issues 'such as race, multiculturalism and [. . .] globalization' (ibid.). Of note is how Robin sees this process as providing foreign students with ways to negotiate some of the emotional, familial issues which emerge from sharing their experiences; that is, as providing an outlet to speak and ease some of the tensions of being Other. It is worth mentioning that Robin does not expand on this point, nor on his earlier one regarding the hardships experienced by foreign-born students, which ultimately suggests that all culturally diverse people have some hardship or emotional issues pertaining to their identities. Well-intentioned commentary no doubt, but, as seen in many multicultural studies and programmes, it reads as if all culturally diverse people can be delineated as a unified group with homogenous experiences.

Emily Wexlar Love et al. (2011) report their findings on a research project which examined the impact digital storytelling had on a group of ESL teenagers in the United States. The scholars developed a project in which university students worked with teenage students attending an English-speaking school to create digital stories about their particular experiences. The project grew out of research which indicated that North American youth are commonly the subject of negative stereotyping, an occurrence amplified if the youth are culturally or linguistically diverse (CLDY). The project aimed to counter these negative stereotypes by providing an avenue for the CLDY to 'find their voices' – an aim concluded to have been met (p. 98). Andrea Quijada and Jessica Collins (2009, p. 165) similarly illustrate that standard curricula in New Mexico do not provide space to address adequately 'marginalized young people and their respective communities' and assume all students have uniform learning styles and needs. Quijada and Collins's

---

6. This sets up an interesting paradox, in which people identified as 'other than ordinary' become the target group for an 'ordinary' storytelling practice.

research thus explores media frameworks that allow marginalised members of communities to build, create and exchange knowledge. Such work is added to by James R. Skouge and Kavita Rao (2009), Amber Reed and Amy Hill (2010) and Karen Rodríguez (2010) whose works attempt to use digital storytelling in the classroom to tell authentic, everyday stories of culturally diverse youth, and counter common misunderstandings of cultural minorities.

The approach to voice in classroom-based digital storytelling is paralleled in the literature that discusses digital storytelling in reference to culturally diverse communities at large. Darcy Alexandra (2008), Sarah Copeland and Clodagh Miskelly (2010), Dylan Davis (2011), Higgins (2011), Tiffany Lee-Shoy (2009) and Rosalie Rolón-Dow (2011) all begin their digital storytelling work based on the premise that the genre will give voice to culturally diverse members of the communities they work in; a premise also driving the book *Digital Storytelling: Form and Content* (2017), edited by Mark Dunford and Tricia Jenkins.

Alexandra's (2008) research, for example, examines ways that digital storytelling can be successfully used to provide a platform for undocumented migrants in Dublin, allowing them to share their experiences with others and feel less hidden or invisible. In an Australian context, Lee-Shoy and Dreher (2009) and Davis (2011) work in Sydney/Eora and Melbourne/Naarm, respectively, on digital storytelling projects aimed at allowing culturally diverse community members to both counter and/or add to mainstream media messages and community meta-narratives. This voice-oriented approach also appears in US-based Higgins's (2011) exploration of digital storytelling in culturally divided Cyprus, research that has links to Reed and Hill's (2010) digital storytelling project in East Cape, South Africa (see also Lovvorn 2011; Rolón-Dow 2011; and Hancox 2012).

The majority of the literature suggests that the ability for digital storytelling to enable voice for culturally diverse people is enhanced by the medium's simultaneous ability to build capacity. 'Capacity' here refers to the possession of skills that enables further learning, contact and critical engagement within social contexts. A common argument is that by following the digital storytelling methodology, participants practice technology-based tasks while simultaneously developing research, planning and interpersonal skills (see Copeland and Miskelly 2010; Podkalicka and Campbell 2010; Reed and Hill 2010).

Capacity building is an obvious justification for its increasing popularity in education curricula, but it is also used to petition for the use of digital storytelling in community development work. Those working with marginalised communities argue that the digital storytelling process allows storytellers to not only find their voice but also practically implement it. Burgess (2006, pp. 209–10) summarises this when she writes that digital storytelling mobilises literacies that 'cross the divide between formal and informal learning', comprising learned skills such as computer usage and the ability to construct an effective narrative, with the more familiar modes such as collecting and arranging texts (like scrapbooking) and telling an effective story (as learned in daily social interaction). It is a process of 'remediation' that allows everyday experiences to be transformed into a shared public culture: 'creativity in the service of effective social communication' (p. 210). Several authors discuss this transfer of learned skills into public sharing. Wexlar Love et al. (2011) describe how producing digital stories enables migrant minorities to acquire 'authentic language', as they practice speaking, listening, writing and reading in English alongside their first languages. In turn, digital storytelling is seen to give them the confidence to speak more often in their daily lives.

Scott Nixon's (2009) study found that migrant students' digital stories often researched social issues that they saw impacting on their own communities, such as domestic violence. They then creatively interpreted these issues and imagined possible solutions to them. This process was seen to build the students' 'sociocritical consciousness', which could then be applied in real-life settings (p. 72). Similarly, Reed and Hill (2010) argue that the digital storytelling process gave marginalised youth skills in computer usage and public speaking, providing them new avenues to advocate for their needs beyond the project. Jamissen and Skou (2010, p. 183) found that because the creation of digital stories is a mostly shared process with a final screening, participants were motivated to ensure they could feel proud of their stories. The skills acquired in digital storytelling are thus frequently linked to the capacity to act and feel like a legitimate member of society.

Key issues of digital storytelling

These positive aspects of digital storytelling are troubled by some studies that draw attention to a few underlying problems. The issues of digital storytelling identified in the literature can be grouped into four main categories: (1) timeframe of the production process; (2) flexibility of the digital storytelling model; (3) skills transfer; and (4) identity construction.

Many authors flag a problem with the intensified nature of the digital storytelling workshop model, suggesting that it can prevent participation and restrict meaningful creations. Indeed, in a lot of studies, researchers altered this aspect of the digital storytelling process, allowing the workshops to be spread out over a number of weeks, or even months (Watkins and Russo 2009; Copeland and Miskelly 2010; Podkalicka and Campbell 2010; Rodríguez 2010; Davis 2011, pp. 530–34; Wexlar Love et al. 2011; Hancox 2012).

Often associated with the time-frame criticism is a concern about the general flexibility of the digital storytelling model, in terms of how rigidly or otherwise the methodological steps outlined by the StoryCenter should be followed. Again, many scholars suggest that a pliable digital storytelling process produces more meaningful results (Scott Nixon 2009; Raimist et al. 2010; Reed and Hill 2010; Rodríguez 2010; Davis 2011; Vivienne 2011; Hancox 2012; Kaaire 2012; Vivienne and Burgess 2013). Some authors, such as Donna Hancox (2012), argue that adhering to the genre's steps can sometimes be impossible. Hancox's project involved working with Aboriginal and Torres Strait Islander peoples on personal trauma narratives. She found various aspects of the digital storytelling process inappropriate for the cultural setting. In fact, many of the project's participants refused to participate in the Story Circle sharing and diverged from the standard narrative structures and images of digital storytelling. Hancox's project is an excellent example of the complexity of community-based work and the necessity of remaining self-reflexive as a facilitator. Allowing the process to move in slightly different directions produced for Hancox more meaningful results:

In the end, Simon created the most honest and searing portrayal of his life possible with the tools. But more importantly, the viewer is left with an impression, an echo of how Simon remembers his life. Rather than watching a narrative telling us about his life, the viewer instead experiences Simon's memories and, perhaps, a brief glimpse into the suffering and grief he continues to endure. Thus, the story he created was more a digital process (of remembering, sharing, and even healing) than a digital product. (p. 71)

The same can be said for Vivienne (2011), who facilitated digital storytelling with a group of South Australians identifying as transgender. The way the trans-storytellers used digital storytelling tropes was, according to Vivienne, 'divergent and complicated', variations that ultimately led to stronger storytelling (p. 50).

In contrast to the oft-cited argument of capacity building, some authors claim that the transfer of skills remains unachieved. Davis (2011, p. 539), for example, argues that while up-skilling participants in usable technology is a 'central tenet' of the digital story-telling model, his years of working with the genre had yet to achieve this. Davis is a university lecturer at Melbourne's/Naarm's Swinburne University. In one of his classes he teaches his media students digital storytelling; they then work with elderly members of local communities to develop intergenerational stories. The project has been running for a number of years and is always adapted according to the previous years' outcomes. Yet, so far it has not had much success in transferring the media literacy skills to the elderly community members.

Another interesting point regarding skills transfer has been raised by Anne M. Bjørgen (2010) in her classroom use of digital storytelling. She has observed that while some students find the use of multimodal literacy engaging and excel at digital storytelling, introduction of the new media to those unfamiliar with it can further ostracise marginalised students (pp. 171–72). This contrast can be linked to a socio-economic background that restricts access to technology at home. For students from such backgrounds, new media technology can present a formidable challenge, compounded by having to work alongside students versed in digital literacy and who leap ahead. Despite the romanticised notion of digital spaces being removed from the material realities of everyday life, it is, as Lisa Nakamura (2002, 2007) has well examined in her studies of race and online spaces, a continuation of real life, not a clean break from it; in Henry Jenkin's (2006, p. 3) words, 'not all [digital] participants are created equal'. Bjørgen (2010, p. 172) observes that the introduction of the digital storytelling model causes some students to withdraw further from the social setting.

Finally, some authors point to issues with the ways in which identity is framed by the traditional digital storytelling model. Aneta Podkalicka and Craig Campbell (2010) argue that there are reductionist features of the digital storytelling genre, namely, its use of human rights discourse that claims 'identity recognition' for all participants (see also Hartley and McWilliam 2009, pp. 14–15; Watkins and Russo 2009). The focus on the self in the digital storytelling process is considered to aid identity recognition, though, as Podkalicka and Campbell (2010) argue, creating a 'me' narrative sometimes has adverse effects for the participants. In their work with 'at-risk' youth, they found some participants responded in more positive ways when they were able to 'talk about something else' rather than themselves (p. 8). Often, being able to create a digital story on a different subject saw the participating youth reach out to others to formulate collaborative, creative works, reducing the pressure to 'be' a certain way and ultimately giving them a greater sense of agency as an active member of a larger community. Hancox's (2012, p. 70) project with Aboriginal and Torres Strait Islander peoples also came to a similar conclusion, finding that although narratives that embodied disconnections and uncertainty resulted in digital stories that did not look or sound conventional, the meaning of these stories was far greater for the storytellers and ultimately their 'audience' (see also Rodríguez 2010; Vivienne 2011; Vivienne and Burgess 2013). I explore an example of an unexpected multicultural narrative in Chapter Seven.

'Not migrant enough': Problems in migrant digital storytelling

The four key issues that surface in the literature warrant further exploration, especially since the literature on digital storytelling often focuses on minority ethnic groups and is produced mainly within a white, Western framework. The vast majority of the literature is written from an Australian, North American or UK context. Where it does feature in other geographical contexts it is usually in Western Europe (see Kaaire 2012) or in developing parts of the world as belonging to Western-based projects/social interventions (see Zoettl 2013). These patterns are hardly surprising given the roots of digital storytelling. Nonetheless, it is troubling to witness a high practice rate of digital storytelling and little critical work on how this practice implicates notions of ethnicity and race, notions that so frequently backdrop the projects.[7]

Perhaps one of the main reasons for this gap is the general lack of critical examination of the genre *itself*, as a mode through which certain norms are deployed. The positive claims of digital storytelling are rarely contextualised in a rigorous theoretical framework, and explorations of suggested limitations or concerns are yet to be widely carried out. In many cases, the optimistic understanding of digital storytelling acts as an immediate assumption or beginning point. Richard Bromley (2010, p. 10), for example, asserts early in his study: 'what distinguishes digital storytelling is the way in which it challenges traditional notions of region and community'. This point acts as a framework for his analysis, rather than as a hypothesis to be tested. Similarly, Sarah Copeland and Clodagh Miskelly's (2010, p. 194) introduction of digital storytelling simultaneously functions as the justification for using it in community-based work: 'Given the capacity of the CDS model (Lambert 2006) to be empowering to participants and to cross boundaries, it [digital storytelling] became central to the design of the intervention.' As this statement exemplifies, assumptions about digital storytelling are often based on the founding literature of Lambert, which is problematic since he designed the model and

---

7. As Tiffany Lee-Shoy, in conversation with Tanja Dreher (2009, p. 55), alludes to: how can we think about digital storytelling in narrative structures that are not Western? For Lee-Shoy, who works as a community development officer for Sydney's/Eora's Fairfield district, digital storytelling allows intercultural understandings of minority ethnicities, such as Khmer identity. Lee-Shoy feels it unfortunate, however, that to date she has been unable to utilise narrative forms and storytelling traditions of Khmer identity in the digital storytelling projects.

defined it as inherently enabling and positive. Other scholars that *start* their work with the assumption that digital storytelling is an enabling text include Jessica Fries-Gaither (2010), Rodríguez (2010), James R. Skouge and Kavita Rao (2009) and, to some extent, Jamissen and Skou (2010).

Compounding the assumptive quality of a lot of digital storytelling work is the way in which the genre engenders certain behaviours as commendable. Underlying the discussions about digital storytelling as a 'tool' for voice is, after all, a notion of performance. Digital storytelling can be read in many of the texts as a behavioural tool that optimises, facilitates and negotiates participants' performances. The literature emerging from education disciplines most frequently points to the productive ways the genre can guide behaviour in particular settings. These researchers commend digital storytelling for its ability to activate students' awareness of cultural difference and teach them how to adjust their actions accordingly. Skouge and Rao (2009, p. 55) are explicit about the performance aspect, arguing that the different modes of engagement that digital storytelling incorporates can help build 'civic responsibility'. They expand: 'An essential aspect of digital stories resides in the power of example – the power, that is, to project images of exemplary individuals who can influence other people and make a difference in their lives' (ibid.). It is not made clear what terms like 'exemplary individual' or 'civic responsibility' refer to, but it goes without saying that these agendas will impact the participants' digital storytelling process and their performance in this setting. Instilling responsibility or social performance etiquette is further illustrated by Grete Jamissen and Goro Skou (2010, p. 187), who use digital storytelling to train health students at the University of Oslo, in particular to teach them how to behave in culturally diverse contexts.

In other settings, the framing of performance in digital storytelling is conveyed more subtly, for example, by encouraging participants to use particular images or narrative forms. Alexandra's (2008) project encourages participants to use personal images, despite concerns about anonymity, explaining that they would 'more powerfully elucidate these stories' and lend 'proof' to their narrative performances. Given these subtle pressures, it is hardly surprising that one participant in Alexandra's project changed his digital story at the last minute, feeling it wasn't 'migrant enough' (p. 106). It becomes clear that participants undergo certain forms of behavioural 'shaping' when producing the voice of digital stories, an aspect that I address in detail in Part Two of this book. At the same time, it is clear that how and why this voice and performance are produced is mostly overlooked.

Theo Hug's (2012) article 'Storytelling – EDU: Educational – Digital – Unlimited?' speaks to my concern that current digital storytelling literature overlooks some of the key or, in Hug's term, 'basic critical issues' (p. 20) that the genre gives rise to. Hug provides an excellent account of digital storytelling through the lens of education and literacy, but pauses early in the article to note: 'In view of the rapid proliferation of concepts and practices of digital storytelling it seems acceptably [lit] to step back for a moment and look, how stories about digital storytelling are being told' (p. 17). After summarising some of the main forms of literature on digital storytelling, he too recognises that much of it fails to 'step back'.

Of particular interest for Hug is how the literature refers to digital storytelling as a type of toolkit, involving the circulation of associated words such as 'knowledge transfer' and 'education distribution' (pp. 19–21). Use of this terminology raises immediate concerns for Hug pertaining to Foucauldian notions of discipline and surveillance, in particular, Foucault's theory of 'technologies of the self'.[8]

For Hug, the ways in which we associate narrative with truth raises a critical ethical question. He writes, 'This is not just about orientation, moral judgement and enjoyment, about factual or desirable limitations of the instrumentalization of storytelling, or about blurrings of local or global public and private spheres – this is also about the basic question of storytelling as "truth-telling" ' (p. 21). Hug argues the political urges of digital storytelling projects are often hidden and need to be brought forth (ibid.). He asks: how is power organised within the context of digital storytelling projects? Hug urges scholars to remain critically aware of the way any movement towards 'truth' or knowledge sharing in digital storytelling is always a movement towards *a particular* truth and knowledge. As such he is wary of the genre's frequent use of the term 'self-determination' and suggests 'self-organisational' might be more useful (p. 22). These concerns are taken up at length in Part Two, which examines the types of truth claims made in digital stories about multicultural subjects and the nation at large.

Alternative readings of digital storytelling

In order to carry out this critical work, I draw on the handful of scholars who are rigorously engaging with digital storytelling in cultural studies or the social sciences. In addition to Theo Hug, Australian scholars Jean Burgess, Tanja Dreher, Anna Poletti and Sonja Vivienne examine digital storytelling with a view to consider not only the type of voice that gets enabled but the type of listening that occurs in response. Their work considers who gets to provide voice, how and – importantly – to what end (Burgess 2006). I add to their examinations by suggesting that in digital stories pertaining to ethnicity, the end pursued is a material one, inextricably linked to normative discourses of whiteness.

Australian media and cultural studies scholar Tanja Dreher considers how race is tied up with notions of 'voice'. Working from a political theory perspective, Dreher (2009, 2012) has urged media studies to interrogate notions of 'voice' and the ways in which it detracts from listening. She argues that emphasising process in media democratising movements does not necessarily 'challenge overall inequalities in how voice is valued, nor the unequal distribution of voice as a value within mainstream media and policy settings' (Dreher 2012, p. 159). Further, the issues behind politicised stories are often not meaningfully or productively discussed (p. 163). For Dreher, an inquiry into the 'politics of

---

8. Foucault (1988, p. 18) defines technologies of the self as the various 'operations on their own bodies and souls, thoughts, conduct, and way of being' that people undertake in the pursuit of a 'state of happiness, purity, wisdom, perfection, or immortality'. His earlier work outlined a genealogy of these technologies, focusing in particular on the practices of confession and 'truth telling' as a means of self-discipline that inevitably produced what he terms 'docile bodies' (Foucault 1977, 1978).

voice' is vital, involving the destabilisation of media conventions at all levels – in everyday spaces like digital storytelling, as well as in mainstream spaces.[9]

A prime example of why Dreher's argument is so crucial is evidenced in Pauline Borghuis et al.'s (2010) article 'Digital Storytelling in Sex Education: Avoiding the Pitfalls of Building a "Haram" Website'. The article reports on a Netherlands-based digital storytelling project developed by the authors to be used for sex education. The rationale for the project was that sex education in schools and complementary websites was not appropriate for migrant groups, especially the high number of Turkish and Moroccan youth in Holland. Islam was the main religion practiced by the target group, and the authors argued that the religion acted as a cultural barrier to sex education and made the youth vulnerable to sex issues (p. 236). They considered it their 'responsibility to contribute to the emancipation of Muslim youngsters' (ibid.). While the authors had well-meaning intentions, the drive for the project clearly came from a white, Western set of beliefs. The authors acknowledged their position as 'three middle-aged white women' and yet argued that the project was not in any way linked to questions of race or ethnicity but was relevant only to gender norms: 'A second danger in this project would be to either act or be perceived as "voyeurs", hoping to exoticize "oriental Others" [. . .] But this project has nothing to do with either voyeurism or colonialism [. . .] it is an old-fashioned feminist project' (ibid.). They claimed that their work had no impact or relevance to colonialism in spite of their later discussions of how they learned, as facilitators, to structure their sex-education narratives according to the *ethnic* community in question. Adding to this, the authors noted the importance of having Turkish and Moroccan voices to work on the project directly. They explained, 'We were lucky to have our multicultural aware students at hand. Without them, it would have been far more difficult to achieve the current level of authenticity in the stories' (p. 243). The project clearly deployed certain notions of ethnicity and cultural difference – and it is impossible to project an idea of multicultural voices or ethnic needs without simultaneously

---

9. I hold some concerns, however, about the politics of recognition that is utilised in Dreher's work, and some others who investigate digital storytelling from a political science perspective (see, e.g., Grossman and O'Brien 2011). Dreher (2009) uses the work of Nancy Fraser, Axel Honneth and Judith Butler in conjunction with one another, suggesting that they each approach identity politics in the same way. Fraser and Butler are, however, in an ongoing debate about identity recognition. Fraser (1989, 1997) frequently criticises Butler's use of theory as groundless, arguing that it lacks potential for legitimate political action. Dreher's reliance on Fraser is concerning because Fraser continues to enact the Master-Slave dialectic in her work. The Master-Slave dialectic, as developed through Hegel, suggests that self-consciousness, or our understanding of ourselves as 'individuals', can come only through the recognition of an Other. Thus, the Master can be a Master only if it is recognised by the Slave, and the Slave will, in turn, recognise itself only in relation to the Master. Spivak (2012, pp. 345–47) critiques Charles Taylor's use of the Master-Slave dialectic in his politics of recognition theory, arguing that the recognition it allows remains implicated in a type of moral duty. (Ultimately, the recognition remains racist, albeit 'good-willed'.) The use of Taylor's and Fraser's political theories may reinstate a binary model that prevents the work from moving beyond an 'us' versus 'them' framework.

making reference to the legacy of colonialism. There are thus some deeply embedded issues with this work pertaining to the ways in which white-centric feminism fails to consider its implicit position of power. To suggest that such a project has nothing to do with colonialism is, in this context, an act of neocolonialism. Even though the digital storytelling project *did* produce some affirmative outcomes for Turkish and Moroccan youth, the ways in which 'voice' and 'listening' functioned at a political level to reinstate normative power structures is troubling.

Encouragingly, some studies examine digital stories in relation to normative structures by using critical race theory (CRT). In a similar fashion to Dreher, Jason F. Lovvorn (2011), Rolón-Dow (2011) and Matias and Grosland (2016) use digital storytelling as a practical way of implementing CRT in everyday life. Such work relies on the argument that racism operates through the production and reinforcement of normative metanarratives. These metanarratives are formed on the basis of white privilege and become the overarching historical story for nations and – because they are projected and reiterated so relentlessly – come to be seen as the founding truth of that nation. CRT attempts to deconstruct metanarratives of racialisation that have become embedded within organising structures in society – law, education, capital flows, public policy and so forth.

Lovvorn (2011, p. 97) argues that digital storytelling has three key characteristics that help to effectively spread alternative stories in society and, therefore, destabilise normative metanarratives. First, digital stories are mobile, moving beyond organisations and becoming circulated on the internet, where they are uploaded, streamed, played and forwarded. Second, they are personal, having the ability to 'relate stories of the self in distinctive voices'. Third, they are connective, in that the narrations of the self help to create attachments between the author and the larger social world.

The work is important, but once again in danger of assuming the mode of digital storytelling to be external to the reproduction of racialised metanarratives. Even Matias and Grosland's (2016) brilliant pedagogical use of digital storytelling in education settings begins with an assumption of the neutrality of digital storytelling (via Rolón-Dow [2011] and others). Their work cleverly utilises digital stories to redirect the onus of learning about whiteness and race onto white (rather than non-white) teaching candidates; however, the assumption that digital stories entail critical reflection by the narrator underlies the work (Matias and Grosland 2016, p. 156, 160). I suspect that the critical reflection occurring in the digital stories created under Matias and Grosland's guidance has more to do with their deft skills regarding the teaching of race. As seen earlier, and as Blum-Ross (2015) and Literat et al. (2018) highlight, the facilitator or intermediary of digital participation projects has a far greater impact on their final outcomes than is often acknowledged. Digital storytelling in and of itself does not lead to critical reflection of race.

Furthermore, while the presence and power of metanarratives cannot be denied, the deployment of whiteness also occurs in micronarratives, in the margins themselves. Frantz Fanon's *Black Skin, White Masks* (2008) effectively demonstrates the ways in which false ideas about black persons become part of the collective unconscious, allowing racism to continue in a thoughtless, everyday manner. More than that, Fanon demonstrates that these false, negative projections embed themselves within the black person's subconscious and are consequently lived by the black body as a material reality.

I thus depart somewhat from the CRT-based work by closely examining how whiteness and the negative projection of non-whiteness infiltrate bodies in a way that is both macro and micro/public and private. Following Butler (2009, p. 161), any form of multiculturalism or culturally diverse project that seeks 'a certain kind of subject' actually goes some way towards instituting 'that conceptual requirement as part of its description and diagnosis'. In both cases, there is a sense of 'who' the culturally diverse subject is. In that sense, we must question: 'What formations of subjectivity, what configurations of lifeworlds, are effaced or occluded' within these projects (ibid.)?

Conclusion

Digital storytelling is conventionally defined as a narrative-based, new media genre that utilises home photography, video and a voice-over to emotively present a first-person story in a hyper-short film format. For the purposes of this book, I define two main types of digital stories: individual digital stories and collaborative digital stories. Individual stories refer to the conventional digital story, in which individuals join members of the public to produce a short, two- to five-minute digital story. The story tells a personal experience in the author's own voice and includes private photographs and/or home videos. Collaborative digital stories refer to digital stories that are created by a community group over a relatively longer time period. These stories tend to be much longer and combine the artistic outputs created in sequential workshops into a more abstract interpretation of the community.

The digital storytelling genre has its roots in the StoryCenter in California but has also proliferated in Australia, Canada, the United States and the United Kingdom in the past decade. The literature on digital storytelling is consequently produced mainly within a Western framework. What is interesting, however, is that the scholarship continues to focus on the genre's ability to serve as a 'tool' for the democratisation of media and community narratives, despite the different cultural contexts and settings in which digital storytelling is now being utilised.

A significant portion of the scholarship discusses the genre as an enabling medium for marginalised peoples, including migrants, people with health and disability issues, ethnic and religious minorities, women, LGBTQI+ persons and people from a low socio-economic bracket. However, only a small proportion of the scholarship critically examines the ways in which the genre is *itself* entangled within discursive regimes that ultimately impact the storytellers and the stories produced. An even smaller proportion examines the operation of racialised norms within the medium, despite ethnic minorities frequently acting as the genre's target group.

It becomes clear that digital storytelling and everyday multiculturalism are guided by similar aims and principles in their approaches to cultural difference. The similarities can be grouped into three main characteristics: (1) the attempt to 'bridge a gap' between the ordinary person and the institution; (2) the attempt to tell unheard/marginalised stories and share different perspectives; and (3) the attachment to and use of the notion of a culturally diverse society. These similarities make digital storytelling a useful point of entry into thinking about how notions of multiculturalism and cultural diversity manifest in Australia and comparable nations.

Chapter Three

MEETING IN THE MIDDLE: A THEORETICAL FRAMEWORK

A cross-comparison of digital storytelling and everyday multiculturalism reveals that the two phenomena are guided by similar aims and principles pertaining to the value of shared, diverse experiences. In a way, the pattern in migrant digital storytelling seems symptomatic of the drive towards cultural difference that occurred in the early part of the century, following identity politics debates. Scholars and practitioners alike are drawn to digital storytelling's capacity to express cultural difference at a 'grassroots' level; however, they often move ahead too quickly into empirical discussions of the technology, before asking critical questions of the genre itself. In this way, many of the problems inherent in art practice pertaining to cultural diversity are reinstated.

I attempt in this book to create a pause before this moving ahead – to consider how we might carve out critical spaces in both digital storytelling and everyday multiculturalism as a way to deconstruct cultural difference more productively. So far, I have argued that there is a need to analyse the corporeal manifestations of multicultural life, in particular to consider how discursive regimes construct bodies in twenty-first century Australia and elsewhere according to long-standing conceptions of race. I have also highlighted the tendency in everyday multiculturalism scholarship to analyse multicultural experiences as belonging to one of two separate spheres: the institutional/theoretical or the ordinary/street. Often, scholars study this 'street level' as a means of providing what is considered to be a genuine reflection of everyday cultural encounters. A similar tendency is prolific in digital storytelling scholarship. As a community-based arts practice, digital storytelling is often considered to be removed from the political pressures of mass-produced media or art practice and thus implies an authenticity – as if the genre is a conduit through which the real voices of the marginalised can be expressed.

Everyday multiculturalism must be broadened to include a closer attentiveness to the ways in which everydayness and institutional spaces are interrelated. Although it is important to maintain a focus on the messy middle section of multicultural life (where everyday practices and formalised encounters interact), deliberately trying to fill in a perceived gap between the everyday and the systemic could be counterproductive in deconstructing the racialised body.

I wish, instead, to analyse contemporary formations of multiculturalism in a manner that resists the inclination to posit the institutional and the everyday as distinct arenas of cultural production. Resisting this tendency means analysing digital storytelling as a node of cultural articulation, as an opening 'through which one enters into the context'

(Grossberg 2010a). In this instance, the context is the messy entanglement of public multiculturalism discourses and private everyday encounters.

Chas Crichter, Tony Jefferson, John Clarke and Brian Roberts (1978, cited in Grossberg 2010a, p. 26) emphasise the need to remain aware of the context or 'background' in cultural studies work. This background – or conjuncture, as later termed by Hall – informs the object of study but is often left vague and abstract in analyses. This oversight occurs despite the fact that the background 'is precisely the context which constitutes any possible object of study' (ibid.). When analysing an object of study, especially one like digital storytelling which claims to be everyday, there is a danger that focusing on it will 'displace the context as the real object of concern and investigation' (ibid.). In this case, the analysis could follow other scholars by examining the digital storytelling genre and considering how it represents everydayness. However, in performing this task alone, the attention is misdirected from what precedes and facilitates the productive power of digital storytelling, notably, the normative force deployed by the notion of the everyday, the very 'everyday' digital storytelling claims to reveal. There is a risk, in other words, of performing what Foucault (1978, p. 159) terms an 'ironic deployment' when undertaking this analysis.

How can digital storytelling be used as a way to offer a new understanding of the context? Or, in this case, how can the genre be used to examine the various ways in which racialisation formulates and infiltrates everyday life? To begin, it surely requires a theoretical framework that allows the private and public aspects of subject formation to cross over. The framework I offer henceforth blends three theoretical tools: Foucault's notion of apparatuses of security, Butler's theory of performativity, and affect theory that focuses on the notion of affective economies. The case study analysis in Parts Two and Three will move across these three optics in order to capture the relationships between institutional and everyday power and the power relations of the so-called gap. This movement provides a useful picture of how the material subject is constructed in digital stories according to both public and private discourses of multiculturalism. Further, it provides an avenue for considering the material possibilities available to the 'culturally diverse Australian' in community-based arts.

Multiculturalism as an apparatus of security

The concepts of biopolitics and apparatus of security (AoS) as developed by Michel Foucault provide a useful theoretical frame for analyses of multiculturalism. Most of Foucault's work is preoccupied with developing the notion of disciplinary power, in particular, the ways in which the subject or body is compelled to discipline itself in accordance with certain societal norms. In the *Collège de France lectures* (1975–76), Foucault begins to productively expand the notion of disciplinary power to connect with a broader State power, which he terms 'biopolitics'. This expansion is not, as some critics have suggested,[1] an abandonment of his earlier work, but rather an extension of it into a

---

1. For example, Nancy Fraser (1989, 1997).

more robust understanding of power. Such an understanding accounts for the individual, mundane instances of power alongside and imbricated within the collective, formalised instances of power. In this framework, the human compels itself to become a subject via disciplinary power, but it also becomes an active element of civil society at large by means of the power exercised through biopolitics.

Foucault's biopolitics emerges from his analysis of race struggle. While his study is not a direct attempt to trace racism per se, it inevitably leads him to do so, thus forming the most significant account of racism in his scholarship. Foucault's (2003, p. 258) claim that 'the actual roots of racism' stem from race struggle is useful for thinking about Australian discourses of multiculturalism, ethnicity and cultural diversity; in particular, the strategies of racialisation that haunt these discourses.

Foucault begins by mapping the way race struggle was harnessed and reutilised by the State at the end of the nineteenth century in order to maintain power. He argues that towards the end of this era a turn to class struggle (via Marxism) was threatening to take over all claims to State truth and power, consequently threatening to usurp the sovereignty of the State (p. 80). Emerging simultaneously with this threat of class struggle was a new scientific discourse operating in the West to classify biologically all objects and beings in the world. This scientific discourse became a tool that the State was able to deploy as a new counterhistory: a 'biologico-medical perspective' that ultimately led to 'the appearance of what will become actual racism' (ibid.). This 'actual racism' takes on a particular function for the State, leading Foucault to term it 'state racism'. The discourse of race struggle – originally 'a weapon to be used against the sovereign' – is appropriated by the sovereign (p. 81). With the aid of science, the State is able to deploy a discourse of race that classifies human beings, coding them with certain characteristics that determine their so-called race. In this manner, the State can 'recode the old counterhistory not in terms of class, but in terms of races – races in the biological and medical sense of that term', consequently turning the race struggle weapon 'against those who had forged it' (pp. 80–81).

Foucault argues that State racism emerges as a tactic for the sovereign to continue claiming his legitimacy as the holder of the right to life and death and in order to pursue the colonial project (p. 258). For colonialism to succeed, it was imperative for colonising states to establish a break in 'the domain of life that is under power's control: the break between what must live and what must die' (p. 254). The State had become accountable for its right to decide the life and death of subjects under its control. Thus, as Foucault describes, the State could no longer simply eradicate those who stood in the way of the colonial enterprise by its will alone, although colonialism could not succeed unless the colonisers were able to eliminate those it intended to colonise. The State consequently appealed to racism, using the 'themes of evolutionism' to justify its killing (p. 257). In particular, States used science to create a 'biological continuum of humans', which listed races from strongest to weakest, best to worst (p. 254).

Foucault's work is here analogous to Edward Said's work in *Orientalism* (1978), which describes how colonial discourse is strategically linked to nature by 'the West' in order to racialise people living in 'the East'. As Said explains, colonial discourse creates 'the Orient' – an objectified subject placed in a lowly position against what is inscribed as a superior, white ontological position, 'a concrete way of being in the world' (p. 62). Colonial discourse draws on Darwinism to order human beings and legitimate the order through Western science and coding systems. In short, it constructs a hierarchy that is able to identify those subjects that deserve to die in order to create those subjects that deserve to flourish. The death of the Other can then be sold as a way of creating a healthier and more natural life for the 'rightful' species: only by erasing the 'weaker' races can the colonizing race – the 'superior' race – proliferate (Foucault 2003, p. 255). Foucault writes: 'The more inferior species die out, the more abnormal individuals are eliminated, the fewer degenerates there will be in the species as a whole, and the more I – as species rather than individual – can live, the stronger I will be, the more vigorous I will be' (ibid.). By creating this biologically sanctioned relationship between 'our life' and 'their death', State racism henceforth orchestrates the elimination of certain people in a strategic way. Namely, the State exercises a new method of power that gets applied to human beings as a whole, described by Foucault as a ' "biopolitics" of the human race' (p. 243). Biopolitics introduces normalising techniques such as 'forecasts, statistical estimates and overall measures' (p. 246) to 'affirm' a certain race as the 'rightful' holder of sovereignty. Those that do not fit the calculated average, or that present disturbances to the scientific equilibrium, are defined as less human and targeted as a threat that must be eradicated for the good of the State. By employing scientific rationalisations, the eradication of the impure race can be carried out in a 'non-militant' fashion, for example, through careful management of 'the rate of reproduction, the fertility of a population [. . .] the birth rate, the mortality rate' (p. 243, 255). Regulating these rates increases 'the risk of death for some people' and can also allow for 'political death, expulsion' and 'rejection' (pp. 255–56). These measures do not enact a physical murder but a subjective one; they persecute a person from the domain of what Butler (2004) calls 'livable life', all under the guise of 'optimiz[ing] a state of life' (Foucault 2003, p. 246).

Biopolitics adds useful weight to the understanding of race as a construct, by tracing in detail how this construction gets tailored according to various State strategies to retain power. Foucault's analysis of how State racism can kill through strategic, subjective means is pertinent for contemporary multicultural countries such as Australia, which often deem racism to be 'behind them', largely because physical killing of 'races' (arguably) no longer occurs. Under a biopolitical framework, however, we can consider how struggles continue to occur between subjects who have become racialised by a science originally formulated for the so-called good of the majority of people. Or, in Hage's (2017a, p. 67) framing, how a 'colonial society tries to disavow the savage grounds on which it rejuvenates itself by distancing itself from those who have to be more savage than they are'.

Managerial multiculturalism can be read as an AoS that enacts certain measures in order to streamline cultural diversity and possibly undermine the needs of migrant communities. As outlined, multiculturalism has a complex history in Australia that has rendered ethnic people and their rights visible while also reinstating ethnicity as separate and Other to white Australia. Hage's *White Nation* (1998) examines how Australian multiculturalism has enabled a space for migrant culture, but only as a space that exists *for* white Australia. Using Bourdieu, Hage describes how migrant culture acquires 'a different *mode of existence* to Anglo-Celtic culture' (p. 121; italics original). The move to cultural diversity in areas such as Australian arts practice has worked to complicate this mode of existence and often for affirmative outcomes. However, it can be argued that the celebration of cultural difference through public programmes (multicultural digital story programmes, for example) is also an AoS in action: these public programmes allow the fluctuating 'ethnic' multiplicities to be controlled as an object of power, acting as one means to the biopolitical end. In this schema, governmental discourses on cultural diversity pose a norm for the 'multicultural/ethnic' person and then compel the body to conform to this norm (according to disciplinary power). Ang and St Louis (2005, p. 292) point to this predicament when, with regard to Australian multiculturalism, they write:

> A key plank of state-led recognition of difference is the policy of multiculturalism, which officially sanctions and enshrines ethnic, linguistic and cultural differences within the encompassing framework of the state. In this administrative-bureaucratic context, difference becomes the cornerstone of diversity: diversity is the managerial view of the field of differences to be harmonized, controlled and made to fit into a coherent (i.e. national) whole by the (nation) state.

The cumulative effect of this is the control of an imagined and manageable multicultural community.

I thus seek to extend Hage's (1998) notion of multiculturalism as a technology of the 'national body'. Hage argues that 'rather than being imagined as an essential part of the national body, multiculturalism is imagined as an object performing a function for that body' (p. 150). In other words, multiculturalism, or ethnic difference, becomes that which is 'taken on' by what remains an essentially white national will (p. 149). He goes on to consider how multiculturalism's subject – the migrant or ethnic Australian – becomes an essential element of the national body: it is an 'exterior object' but still 'an interior extension' (p. 150).

The following chapters consider in greater depth this latter relationship, in particular, the strategic deployment of individual bodies within the national body through community arts projects, such as digital storytelling. As Michael Lambek and Paul Antze (1996, p. xx) explain, experiences of nationhood and ethnicity are 'linked to popular narratives and ceremonies, which are linked to newspaper accounts and thence to official histories, museums, boundary disputes, and sponsored ceremonies, which are linked to theories propounded by historians, political scientists and other experts. The writer of the "simple" life history often unintentionally reproduces the assumptions and biases contained in these links'. The digital story is a 'simple' life history of an ordinary Australian, but this ultimately feeds into the imagined community of Australia. In her analysis of the 'Demidenko affair', Gunew (2004, p. 76) further supports this, noting that ethnicity 'conceived as minority or apprentice national subject-in-process, is always a performance and, significantly [. . .] this performance is framed by a decades-long reception of such "multicultural" texts and subjectivities'.

In the following analysis, I examine how this imagined Australia and thus the AoS of multiculturalism is linked to whiteness. The notion of whiteness employed here draws on that developed in the 1990s – beginning in North America and Europe through scholars Toni Morrison (1992), Ruth Frankenberg (1993) and Richard Dyer (1997), and continuing in an Australian context through the foundational work of Hage (1998) and Aileen Moreton-Robinson (2000). Such work critically analysed the ways in which whites become racialised as the invisible but dominant centre of social and cultural life. Hage (1998, p. 20) argued that whiteness is not a biological fact but a racial position, accumulated through the fantasy of white superiority 'borne out of the history of colonial expansion'. This idea frames the following exploration of how digital stories that focus on 'cultural diversity' in Australia animate scripts of ethnicity that reinforce or destabilise the dominant discourse of whiteness. In this way, the analysis follows John T. Warren's (2003, p. 20) argument that studies on whiteness ought to cease placing 'identity in the materiality of [...] bodies', or on the 'fact' of the subject's whiteness. Instead, they should explore how subjects 'use or site a discourse that works to promote and maintain white privilege and power', how it is that the materiality of 'race' is coercively produced.

With this in mind, I position the formal, or governmental, notion of Australian multiculturalism as a type of AoS, which organises certain Australians in particular ways. As an AoS, multiculturalism asks: what is the most efficient, economical way of managing ethnic subjects as a *whole*?

Ethnic performativity in digital storytelling

The second theoretical optic utilised in the following case study analysis is Butler's concept of performativity. The addition of this theory is important because power does not create subjects by coercing them from above. Power is certainly exercised through multicultural policies and programmes, but this involves an insidious, disciplinary form of power that works to turn some Australian bodies into an active element of the multicultural nation at large. Utilising AoS in conjunction with performativity avoids the problematic approach to multicultural policy as a 'cause' and the multicultural subject as an 'effect' which plagues many critiques of multiculturalism (Khan 2011, 2015). The analysis adopts Butler's approach to gender/sex in order to interrogate the relationship between ethnicity and race. Specifically, it asks: how does the performance of 'ethnicity' in digital storytelling reinstate the regulatory force of 'race'? The following analysis is guided by this question, in order to examine the ways in which the authors of digital stories are constituted through corporeal acts deemed 'ethnic', and how the persistence of these acts via performativity reinforces racial categories.

Following the work of Gunew in *Haunted Nations: The Colonial Dimensions of Multiculturalisms* (2004), the following analysis of digital stories uses Butler's theory of performativity to trouble the boundaries of the classificatory terms 'multiculturalism', 'ethnicity' and 'cultural diversity'. Gunew interrogates how it is that 'the ethnic' comes to be known in a subjective sense through ethnic discourse, and she also questions how the deployment of this discourse creates and affects bodies in literal and meaningful ways. Gunew suggests that ethnic identity extends beyond a question of subjectivity and culturalism to one of corporeality, interrogating the ways in which the ethnic subject comes to know itself as 'ethnic' at a body-politic level.

Butler (1993, p. 9) develops the theory of performativity using Foucault's idea that the body is an effect of power in which power does not come from an agent, a state of nature or a single act: 'There is no power that acts [. . .] only a reiterated act that is power in its persistence and instability.' Key to the theory of performativity and thus to this book is the argument that the subject does not passively accept and pass on norms, but actively cites and reproduces these normative elements. Power is not an autonomous agent that acts *upon* subjects, but a cumulative force that works *through* discourse: the 'reiteration of a norm or set of norms' that acquire 'an act-like status in the present' and conceal 'the convention of which it is a repetition' (Foucault 1978, p. 155; Butler 1993, p. 12). Butler (1993, p. 19) summarises this when she writes: 'Discourse gains its authority by citing the conventions of authority [. . .] the norm of sex takes hold to the extent that it is cited as such a norm, but it also derives its power through the citations that it compels.' It is this perpetual reiteration propelled through discourse that Butler terms 'performativity', the citational force by which 'discourse produces the effect that it names' (p. 2).

Butler's (1997b, p. 402) theory of performativity emerges from her analysis of the sex/gender dichotomy, which seeks to implement a more radical interpretation of phenomenology's 'doctrine of constitution'. What Butler takes from phenomenology is its focus on 'the mundane' ways individuals 'constitute social reality through language, gestures, and all manner of symbolic social signs' (ibid.). What she rejects, however, is phenomenology's persistent focus on a 'social agent' driving the constitution, opting instead for a Foucault-inspired focus on the subject rather than the individual. In other words, in phenomenological studies, the individual is still considered to be the primary site of agency; a 'beneath' underlies the layers of construction, a 'Self' that acts. What's more, Butler seeks to expand on the theory and use of the term 'acts' to mean both 'that which constitutes meaning and that through which meaning is performed or enacted' (p. 403). Specifically, she aims to examine how the gendered subject 'is constructed through specific corporeal acts'; how the persistent performance of these acts works to create a 'regulatory fiction' that is 'gender'; and, importantly, how a focus on this 'gender fiction' diverts our attention from quite possibly the most blatant regulatory fiction of all – sexual difference (p. 403, 412).

The theory takes particular interest in how this citation of intelligibility gains its momentum at the level of the body, under the 'elegance of the discipline' that Foucault (1977, p. 184) describes. As Foucault stresses: 'For the disciplined man, as for the true believer, no detail is unimportant' (p. 140). For Butler, gender is a series of predetermined possibilities and details – details that are practised and repeated by bodies so incessantly that they materialise as reality. Gender thus becomes an embodied stylisation – 'the mundane way in which bodily gestures, movements, and enactments of various kinds constitute the illusion of an abiding gendered self' (Butler 1997b, p. 402). As Butler summarises, the existing sociality one is born into has created possibilities for the body, but these are performed and materialised by the body so 'one is not simply a body, but, in some very key sense, one does one's body' (p. 404). Gender reality is thus performative in that 'it is real only to the extent that it is performed' (p. 410).

A sexed or gendered identity comes to be performative in that to make a statement such as 'I am a feminine woman' or, indeed, 'I am *not* a feminine woman' requires one to cite the norms of 'femininity' and 'woman-ness'. Citing these norms reinstates not only their authority but also them as the norms that others will be compelled to cite as well. A useful analogy I find for performativity is that of a perpetual baton-relay in which the norm is accepted and passed on from runner to runner (subject-to-subject), inevitably contributing to the 'signifying chain' of identity, whereby the 'political signifier', for example, 'woman', is 'resignified' (Butler 1993, p. 220).

Performing this state of 'realness' is what Butler (1997b, pp. 404–5) refers to as the 'corporeal project' – or the process by which an individual compels its body to 'conform to an historical ideal [. . .] to induce the body to become a cultural sign'. In other words, there are historical possibilities for a 'woman'; norms which one does and norms which through their doing contribute to the 'signifying chain' of 'woman'. Significantly, this doing of the corporeal project – and, in turn, of 'woman' – always returns to the question: am I reflecting my sex or otherwise? If I do not 'do femininity well', some may suggest that I am acting in an 'unnatural' manner, or in a way that is 'untrue' to myself. Others, such as those that argue that gender is construction, would likely say it does not matter how I 'do' my gender; that I can interpret my 'woman-ness' in any way I wish. But, in fact, it does matter, for both lines of argument – even the latter – lead us back to the finite origin of 'sex' (sexual difference), the benchmark for the 'construction' of gendered acts. We thus see that gender discourse needs to position sexual difference as a cause to create the gendered subject and, inevitably, our sense of 'self' – for even when we act in discord to the gendered norm we reaffirm its ties to 'sexual difference'. Butler's argument is shown here to clearly mirror Foucault's (1978, p. 155) claim that it is always 'through sex that each must pass in order to have access to his own intelligibility'. What this means is that there can be no expression of sex through gender that is not a 'further formation' of that sexed body (Butler 1993, p. 10). In fact, there can be no expression of sex at all – only performativity (Butler 1997b, pp. 411–12). We become actors perpetually acting, taking the gendered script as life itself: 'the mundane social audience, including the actors themselves, come to believe and to perform in the mode of belief' (p. 402). Thus, through the corporeal project we dramatise a set of possibilities we believe to be linked to sex (either as reflective or oppositional) into a physicality, and through this process conceal the fact that these possibilities have no actual referent to a 'sex' at all.

The following case study analysis considers how 'multiculturalism' is displayed through various performative actions in digital stories and, further, how these displays embed themselves as everyday. In this way, the analysis has parallels to Stella Bruzzi's (2006) analysis of documentaries as 'performative acts', recently adopted by Smaill (2010, p. 19), who argues that as screen technologies become more advanced, documentary moves further away from the original 'conventions of observational and expository form' and becomes increasingly performative. While this book posits that, like documentary, digital stories are performative acts, it departs somewhat from Smaill's application of Butler's performativity. In particular, it does not see digital storytelling as being more or less performative. It argues, instead, that there is no outside to the performative in the digital story: it is all performative, albeit sometimes less overtly so than others. The analysis in Parts Two and Three assesses how normative or counter-normative the performative is in the production and consumption of the digital storytelling case studies.

Using performativity in this manner adds to the everyday multiculturalism work of Noble and Poynting (2010, p. 502) who are also turning their attention to the 'walking and talking' that occurs *during* the development of subjectivities. In a similar approach, the digital storytelling analysis will consider how it is that we, as creators and consumers of digital stories, are thrust into 'walking and talking' in ways that create particular subjectivities and, importantly, compel us to keep walking and talking them as depictions of 'the everyday'.

Affective economies in digital stories

The third key theory used for the following case study analysis is affective economies. As highlighted in Chapter Two, the subjects performing digital stories are disciplined according to particular methodological steps that aim to ensure the finished product is persuasive and engaging. In order to track the operation and intent of this persuasiveness, the analysis needs to pay attention to bodily 'saying' in the digital stories. This task entails the examination of the discursive elements of the stories – the narrative, the visual aesthetics and the sound components – but it also involves examination of the non-discursive elements, that is, what the assemblage of all the discursive elements *feels* like. As Grossberg (2010a, p. 18) asserts: 'Knowledge always depends on a visceral relevance.' Affect theory provides a methodological tool to examine this visceral relevance of digital storytelling. It also helps to address the intrinsic presence and power of emotions that, as Hug (2012) identifies, is largely overlooked in digital storytelling literature.

I argue that it is via the force of the performative that affect gets propelled into and implicated in certain forms of materiality. Via the analysis in the following section, I offer a new, more specific way to consider the connection of performativity and affect and demonstrate its relevance for projects where identities are (re)articulated. This move follows Gunew's extension of the linguistic model of performativity into the realm of bodily acts. Although predominantly interested in the ways the English language choreographs bodies, Gunew's (2004, p. 12) analysis considers ethnic performativity not merely in relation to spoken language but also to 'bodied language', or 'a repertoire of gestures which indicate belonging, or otherwise'. For Gunew, all 'displays of ethnicity', including but not confined to language, 'might be perceived as performative', and performative for particular desires and audiences (p. 10). Gunew is here pointing to the incorporation of affect in analyses of the performative. She reads Butler's performativity as operating through the speech act. This book's reading of Butler, especially of her later work (2004, 2006, 2008, 2009), suggests that performativity does include these affective elements, although they are not directly labelled as such by Butler until her later work (see 2015). Indeed, it is perhaps because affect is an 'indirect' structure of organisation that this is the case. Like performativity, affect is an energy that gets harnessed and channelled in everyday life and helps to demarcate subjects.

A variety of approaches and definitions of affect have emerged in the past decade. These range from the heavily positivist or biological approaches of psychological and psychoanalytic inquiry to the assemblage work between human and machine as found in cybernetics or the neurosciences (Seigworth and Gregg 2010).[2] Patricia Clough (2007) argues that the use of affect theory in this manner is indicative of a move in critical theory from discipline and representation to control and information; and from questions of production and consumption to the circulation of affect. Generally speaking, this move asks how life itself is being commodified and reorganised, allowing us to begin thinking about how certain bodies are inscribed with affective meaning and ultimately become livable or unlivable. As Clough writes:

> There is a marking of populations – some as valuable life and others as without value. Increasingly it is in these terms that differences such as those of ethnicity, race, gender, class, sexuality and nation are materialized. Some bodies or bodily capacities are derogated making their affectivity superexploitable, or exhaustible unto death, while other bodies or body cap-acities collect the value produced through this derogation and exploitation. (p. 25)

The understanding of affect as both controlled and networked can easily be linked to the Foucauldian framework of power in which power at the level of the body and power at the level of State control is intertwined.

With this in mind, affect is used in this book to broadly describe energy before it becomes matter, that is, the sense of energy one experiences before one is able to put that experience/feeling into words. Affect includes feelings, but it also involves all other forces of energy that move between objects and bodies. Affect is used in this manner to describe the in-between state – that which is moving between objects and bodies but is yet to impose definitive impressions upon either. As Greg Seigworth and Melissa Gregg (2010, p. 14) outline, affect 'arises in the midst of inbetween-ness: in the capacities to act and be acted upon'. They argue that while affect is not necessarily forceful in itself, the study of affect is about forces between bodies, including those subtly deployed. Examining this in-between space is important in digital stories which deliberately work to create a relationship in terms of an implied viewer and narrator or implied author. After all, the digital story utilises a range of techniques to connect the public to an individualised story or experience and vice-versa. This relationship is encouraged by subtle combinations of visual, audio and narrative techniques that attempt to draw out, or, to use Anna Poletti's term, 'coax', a particular type of attachment between the author and viewer. Poletti (2011, p. 81) expands:

> The digital storytelling movement is clear in its desire to make a contribution to the public sphere, and what marks that contribution as an attempt to create an intimate public is its insistence on the pre-existence of 'story' and the universality of themes such as 'life, loss, belonging, hope for the future, friendship and love' (Burgess 2006, 212). These themes, posited

---

2. For example, the investigation of how affect operates in life technologies such as artificial intelligences, robotics and other inorganic objects (Seigworth and Gregg 2010, pp. 6–7).

as self-evident but actually the product of the movement's own discourse, are presented as the common historical experience shared by the participants.

Poletti is using Berlant's (2008) notion of the 'intimate public' here as a way to describe how digital stories create an intimacy between narrators and implied viewers (the public). She suggests that the themes of universality or humanness animated by digital stories to create an intimate public are the effect of careful storytelling. This process raises concerns because it endangers – even eradicates – alternative stories that do not fit these particular notions of intimacy.

Some of the digital storytelling projects described earlier illustrate the coaxing of this intimate public. Helen Klaebe's (2006) master's study, for example, aimed to share the stories of ordinary people in the neighbourhood of Kelvin Grove, United Kingdom, and used digital storytelling as the medium to do so. Throughout the book, she discusses how the project had to 'coax' certain stories out of the participants and craft them in ways that remained interesting yet authentic. Even in projects committed to social justice outcomes we see this coaxing and narrative control manipulating the result. The digital storytelling literature review shows that many researchers experience frustration/disappointment when the stories they feel to be most important or to reflect the biggest community issue are not told by the digital storytelling participants. Thus, digital storytelling is affectively and normatively organised, and the outcome is impacted by a range of circumstances, including the participants' agendas and the context within which they digitalise them. Arguably, digital stories may be understood as performative of a complex set of affective and normative combinations. As Nigel Thrift (2004, p. 58) argues, affect has become an everyday yet 'actively engineered' aspect of our daily landscape and needs to be viewed as 'a set of performing relays and junctions that are laying down all manner of new emotional histories and geographies'.

How does affect become structured and oriented in the digital stories? Further, how does this structure and orientation allow the fictitious construct of race to be 'made live' through what Anoop Nayak (2017, p. 290) terms 'felt intensities'? A useful way to explore these questions is through the utilisation of Grossberg's (1987) concept of 'affective economies', which refers to the circulation of emotion and energy between people, images and things. Grossberg argues that these economies 'articulate affective struggles into a limited set of structures', restricting the way affect can be harnessed politically (p. 41). Utilising affect theory in this way allows for a rigorous and multidimensional framework for dissecting the spaces between the author and viewer of digital stories, or, stated differently, the spaces in which the performative is passed over.

Performative relays tend to be mundane and inconspicuous, so that, as Cvetkovich (2007, p. 464) describes, racism and other 'structural forms of violence [. . .] become invisible and normalized within our daily lives'. It is, therefore, crucial to consider how affect forms a performative loop between the authors and viewers of digital stories (in both everyday and institutional settings). Embedded within these performative loops are ideas or emotions and a force that lays down the boundaries of our subjectivities. When Cvetkovich (2003) calls for the consideration of 'buried traumas', she is urging the location and illumination of micro or alternative stories of loss and difficulty, *as well as* the violence and traumas that might actually be embedded within the performative loop of these micro stories themselves.[3] I argue that this task needs to be carried out in less obvious fields, including those considered 'organic', or somehow more 'expressively free', such as the arts realm, grassroots community work and, in this instance, digital storytelling. Such a project connects to Cvetkovich's (2007, p. 464) injunction to think beyond the usual understandings of trauma as catastrophic, and begin to develop a map of everyday trauma that focuses on 'the everyday and the insidious'. By placing macro and micro registers of affect alongside one another, I hope to avoid what Nayak (2017, p. 290) warns multicultural scholars against when he writes: 'The sonic melody of multiculturalism advanced through the convivial turn can risk deafening us to some of the scratchiness and bumpiness that lie in the grooves of many encounters with difference.' As Nayak illustrates, the daily 'scratches, bumps, crackles and hisses' that occur in everyday encounters of racism are tied to and often amplified through a geopolitical lens, so it is important to consider the 'multi-scalar' elements of affect (p. 291, 295).

While the case study analysis draws on European categories of affect theory, it avoids any understanding of affect as biologically derived or universally translatable. As Gunew (2009) stresses, and as work by Helen Moewaka Barnes et al. (2017), Vinay Dharwadker (2015) and Divya Tolia-Kelly (2006) among many others illustrates, affect studies have a tendency to understand affect as manifesting in the same fashion across all people, even though there are clearly differing taxonomies and interpretations of affect within and across cultures.[4] I try to ensure the concept of affective economies remains flexible by considering the ways in which these economies might be modified. This is not to occupy the view that affective regimes can be fully opened for the liberal flow of affective forms – like discursive norms, affects remain limited in the sense that they are produced within particular cultural systems. However, as Butler (2004, p. 15) describes in her discussion of normative constraints, persons are not 'in those constraints as something is "in" a container: [they are] extinguished by constraints, but also mobilised and incited by constraints'. If we take the affective economy to refer to the movement and structure of various energies between bodies and objects, then it becomes possible to explore the ways in which this economy might be reorganised to create new affective outcomes.

Such a task is inspired by Foucault's (1978, p. 9) argument that 'it might be possible to think differently rather than legitimating what is already known'. Understanding the affective dimension can provide a new means of rearticulating knowledges by retexturing our understandings of 'the complex regulation of bodily subjectivity', an ever-pressing task in a globalising world (Antwi et al. 2013, p. 1). In Part Two, I undertake a close reading of some digital stories, considering how the authors perform the multicultural subject, according to dominant norms of whiteness. I then extend this by considering

---

3. This is indicative of Berlant's (2011, p. 7) argument that screen media is archiving new, alternative stories, including those that are being lost from the historical record, but is also tracking 'what happens in the time that we inhabit before new forms make it possible to relocate within conventions the fantasy of sovereign life unfolding from actions'.

4. This issue was robustly workshopped at the colloquium *Feeling multicultural: Decolonizing affect theory*, held in 2006 at the Centre for Women's and Gender Studies, University of British Columbia, Vancouver, 25–27 June, and convened by Sneja Gunew.

how affective economies add to (and, indeed, take from) these particular performances. This analysis leads the book to consider how digital stories can allow for extensions of performativity and affect as political forces of change: capable of disrupting and resisting norms of whiteness to create alternative realities of everyday multiculturalism detached from racialisation.

Conclusion

Essentially, the theoretical framework I have proposed here for the analysis of migrant digital storytelling attempts to draw attention to a tension between '(a) expanding the existing normative concepts of citizenship, recognition, and rights to accommodate and overcome contemporary impasses, and (b) the call for alternative vocabularies grounded in the conviction that the normative discourses derived from liberalism and multicultur-alism alike are inadequate to the task of grasping both new subject formation and new forms of social and political antagonism' (Butler 2009, p. 146). Indeed, this tension is how I would like to position everyday multiculturalism: as a scholarship that attempts to create an alternative form of multiculturalism, one that deals with the limiting notions of identity, as well as the problems of detachment that liberal multiculturalism creates. Some approaches to multicultural studies claim that the answer to this predicament lies either in the reduction of the multicultural subject 'to a single, defining attribute' or in 'the construction of a multiply determined subject' (p. 147). This either/or tendency is exemplified by Araeen (2010a, p. 34) who asks: 'The question remains: what do we really want? Should we adopt a model of cultural diversity that brings us all together in a cohesive whole, or accept the attitudes that promote the division of society into unrelated fragments?' The 'answer' need not be one or the other, since both still do not address fully the question of the human and how these approaches foreclose possibilities for the subject. As Butler (2009, p. 147) remarks, if we continue to employ an approach of one or the other, then '[we cannot be sure] we have yet faced the challenge to cultural metaphysics posed by new global networks that traverse and animate several dynamic determinations at once'. The intention of the three-tiered framework is to try to avoid this one or the other approach and attempt, instead, to meet somewhere in the messy middle of the conjuncture, from which we can then move inwards, outwards and across.

Part Two

MULTICULTURAL BODIES

This section closely analyses digital storytelling case studies in terms of their narrative structure, aesthetic techniques and audio components so as to illustrate how migrant digital stories manifest in accordance with normative whiteness. Digital stories produced via the Australian Centre for the Moving Image (ACMI) form the focus of the individual digital storytelling case studies, and the *Junk Theory* (*JT*) project facilitated by community-based arts organisation Big hART is the focus of the collaborative digital storytelling analysis. *Junk Theory* was a creative response to the 2005 Cronulla race riots in Western Sydney/Eora, Australia. A lot has been written about these riots, but no scholarly attention has been paid to this significant artistic, community response. The prominent use of the face and hands in both kinds of digital stories is explored, illustrating how the genre deploys certain notions of 'humanness' in relation to whiteness. This allows for a discussion of how everyday multiculturalism can normatively structure both the individual body and the body of 'the nation'. The analysis reinforces the argument I made in Chapter One that scholarship on everyday multiculturalism and new racism understates the corporeality of racialisation and illustrates how residues of biological racism continue to haunt digital projects – and, indeed, contemporary cultural theory.

Chapter Four

EVERYDAY ETHNICITY IN DIGITAL PUBLICS

All organized narration is a 'matter for the police'.

– Derrida (1979)

Digital storytelling is a useful vehicle for bringing marginalised voices into the public domain and allowing ordinary people to creatively share their experiences. However, there are several aspects of the medium that need to be analysed before it can be deemed an effective mode for destabilising dominant discourses. Digital storytelling is commonly positioned as a tool for enabling voice and worthy behaviour but tends to overlook how and why these aspects are enabled. And yet, like all forms of representation, the mode of digital storytelling undoubtedly constrains the terms of the speaking and ultimately the representation of the speaker, whether the speaking comes from an individual or a community perspective. The task for my analysis then is to consider how the genre operates as a technological form in the Foucauldian sense – a form that deploys particular notions of ethnicity – and consequently how it impacts the formation of 'the ethnic' in Australia and comparable nation-states. The following chapters will consider how it is that the genre informs, resists and/or reproduces racialised notions of the subject within the context of everyday Australian narratives.

The individual digital stories chosen for analysis here are two films produced at ACMI: Sam Haddad's *Loving Lebanon and Australia* (*LLAA*, 2007) and Fatma Coskun's *New Life, New Country* (*NLNC*, 2007). I have selected these films because, after viewing the 32 ACMI-produced migrant digital stories found online, certain patterns emerged pertaining to stories about migration and/or cultural diversity in Australia. These patterns included: (1) three distinct narrative sections, (2) a linear movement from past to present/bad to good, (3) the condensing of convoluted experiences into a palatable trajectory and (4) a summation of the whole experience of one-off migration. The two films *LLAA* and *NLNC* exemplified the typical migrant digital story of those found not only in the ACMI collection but those produced via StoryCenter (United States), Pier 21 (Canada) and BBC's Video Nation (United Kingdom) collections.

In this chapter, I examine how norms of ethnicity and whiteness are animated in the individual digital stories. In doing so, I aim to reach a greater understanding of the conjuncture of everyday multiculturalism, in particular, the material ways so-called ethnic and non-ethnic subjects are enmeshed in Australian power relations pertaining to whiteness. How the authors perform their ethnicity in their respective digital stories is an exercise of power that draws on previous acts and will compel future acts – not only in digital stories but in daily life as well. Power is thus 'a relationship between partners, individuals and collectives', but it is also 'a way in which certain actions modify others' (Foucault 1982, p. 788). Vivienne and Burgess (2013, p. 285) note that digital platforms are 'less tangible' than some forms of art production, but 'nevertheless constitute an archive that is representative of social negotiations around gender, sexuality and fluid identity'. The archive created by organisations such as ACMI has recurring material effects, illustrating not only the various possibilities available in digital exchange, but also the realisation of particular possibilities in everyday life (see Navarro 2012, p. 142). ACMI, like the StoryCenter and comparable digital storytelling institutions, is unavoidably implicated in the creation and deployment of possibilities for 'ethnic' identities and contributes to the story of the nation.[1] Each organisation's framework for producing digital stories is important to consider because it impacts the story that is both told and heard about the respective 'multicultural nation'.

In the following section I analyse how national storytelling about multiculturalism takes place at ACMI in the relationship between individual participants and public discourses of race, in particular, the discourse of whiteness. I consider how Sam and Fatma animate 'the multicultural subject' and thus how digital storytelling's particular structure can both reaffirm and/or resist the normative notions of whiteness when carried out in Australian communities. My work here adds to the scholarship of Burgess (2006), Dreher (2012), Vivienne (2011) and Vivienne and Burgess (2013) to consider who gets to provide voice, how and – importantly – *to what end*.

I should restate here that I am not interested in analysing whether the digital stories reflect 'good' or 'bad' forms of contemporary media art; I am interested, rather, in how the digital stories engage with everyday multiculturalism and what kind of bodily information this produces in relation to 'race'. By examining the narrative, aesthetic and audio aspects of the digital stories, and the ways these elements are produced and placed, I work to trace the simultaneous production of a separate material outcome – the ethnic body. To do so, I draw on material publicly available on the relevant programmes and stories, including online press releases, descriptions and media coverage, as well as interviews with ACMI's (then) programme facilitator Helen Simondson.

Sharing my story: ACMI's digital storytelling programme

ACMI's digital storytelling programme is useful for analysing the notion of everyday multiculturalism. First, the programme prioritises 'on-the-ground' happenings or ordinary stories, mirroring the central concerns of everyday multiculturalism. ACMI

---

1. See Zoettl (2013, p. 210), who emphasises the role institutions play in creating digital stories, and the ways in which this involvement implicates both the digital form and its discursive outcomes. The impact of intermediaries in digital participation projects is studied in detail by Berliner (2018), Blum-Ross (2015) and Literat et al. (2018).

uses the basic principles of the StoryCenter's model that purposively connects digital media, popular culture and the storytelling of everyday life: 'We approach the storytelling part of our work as an extension of the kind of everyday storytelling that occurs around the dinner table, the bar, or the campfire' (Lambert 2009, p. 14).

Second, ACMI collects and publicly distributes stories considered representative of Melbourne's/Naarm's culturally diverse migration patterns and experiences, thus creating a digital memorial of multiculturalism. There is an implied understanding that the stories produced are authentic: reflecting real, on-the-ground experiences of migrants, with a special focus on non-Anglo-Celtic Australians. In this fashion, ACMI is using Lambert's digital storytelling model to engage the public and encourage ordinary people to contribute to the narrative of Australian multiculturalism.

ACMI has its roots in the State Film Centre – first established in 1946 to maintain a film collection for public use. The State Film Centre became a leading library of Australian and international cinematic works and was pivotal in building Victoria's film industry. As technology evolved, the centre widened its collection compass to include films from emerging and student film-makers and began to shift its focus from film archiving to film-making advocacy and education (ACMI 2013; Culture Victoria 2013). Plans to develop the centre into what is now known as ACMI began in the 1990s, instigated by rapid technological advancements that were redefining the moving image and its creative potential. Envisioned to become an internationally recognised hub of screen cultures, ACMI was purpose-built to foster interaction with moving images of all forms – film, television and digital media – a goal supported by the instalment of the 2001 Film Act. ACMI opened in Federation Square, the so-called heart of Melbourne/ Naarm city, on 26 October 2002, and has since become an iconic Melbourne/Naarm landmark (ACMI 2013).

Although the role of ACMI has developed since its days as the State Film Centre, the institution continues to play an important archival role. Today, it houses the nation's largest collection of moving image documents, which has diversified in form to include film, home video, web content, gaming and other hybrid forms of digital media, such as v-blogs and digital maps. Like all cultural institutions, ACMI is designated a particular responsibility for its locale: holding and creating certain forms of knowledge and shaping stories told and received about Melbourne/Naarm and the nation. This responsibility has been refashioned over the years to allow the public to contribute more directly to the evolution and distribution of Australian knowledges and stories.

Developing an engaging link between the cultural institution and the public became particularly crucial during the 1990s. At this time, the curatorial practices of cultural institutions – especially museums – came under increased scrutiny, criticised for using Western scientific discourse to project purportedly authoritative and ultimately monolithic representations of the subject being collected and exhibited (see Sherman and Rogoff 1994; Kwon 2002; Buskirk 2003). Cultural institutions had long been working within a rigid positivist paradigm that compressed shifting multiplicities of knowledge(s) into singular perspectives and linear narratives. As postmodern thinking began to take hold in the 1990s, ACMI also developed more engaging relationships with their audience and reconsidered knowledge presentation and creation in a more dynamic form.

Refashioning ACMI's public engagement required careful planning because although the institution wanted to foster public engagement, it was also determined to be an international leader of moving image technology – two aims that did not necessarily complement one another. The technological boom had occurred and was quickly snowballing; however, the majority of Australians were only just beginning to dabble with the technology, struggling to keep up with the constant developments. As ACMI's former Director of Public Programs Helen Simondson (2012b) outlines, most Australians were intrigued by the advancements in web technologies and desktop publishing, but did not know how to integrate the advancements into their lives, or where to begin to learn about them. There was thus a gap between public interaction and quality technological outputs that needed bridging, requiring a programme that would provide access to moving image technology and simultaneously up-skill participants in visual media literacy.

Working under the banner of 'lifelong learning', ACMI set about designing a programme that 'facilitated co-creative content, rather than an entire user-generated model' (Simondson 2012b). The ACMI building was purpose-built to allow moving image professionals to interact with its audience. This interaction enabled the creation and distribution of moving image outputs that were meaningful for both the public and ACMI: the public could actively contribute to the making of moving image stories, and ACMI could, by facilitating and co-creating the work, maintain a certain quality control over the productions.

Co-created moving image content has mostly been facilitated by ACMI's Public Programs, which include a range of public exhibitions, community projects, workshops and seminars. ACMI's longest-standing and arguably most significant Public Program is its digital storytelling programme, developed in conjunction with the centre's reincarnation. After meeting Lambert in 1998, Simondson was convinced that adopting the StoryCenter model would complement ACMI's dual aims of public engagement and quality moving-image production. She was particularly drawn to the model because it required that participants use their own content and memorabilia, such as personal photographs and home video. This aspect meant it would not be necessary for ACMI to create all elements of the production in-house, essentially simplifying the task at hand. Furthermore, allowing members of the public to contribute their own content would become the archival bridge ACMI sought to create – linking the individual member to the cultural organisation in an ongoing relationship and dialogue. ACMI thus set about learning digital storytelling skills directly from Lambert, who visited the institution to workshop the model with staff.

The digital storytelling programme was launched in 2002 and became one of the first formal avenues for Australian people to directly influence the stories told and shared about themselves and their communities through digital media. ACMI was the first major institution to adopt specifically the StoryCenter model, which has since proliferated in Australia and many other parts of the world. Indeed, Lambert credits the institution as a key driver of this proliferation. He describes the StoryCenter as 'limping through 2001 and 2002' and believes the work it did with the BBC and ACMI over this period was a 'breakthrough' for the genre (Lambert 2009, pp. 34–42). The significance of this relationship is proven by the number of digital stories ACMI has co-created – in a little over a decade, ACMI has assisted in the production of almost one thousand digital stories.[2]

ACMI raised awareness of the genre in Australia by appealing to three main target audiences: members of the general public, organisational trainers, and specific communities or 'clusters' of people. Any person can learn digital storytelling skills from ACMI facilitators via public workshop programmes, which are held by appointment and cost approximately five hundred dollars for three days.[3] The trainer-to-trainer workshops allow ACMI staff skilled in digital storytelling to teach other workers how to run digital storytelling workshops. These workers then take the workshop structure back to their organisations and run digital storytelling workshops with their staff/clients/audience. This process has enabled more people to become involved in the genre and learn about moving image technology.

The community workshops involve a co-creative agreement between ACMI and a community organisation or advocacy group, for example, between ACMI and the Jewish Museum, or ACMI and the Lebanese Community Hall. While ACMI often approaches these organisations or groups in the first instance, there are times (especially as knowledge about digital storytelling increases) that the community group drives the relationship.

ACMI's appeal to community groups has been instrumental to its success. The participation of community organisations helped its digital storytelling programme get off the ground: first, by providing start-up capital; and second, by encouraging more organisations to participate. The community digital storytelling programme runs on funding that the community groups must raise themselves. It costs approximately ten thousand dollars for each three-day workshop, which includes the cost of technical production, script-writing assistance, post-production and distribution (Simondson 2012a). The community representatives often seek funding from government or other relevant bodies for the project. Simondson notes that ACMI's first migrant digital storytelling project, *La Voce del Popolo* (2003), received positive feedback from the Victorian government and encouraged the State government to fund similar community-based projects.

One of the first tasks carried out by ACMI for the digital storytelling programme was to identify groups of people in Melbourne/Naarm and greater Victoria that might have similarly themed stories. This task was crucial not only for funding reasons, but also because little knowledge existed on digital storytelling at the beginning of the ACMI-based programme. Before the programme could begin, ACMI needed first to educate and promote the genre to the Australian community. Simondson and her team identified a range of themes, or 'clusters', of stories that included health, disability, youth and the elderly, and then contacted service or advocacy groups associated with these clusters. Many of the community representatives contacted recognised the potential for

---

2. As of January 2016, ACMI had a total collection of 915 individual digital stories that could be viewed on site in its public viewing library. I was able to locate 32 of these online, on the ACMI website, Culture Victoria website and YouTube.
3. As of 2012.

the individual digital stories to collectively tell a bigger story. These representatives saw the programme as an opportunity to showcase their community and therefore aid particular organisational aims, such as community engagement, advocacy and fundraising. Simondson (2012a) notes that many of the final outputs act as promotional videos or clips for the community they represent. For example, some of the stories from the Lebanese Community Project might be used by the Lebanese Hall to support funding applications or to provide information about its members on its website.

The clustering process links certain Australians to various identity-political categories, for example, women, youth and ethnic minorities. Migration was one of the first themes to be pursued by the digital storytelling programme. Projects resulting from this theme involved the demarcation of particular Australians, according to understandings of ethnic experiences, for example, *Stories from the Lebanese Community* (2007), *Stories from the Jewish Community* (2007), *Enduring Stories: Migrant Stories* (2007) and *La Voce del Popolo (The Voice of the People): Stories from the Italian Community* (2003). Social demography organises other stories, including *Western Stories* (2005–2006), *Craig Family Centre Stories* (2005) and *Building Better Lives* (2010), and features disadvantaged community members, including disabled persons and, very often, migrants.[4]

Whether ACMI is workshopping digital storytelling skills with individual members of the public, a community group or trainers, the structure remains mostly the same and is facilitated according to the conventional three-day programme framed by the StoryCenter. ACMI will often organise a briefing event in advance of the workshop commencement date. This briefing allows people to familiarise themselves with the structure of digital stories and begin to consider potential storylines. The Seven Steps of Storytelling are then facilitated over the three days. The first day begins with the Story Circle in which people develop their basic scripts or story ideas into clear narratives. Sessions on each step of the production process are delivered across the remaining two days to the entire working group, for example, how to edit, or how to do voice-overs.

These steps are designed in accordance with the StoryCenter's Seven Steps, moving the author successively from script development through to image and sound editing. While everyone in the project is involved in these mini-sessions, they are necessarily at the same stage of production. ACMI endeavours to keep everyone working at a similar pace, however, it inevitably takes some people longer than others to master certain skills. Simondson notes that some people also find it emotionally harder to articulate their story and consequently spend longer periods of time on script development.

At the end of the third day, the workshop trainers screen each person's story to the group at large, regardless of how complete it is. The trainers see this shared screening as one of the most important aspects of the process, arguing that it allows participants to feel a sense of closure and fosters the personal 'transformation' element that the genre strives to accomplish (Simondson 2012a). Following the workshop, ACMI staff spends a

---

4. This reflects many of the projects carried out via the StoryCenter in the United States and its partners in Canada and the United Kingdom via the Museum of Immigration (Pier 21) and the BBC, respectively.

few days on post-production, which includes adding the credits and end titles and cre-ating a DVD package.

Methodologically, ACMI has adopted the StoryCenter model, clearly illustrated by the similarities between the stories available on the organisations' respective websites, which reflect the model. However, unlike the StoryCenter and the BBC series *Video Nation*, ACMI's core aim is to produce *high-quality* moving image stories. The StoryCenter and other digital storytelling practitioners focus primarily on the *process* of digital story making, ACMI's focal point is the end-product, or creating 'the best quality digital story' (Simondson 2012a).

While mediation occurs in all digital storytelling work, it could be argued that inter-vening to control quality jeopardises the 'authenticity' of the stories. Simondson is well aware of this potential problem but does not dwell on it. Her goal and responsibility as ACMI's public programs director is to impart some of the knowledge the institution has regarding moving image to the public to enable ordinary people to up-skill in the medium. She states: 'We've always worked towards making the best content possible because we're a moving image organisation, fundamentally we're really interested in how moving image stories are put together and we have a lot of skill base in that and a lot of knowledge to impart in that' (Simondson 2012a). This position contrasts with the StoryCenter's position and that of many contemporary digital storytelling practitioners that focus heavily on process rather than end-product.[5] As Simondson acknowledges, the StoryCenter approach entails a stronger social justice and community empowerment agenda – in fact, it has recently embedded an anti-racist philosophy into its agenda. ACMI engages with social justice in some ways, but its agenda prioritises moving image quality.

'Quality' for ACMI means sleek design and professional presentation of moving image outputs. ACMI works to maintain a high-quality product by ensuring particular production and methodological elements are in place, including highly skilled staff in the art of narrative and scriptwriting, close supervision of the community's use of tech-nology, specific ordering of workshop steps and collaboration between facilitators and participants where necessary. Finally, the post-production process allows ACMI staff to tweak the final presentation of the digital story.

Distinguishing between the social justice agenda of the StoryCenter and ACMI's quality agenda follows the rationale that prioritising social justice or community democ-racy will likely be detrimental to the quality of the digital story. If we trace the logic used by Simondson to differentiate these approaches to digital storytelling, we begin to see not only the ways in which 'quality' informs ACMI's digital storytelling programme, but also how notions of 'quality' are embroiled in discourse pertaining to community-based arts projects at large. In particular, it illustrates an ongoing tension between concepts of community, art and quality.

---

5. For example, Curious Works, a well-established not-for-profit organisation that works with Australian communities on new media projects, including digital storytelling projects (Curious Works is discussed in Chapter Seven).

Simondson echoes a long-standing sentiment that artistic practice relating to community aspirations operates in a field removed from artistic excellence. This sentiment has a complex, shifting history in Australia, which Hawkins (1993) does a thorough job mapping and that Khan (2011, 2015) more recently readdresses. Hawkins utilises Bourdieu (1980) to explain that, historically, aesthetic value has been determined by society's elite, according to a Western system of thought. Ultimately, this value system produced 'others' who were excluded from participating in this artistic realm. Community consequently acted as the 'convenient category in which to group all those left out in the cold by the restricted and elitist definitions of value constituted by the discourse of excellence' (Hawkins 1993, p. 13). Since 'community' has acted as the site of political struggle and investment, community-based arts has conventionally privileged process over product (Khan 2011, p. 4). As Khan argues, community-based art has emphasised 'the *participatory* nature of these processes', arguing for 'their purportedly *transformative* effects' and involving in turn a 'tension surrounding the role of the expert in these processes' (emphases in the original).[6] ACMI is clearly embedded within these tensions – on the one hand, it acts as the 'expert' for digital media; on the other, it works to activate and empower communities.

Regardless of ACMI's quality control element, it remains the case that certain notions of community inform every aspect of its digital storytelling programme. How community is defined and mobilised by ACMI, as well as what implications this mobilisation has for the genre and the community it represents, requires close attention. While 'community' might seem implicit in this 'everyday' genre, the use of such terms has, as outlined earlier, a tendency to operate in fluctuating ways. Chapter One described how the popularity of terms such as 'everyday' in arts programmes has become indicative of an overall attempt in Australia and the broader West to capture power relations as they are materially lived. As such, ACMI not only relies on everyday communities and their stories, it also contributes to particular formations of the everyday person and the community within which they are embedded.

While the organisation is not as flexible or as critically engaged as some digital storytelling practitioners, its approach remains embedded within an ideology of community empowerment and democracy – it encourages individual participation in order to enable broader community aspirations, including the desire for recognition, justice and inclusion. This approach stems from the common community-based arts argument that art and culture should focus on process rather than output (Hawkins 1993, p. 157). By focusing on process, community-based art programmes attempt to foster 'spontaneous cultural practice', valuing meaningful daily experience, encouraging reflection on everyday life and providing greater opportunity for new, meaningful relationships to develop (p. 21, 157). ACMI's digital storytelling programme clearly appeals to community groups in an

---

6. The flipside argument is that any art that emphasises professionalism or excellence in accordance with the conventional notions found in art history is not authentic and somehow undermines the cultural values and aspirations of communities.

attempt to create more genuine relationships between 'artist' (in this case, the visual literacy expert) and 'audience', namely, the general public (see p. 116).

ACMI has established some tactics for its work with community groups that appear to negotiate the tenuous position the organisation occupies as both an advocate of everyday community art and a producer of high-quality artwork. In particular, there is the use of a trust figure and copyright control in its digital storytelling programme. The trust figure is a person who is well known and highly regarded by the community group and who acts as its spokesperson. By liaising with this representative, ACMI is able to structure its approach in a way with which the selected community group will have an affinity and will, in turn, feel more comfortable and safe in sharing stories. The use of the trust figure also helps ACMI convince individual community members that they have 'a story worth sharing in public', the realisation of which is, in many cases, 'an acquisition of agency' (Vivienne and Burgess 2013, p. 286). This agency is further harnessed by participants when they dictate how the stories they co-create with ACMI will be used. The authors retain copyright of their stories and decide whether or not the stories will be distributed online, in public arenas, or used solely as personal memorabilia.

The use of the trust figure is a logistical tactic that also assists ACMI's goal of producing high-quality moving image products. ACMI does not have the capacity to mobilise communities, for example, via community consultations, information sessions and so on. Without the trust figure, Simondson (2012a) feels community groups would be less likely to commit to the full three days of the workshop, and it would also be difficult to gather adequate content for the production of digital stories. Furthermore, ACMI can more easily brief trust figures on what kinds of ordinary stories make for 'good' digital stories. The representatives usually know what community stories will be the right fit and length for the ACMI programme. Much of the 'filtering' therefore gets carried out in advance of the workshop (Simondson 2012a).

ACMI clearly strives for ethical community practice so as to enable what Zizi Papacharissi (2010) describes as the 'digitally enabled citizen'. Nonetheless, it remains the case that the digital story *form* acts to legitimise the authenticity of the story/experience presented by the produced digital stories. Simondson differentiates the process of digital storytelling from other ACMI-led community-based media projects, suggesting that the latter projects involve more production, professionalism and, ultimately, control. This distinction reflects the common viewpoint evidenced in digital storytelling scholarship – namely, the digital storytelling genre is a hands-on form of media making and is, therefore, less susceptible to issues about authenticity. ACMI's digital storytelling programme carries this judgement even though it clearly creates a particular environment for storytelling in the workshops and organises the set and script for its stories to some degree.

The following section takes two digital stories created from one of ACMI's *Migrant Stories* projects to consider how the individual stories reflect broader understandings of multiculturalism and cultural diversity in Australia. Digital citizens are certainly enabled by the creation of these stories. But what kind of citizen is enabled, and on whose terms?

Ethnic performativity in individual digital stories

The following discussion focuses on two digital stories that illustrate the common patterns evidenced in the ACMI-produced migrant digital stories. Sam Haddad's *Loving Lebanon and Australia* and Fatma Coskun's *New Life, New Country* are both typical of a digital story co-created with ACMI in order to 'document diverse voices' (Simondson 2012a). The stories were gathered in community-based workshops – the first from the project *Stories from the Lebanese Community*; the second from *Enduring Stories: Migrant Stories*.

LLAA describes Sam's transition into Australian life after migrating from Lebanon in the 1970s. His transition was often difficult, especially in the beginning, but the story finishes on a proud, satisfied note. Fatma's story also provides a summary of her migration experience, beginning with the difficult decision to leave her home and family in the small village of Corum, Turkey, and ending with her happy life in Australia today.

The stories are structurally and aesthetically typical of the migrant digital story, involving linear movements through clear beginning, middle and end sections; the seamless condensing of tumultuous migration experiences, and recognisable signposts such as family photography and personal voice-overs. As Chapter Five will demonstrate, these typical digital stories also circulate particular affective economies.

Narrative structure

Individual migrant digital stories tend to be divided into three parts, indicative of the journey narrative of the genre. The respective narratives of *LLAA* and *NLNC* are segmented as follows: an opening (or introduction), a main event where 'something happens' and a conclusion or resolution. In the first section, the narrator introduces themselves by using 'I am a .../I am the ...' statements, or, in past tense, 'I was a .../ I was the ...' statements. Importantly, the opening consists of clear statements that subjectively position the narrator. For example, Fatma opens her story with the statement: 'I was born the seventh child of poor farmers.' In the second, or bridging section of the culturally diverse digital story, a journey through time/place/culture and, ultimately, 'sense of self' occurs. This part can be viewed as a type of liminal space whereby the subjects of the stories grapple (sometimes more directly than others) with being 'neither here nor there' in terms of place, temporality and identity. The 'moment of change' identified by the author in the Storytelling Circle is often placed right before this section; acting as the catalyst for the transitional phase. It is the stage when the question 'who am I?' is typically tackled.

Movement through a liminal space is very obvious in Sam's *LLAA*, which, with the help of various aesthetic and audio techniques, sharply cuts from a fairly mundane and peaceful opening to a serious and difficult section, or what Lambert would likely refer to as Sam's 'moment'. This moment is queued not only by the change in music and the lowered tone of Sam's voice, but by a verbal indication – after describing how much he enjoys his dual cultural affiliations, he suddenly says: 'but it wasn't always like that.'

Sam's moment of change is a violent one, involving an altercation with a co-worker at his first Australian job. Sam retells how, following relentless taunting about his ethnicity at his new job, he lost his temper and punched the bully worker in the jaw. This scene is a moment of foreboding in the digital story; however, it quickly transitions to a lighter representation of Sam and the Australian lifestyle. Sam proceeds to relate how this violent act won the respect of many of his new co-workers, who then began to socialise with him at work and after hours.

Reflecting the narrative structure of most stories in this collection, *LLAA* then moves into a third and final section by returning to the opening statement/position and redefining it according to the experience of crossing the liminal space. The author reaches some form of conclusion about themselves: Now I am 'this' or 'that'. In *LLAA*, this third section is once again sharply cut to, transitioning suddenly from the confusion of the violent incident to a sequence of happy and rewarding stories with accompanying pictures. In this closing section, Sam describes how he went on to achieve many things and today respects and enjoys the Australian way of life alongside his Lebanese heritage.

The movement through these three sections is also evident in *NLNC*. However, the liminal space is represented far more subtly, almost to the point of non-existence, with the before and after sections strongly emphasised instead. After a brief summary of her life from birth to marriage, Fatma describes how she and her husband decide to migrate to Australia due to financial hardship in Turkey. She touches on the emotional difficulty of saying goodbye to her mother and father, and the issues faced during the migration application. The parting with her father is shown to be particularly difficult for Fatma. Proportionately, the digital story spends a significant amount of time focusing on this separation and she explains, 'We became even more sad when my father with tears in his eyes said, "I wish I could help you. Go work hard and be happy."' She closes this scene with the haunting statement: 'It is impossible to forget the look on his face.'

Fatma and her husband are initially called from the immigration 'waiting list' by mistake, and for a day they believe they will have to stay in Turkey, despite having sold their home and material belongings. Fatma feels suspended, knowing she has nowhere to return to and, as yet, nowhere to move onto. The immigration department spends a day considering their application and finally decides to approve it. Fatma and her family are in Australia within 24 hours. She explains her high level of anxiety about the new country and what lay ahead. These worries and tensions are briefly mentioned but quickly dismissed. In a similar way to Sam in *LLAA*, Fatma cuts abruptly to the present time where life with her family is happy and financially stable: 'Time flew and twenty years went by . . .' Before she concludes, she describes the event of her parents visiting her in Australia. It is represented as a joyful time, and there is a sense that she is comforted by her Dad's approval of the country. Fatma concludes her story in a similar fashion to Sam: 'We had no problems anymore . . . We are very happy. We love Australia very much.'

The narrative resolution for both Sam and Fatma is that they have achieved success and happiness in Australia in spite of the difficulties involved in migration. For viewers, the stories provide a brief insight into the migration experience, in particular, the emotional and practical difficulties faced when leaving a home country, adjusting to a new way of life and attempting to juggle different cultural values in a new place. They give a sense of the bravery required to make such a move and pay homage to what is, in most cases, a working-class group of people who contribute to the Australian labour market with gusto. In their analysis of queer digital stories, Vivienne and Burgess (2013) argue that the act of paying homage to an identity journey via a digital story leads to an important transformation. They write: 'Making a digital story involves a journey that is both conscious and unconscious, in many cases a trip from marginalization to advocacy and cultural engagement' (p. 288).

Both narrators of *LLAA* and *NLNC* undertake a transformative passage. The sequencing of events and the careful editing of techniques move Sam and Fatma from a place of displacement and even desolation to a place of security and success. They become agents of 'themselves' but also agents for marginal ethnic cultures inside the dominant Australian culture. Sam, in particular, emphasises his continual involvement with the Turkish community in Australia, projecting pride as he describes his role as a community leader and representative. Simondson (2012a) describes this transformation as inherent to the ACMI programme:

> If you think about people getting to that point where they are dealing with quite personal things, and that [these things] are a point of their life that mark them, the transformation comes in the making content . . . so, often people will be very teary and it's really, really hard to tell their stories, and . . . and they wonder whether they're going to be able to do the voice-over without tearing up . . . but . . . they don't often do that because by the time they get to that stage they're actually constructing their story, so there's . . . there's sort of some kind of process in the revealing and sharing and writing and distilling it and *then* [emphasises word] actually literally having to do these processes that construct the story to make it. And then there's the . . . this incredible *pride* [emphasises word] when they view the content and realise they've produced something and that they've produced something that has resonance and means a lot to them and . . . it says a lot about . . . the writing of that script . . . The scripting process is really important, you know . . . It wouldn't be transformative if they stood and talked as an interview to a camera, it's not the same thing.

Here, Simondson sheds light on the highly emotive and tumultuous nature that the digital storytelling transformation takes. However, in the typical digital story, the transition from new migrant to settled Australian (a prodigious transformation in reality) happens relatively smoothly and swiftly. As such, the typical migrant digital story acts as a tool of assimilation into a white Australian narrative. *LLAA* and *NLNC* are premised on the view that, while difference constitutes Australia, the difference is relatively small and, inevitably, 'ethnic Australians' share similar values and pursue similar aspirations. Certainly, the stories allow for an opening in dialogue and connection that might otherwise remain closed. One of the issues of this narrative format, however, is that the authoritative signpost is always and so obviously Australia – specifically, an imagined white Australia – and this makes it difficult for Fatma and Sam to move beyond the structure that binds their respective digital story narratives to the normative narrative of Australian multiculturalism. This narrative reads: *we* [white, Anglo-Celtic Australia] opened our doors to give *others* [non-white, non-Anglo-Celtic migrants] a 'fair go'; *we* acknowledged that it was hard for *them*, but by working hard and assimilating to *our* values they succeed and *we* are thus a happy, multicultural nation. Obviously, this is a simplified version of what has been a complicated, messy history, but it remains the case that this informs the celebratory rhetoric of multiculturalism in Australia and, indeed, other Anglo-settler nations.

The three-part narrative that informs both Fatma's and Sam's digital stories can be seen to correlate broadly to the three key points of Australia's multicultural success rhetoric, and the ways Fatma and Sam are positioned as multicultural subjects. Fatma and Sam discuss the difficult decision to migrate to Australia, and the hardships faced once they do decide. They are shown to work painstakingly in factories upon arrival; in fact, Fatma tells us that she and her husband began working the day after arriving in Australia. After travelling through this confusing, neither-here-nor-there period, they come to love the Australian way of life. Fatma states: 'Because we were working, we did not have any financial problems … we could afford whatever we wanted … We had no problems anymore. We are very happy.' Similarly, in the final sequences of the digital story Sam describes: 'This accident [the physical fight with his co-worker] helped me develop values about mateship [and] tolerance … Australia took me into her arms and taught me to respect others.' What emerges then is a subjective positioning of Fatma and Sam that mirrors the normative narrative: they take the opportunity to migrate to Australia; it is very difficult and at first they are troubled by the differences and uncertainty; however, they work hard and adopt Australian values and are, in turn, fulfilled.

The particular ordering of the narrated scenes in the stories thus works to create a linear movement of time and space and generates an understanding of Australian history as cause and effect. This ordering simplifies the complexities and nuances of the migration experience, smoothing over the disjuncture caused by migration and that results in a constant oscillation between past and present/there and here/then and now. At no point in *NLNC* and *LLAA* does the back-and-forth movement between home and away cease for Fatma and Sam. Both the characters represent 'completeness', however, there is constant referral back to the homeland – explicitly through Sam who shows pictures of himself celebrating Lebanese cultural traditions while surrounded by the Australian flag; implicitly through Fatma who points to an unresolved discord in her father-daughter relationship.

Describing her parents' visit, Fatma focuses on her father's reaction: 'When my father left he was smiling. He said, "Daughter, I wish you had invited us here twenty years ago. How beautiful this country is. We would live here. We would not go back."' Although this scene is painted as a moment of pride and triumph, there is a tension that hovers above the narrative, forming an unspoken discomfort that alludes to unfulfilled wishes, longings and regrets. This tension is reinforced because Fatma's recently spoken words, 'It is impossible to forget the look on [Dad's] face', still resonate. What emerges in *NLNC* is a sense that Fatma is inhabiting what Phanuel Antwi et al. (2013, p. 5) term an 'anxious entanglement' of two conflicting narratives and the related affects: 'the happy fictions of success and inclusion' that dominate accounts of multiculturalism and 'the various interruptive texts and textures that emerge from the accumulated everyday experience of various forms of structural violence.' The memory of her father and his aspirations constantly interrupt the easy flow of Fatma's narrative.

Aesthetic techniques

The selection and placement of images is a vital part of the digital storytelling genre and, in the cases of *NLNC* and *LLAA*, for the performance of ethnicity in the Australian context. In a similar way to the speech act, images perform a type of cumulative symbolism. Digital stories build on one another not just in terms of narrative tendencies but also in terms of the visual signposts used. Patricia Holland's (1991) work on photography demonstrates the ways in which everyday snapshots help us to make sense of the world and ourselves within it. Snapshots also help to keep some sense of cohesiveness alive in an increasingly fragmented world – a particularly relevant feature for migrant Australians who, as discussed, live within a fractured framework of place and time.

Overall, Sam and Fatma mostly use images that have a clear and obvious referent, or what the genre refers to as explicit imagery. These types of images represent whatever it is the authors are referring to verbally in a direct manner; for example, Fatma uses personal family pictures when introducing her family members, and a personal picture of her workplace when she refers to her Australian job. Likewise, Sam uses pictures of his former homeland Lebanon when he mentions his birthplace. The use of this imagery reflects the aim of digital stories to 'show rather than tell' and assists the viewer to build a cohesive understanding of Sam and Fatma as migrant Australians.

While moving image, most commonly home video, is sometimes used in digital stories, *LLAA* and *NLNC* use only still imagery, drawing on photographs from private collections and publicly available images, including ACMI's image library. One of the first images Sam uses when talking of Lebanon has the feel of a coloured encyclopaedia image. The picture is of a people-less space filled with ruins that, together with Sam's verbal narration, leads the viewer to ascertain this place to be 'Lebanon'. Similarly, Sam uses a black-and-white picture of a large ship coming into port when he mentions his Australian arrival. This particular image is used in many other digital stories co-created with ACMI about migration and is also reminiscent of photographs popularly used in public documents to represent Australia's post-war migration.

The images are selected and manipulated in a way that invites the viewer to 'come along for the journey' – a very particular journey that moves the subject along a trajectory of performance, the ending of which is, in one way or another, a 'performative accomplishment' (Butler 1997b). Pictures of mementos like passports or postcards are frequently used in the migrant digital story and are evidenced in both *NLNC* and *LLAA*. These obvious images make immediate sense to viewers as they represent travel on a global scale: one cannot legally leave a country or enter another one without a passport, thus making it a global (and nationalistic) document of mobility, surveillance and national borders. Similarly, Sam persistently uses images, including the Australian flag and the Lebanese flag, indicating his movements from one nation to another. As the story moves from photos of ruins at Lebanon to pictures of Sam shaking hands and signing his citizenship documents surrounded by Australian flags, the narrator's successful journey from Lebanese to Australian is ratified.

Two other aesthetic techniques aid the affirmation of the journey narrative: the shift in image style over the course of the digital story from black and white to colour; and the use of the slideshow format. Both *NLNC* and *LLAA* use imagery that shifts from black and white to colour. This technique is indicative of technological changes and the evolving uses of photography, thereby conveying the temporal distance that Sam and Fatma have travelled. However, the shift in aesthetic also moves the journey of Sam and Fatma as subjects from a distinct past to a distinct present or future, aided by the use of the slideshow format. The images tend to slide across the screen in the same direction as a Western viewer is taught to read, namely, from left to right. We thus move both temporally and geographically with Sam and Fatma along a historical timeline: leaving a strange and distant past and place (Lebanon/Turkey) for a familiar, close and contemporary present/future (Australia).

It is also noteworthy that the pace at which these photos slide across the screen increases towards the end of both Sam's and Fatma's narratives, that is, towards the present Australian life. In many other migration stories co-created by ACMI, this heightening pace is carried out by stacking images in a collage fashion, or by using several images on a page which are consecutively highlighted by the use of zoom effects. These techniques transport the viewer speedily through the story, rapidly transferring many pieces of information. Holland's work on the family photograph album is relevant for contemplating the use of sliding images. She describes the ways that the family album is arranged conscientiously to produce corresponding historical moments: 'The principles of selection and arrangement are exercised to tell a story of progress or decline, to construct a sense of period and to hint at major historical shifts' (Holland 1991, p. 10). For Sam and Fatma, the technique also implies a form of quasi-mobility across time and place.

The quality of the photographs used in *NLNC* and *LLAA* are by no means professional, nor are they supposed to be. It is common that photographs and moving image segments used in digital stories are worn out and of poor quality in terms of focus, framing and so on. This quality is especially true for digital stories which narrate a historical event, and thus use older photographs which are not privy to the technological advancements afforded to contemporary images taken with a digital camera or mobile phone device. In *LLAA* and *NLNC*, the photos are mostly drawn from personal archives and are often blurry or tattered. Indeed, it is important for the genre to utilise these private everyday snaps – and not only because of the aforementioned access and resource management points.

Use of these images also gives the digital stories an authentic feel and creates a certain intimacy with the viewer. This intimacy is aided by the heavy use of familial photographs in the digital stories. Family is a common trope of the identity narrative, and personal photographs of the family are often used as a grounding point for the home. By showing us family pictures we, as viewers, are admitted into Sam's and Fatma's private realms. It is important to remember, however, that regardless of how private the collections appear, they are always 'thoroughly public' – even before their display in the digital stories. This dynamic is, as Holland (1991, p. 3) explains, a result of the public conventions of the image to which they adhere – the pictures are taken in a way that is dependent on shared understandings of 'the family' and ultimately how they will be received. The personal histories that they document thus belong to broader narratives of ethnicity, gender, community and nationhood, which enable the possibility of the private identity: 'Family photography is not expected to be appreciated by outsiders, yet there is a need to produce the correct pictures as if the audience were the public at large' (p. 7). This underlying expectation goes some way towards explaining why the familial images in *NLNC* and *LLAA* – in fact in most of the digital stories watched across the main 'home-bases' of digital storytelling – look aesthetically similar and feel so familiar.

Both authors, though Sam especially, utilise implicit imagery to create an intimate space and performative loop between the viewer and the author. Fatma's use of implicit imagery is subtle and less choreographed than Sam's. There are two key moments in Fatma's story that utilise implicit imagery: the first when describing the farewell from her father; the second when her family awaits news from the Immigration Department. In the first instance, Fatma uses a black-and-white photograph of her father when she begins to speak of saying goodbye to her parents. The photograph features her father sitting, slumped and looking downwards. The details of his face are clearly observable, and his expression seems sad and distant. As if to highlight the emotions of this expression, the story zooms in on his face. Zoom effects are regularly used in digital storytelling, carefully timed to prompt the viewer to focus on a particular moment, subject or character. Frequently, the zooming will occur on the photographed face of the subject in question, drawing the viewer close to their expressions and their eyes in particular.

There is a humanistic element to this that draws strongly on social justice documentary and dead-pan photography of the 1970s (Smaill 2010). These genres use portrait pictures, often in black and white, and often focusing on the eyes, as a way to translate emotion and universality. We are thus drawn towards the emotionality of Fatma's narrative. The story then moves to a picture of Fatma's father holding a small child in his arms. It is unknown who the child is, but the picture conveys the father-child relationship and thus the emotionality tied to Fatma's separation from her father (Figure 4.1). She closes this segment with the line: 'It is impossible to forget the look on his face.' Interestingly, the accompanying picture for this statement is of a people-less landscape, presumably near her village. Regardless of the actual place represented here, in this instance it signals loneliness and a sense of the unknown for Fatma.

The second moment of Fatma's implicit imagery is when the Immigration Office explains to her and her husband that it made an error and should not have called them for migration to Australia. She exclaims, 'How could we go back!' and the frame switches from the jubilant tourist shots taken near the Immigration building to an image of Fatma bundled up outdoors, amid heavy snow. A similar photo of Fatma in the snow was used earlier in the story when the hardships of life in Turkey for herself and her husband were described (see Figure 4.2). The repetition builds the idea that Turkey is cold and restricting, and a hint of the Australian fantasy – warm, sunny and 'easier' – is subsequently conveyed.

Sam's use of implicit imagery is most clearly seen when he retells the violent altercation he had with his co-worker. The narration of this section is accompanied by a sequence of images featuring 'present-day' Sam. The sequence begins with a picture of Sam's feet, wearing leather shoes, on grass. The next image is of Sam's face, gazing distantly into that which is off the frame. Explaining his new job, he states, 'I got along

Figure 4.1 (Left) Screenshot from Fatma Coskun's digital story *New Life, New Country* (2007), featuring Fatma's father; (Right) screenshot illustrating father-child relationship in Fatma's digital story.

Figure 4.2 (Left) Screenshot from Fatma Coskun's digital story *New Life, New Country* (2007), used when Fatma describes the hardships of life in Turkey; (Right) screenshot used when Fatma describes her family's suspension in Turkey.

very well with most people there', and here a picture of his hands resting on the small of his back is shown, his fingers interlaced. Other close-ups of his face are then used until he begins describing the co-workers who teased him, calling him 'wog' and asking him, 'Where is your sandals?' At the mention of the sandals, we are again taken to an image of his *enclosed* leather shoes. 'I did not bother answering', he says, 'I kept to myself.' Here again, pictures of Sam taken from behind are used. We can see his back and legs, but no head, and his arms remain resting on his lower back, joined by his clasped hands. Sam then describes: 'After a while I could not take it anymore', and the frame zooms in on his clasped hands. 'So I punched one of them . . . I broke one of my fingers and his jaw', he

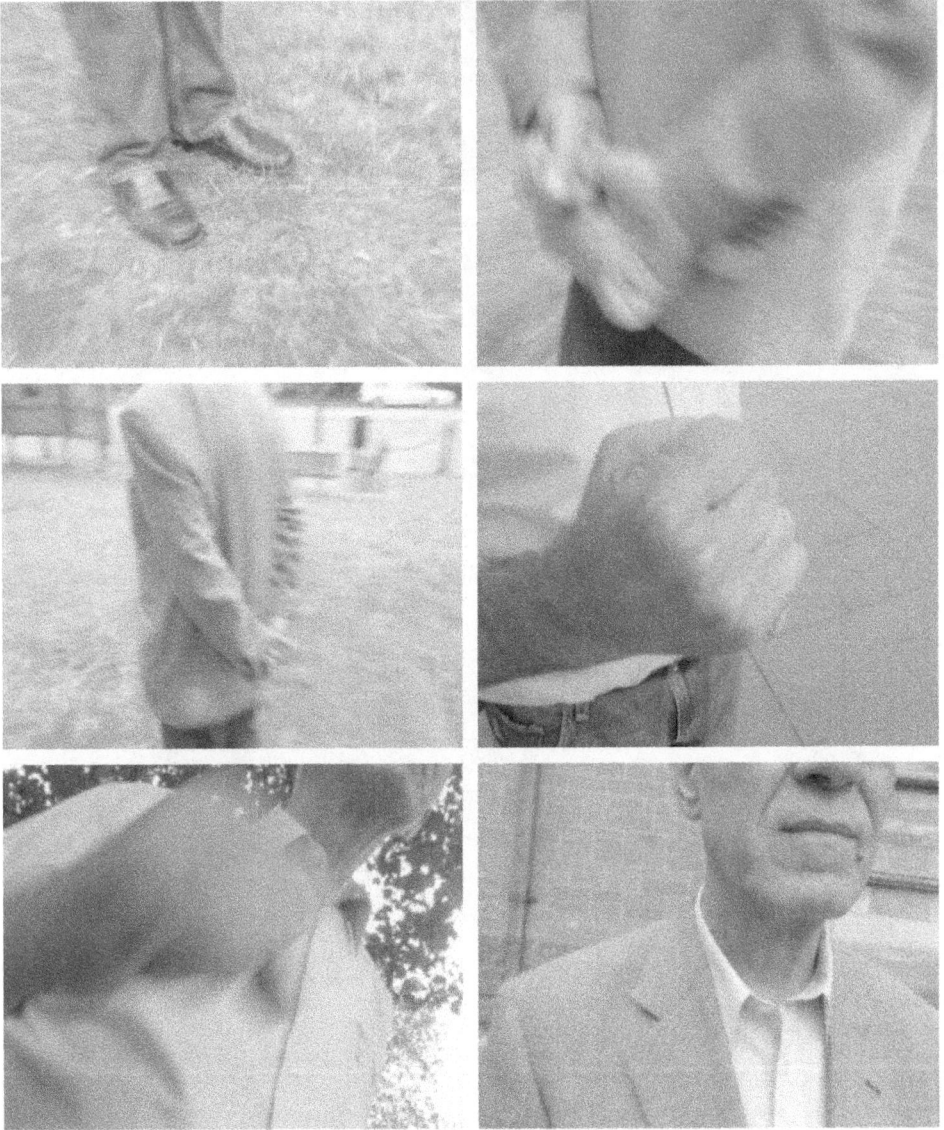

Figure 4.3 (L-R) Screenshots from Sam Haddad's digital story *Loving Lebanon and Australia* (2007), showing the sequence of shots used by Sam when narrating his work altercation. Courtesy of the author.

asserts. As he describes this rupture, there are three pictures of his fist going through the motion of punching, then images of his face again – two taken close up and cut off below the eyes so that the focus is on his jaw and lips. This sequence all happens in the space of seconds (Figure 4.3).

Figure 4.4 Screenshot from Sam Haddad's digital story *Loving Lebanon and Australia* (2007), showing Sam at the pub as his digital story shifts to its happy ending. Courtesy of the author.

The combination of words and images is particularly affective. First, the use of Sam's face continuously returns the viewer's attention to the 'person' behind the body. The shots featuring his hands clasped behind his back convey his initial withdrawal from the workplace and Australian life. It is reminiscent of the saying 'My hands are tied behind my back', used to suggest that one is unable to act in the way one wishes. Sam is, essentially, silent and powerless. Mobility arrives for Sam when he loses his temper and punches the co-worker. The image that focuses on the lips seems to go hand-in-hand with the idea that Sam has utilised his 'voice'; he is no longer being silenced. Sam then describes how most of the workers took his side, acting 'polite' and 'understanding'.[7] He quickly moves on to describing how he became friends with his co-workers after the alter-cation, socialising with them outside of work: 'From that time on they were fighting each other, who was going to take me to the pub and invite me to their parties and barbeques.' A picture is shown of Sam walking into a pub, his hand on the door. We see his reflection in the glass of the door and are led to believe that Sam is about to move beyond the lim-inal space, into a (now) welcoming Australia (Figure 4.4).

What this troubling snippet reveals is that the unexpected outburst of violence became a marker of certain norms that enabled Sam to feel a sense of belonging in Australia. Through this action, he proved himself worthy as 'one of the blokes' and is now

7. Interestingly, the image he chooses to use here seems at odds with the accomplishment he is describing. The street is full of people and the whole background has been overexposed – it is glaringly white and very blurry, so that it looks confusing and confronting, rather than safe and relieving. This incongruent image placing is taken up again in Chapter Six.

permitted entry into white social happenings. Sam goes on to list his accomplishments in Australia, including (ironically) his acquisition of a Justice of the Peace qualification. Given that Australianness is normatively defined as white, male and heterosexual (see Taylor 2006; Dunn 2006), it seems clear that the punch was a successful performance of white Australian masculinity, subsequently allowing Sam honorary access to this sphere. Suddenly, the digital story moves from melancholic music and narration of daily sorrow to happy photographs of Sam and his new friends at the pub, as well as to a description of how he has blended aspects of his Lebanese culture into Australia – in Sam's words, 'this wonderful multicultural society'. The Australian national anthem begins to play as a second audio layer and really brings this sentiment home. There is no time to ponder the initial problem of Sam's experience of everyday racism, nor the undoubtedly complex transition of going from outsider to insider in (what is portrayed as) a virtual instant.

Sound techniques

In both films, and in most individual digital stories analysed for this research, the music and sound effects correlate to the three main sections of the assimilationist migrant narrative. At the start of the story, the music generally has a steady pace and a happy tone. This pace either dramatically quickens or dramatically slows down when the character's 'moment' hits. The liminal space of the narrative is accompanied by music with a sombre or dramatic tone. Towards the end, the music once again lifts – often both in tempo and in volume.

Sam's use of music is particularly effective for conveying his success. It begins with a melancholic instrumental version of *Waltzing Matilda*, far slower than the original and carrying a deeper tone, perhaps an octave lower. The iconic Australian folk song by Banjo Patterson performs the ideal backdrop for an Australian story, but because it is slowed down it seems to convey the problem of subjectivity faced by Sam: the song, like Sam, is 'technically' Australian, but something about it is not quite right, it is a different, sadder Australian version. Towards the end of *LLAA*, this song transitions into a new iconic audio symbol: the Australian anthem, *Advance Australia Fair*. The transition is emphasised by a shift in volume and careful selection of a snippet of the anthem – the moment where the instruments merge triumphantly, just after the final bridge. The shift in Sam's subjectivity – from a troubled migrant to a happy, settled Australian – is reinstated. His message is made clearer to us through the use of this music: he is proud, he is Aussie!

The other important sound element of digital storytelling is, of course, the voice-over. In *LLAA*, Sam's voice-over is given in English, whereas Fatma speaks in her first language with subtitles provided. The use of the author's own voice is possibly the most important attribute of the digital storytelling genre, working to create a sense of the everyday and an intimacy between author and viewer. The use of the voice-over is a technique that can be linked to documentary. Smaill (2010) explains that the voice-over was pioneered by political documentary film-makers like John Grierson, who worked to bring the physical presence of working-class subjects into film in a more discernible way, in particular by focusing on their bodies and incorporating their own voices. The move corresponded with new technological developments which allowed voice to be heard simultaneously with what was seen on screen: 'If we are showing workmen at work, we get the workmen to do their own commentary, with idiom and accent complete. It makes for intimacy and authenticity' (Grierson 1934, cited in Smaill 2010, p. 53).

Smaill (2010) also links the voice-over to the introduction of what she denotes as a form of 'victim documentary', which focuses on perceived social issues and uses various techniques to create empathy from the audience being addressed. Part of the attempt to create empathy involves giving the subjects affected by the social problem 'an opportunity to speak directly to the camera about their own experiences, in their own environment' (p. 56). This technique set the foundation for personal testimony in documentary, and today it is a fundamental aspect of articulating subjectivity in most documentaries and digital stories.

Speaking is a highly performative act. The verbal statements made by the authors respectively interpellate Sam and Fatma within the terms of language that enable 'a certain existence of the body' (Butler 1997a, p. 5), and illustrate a particular exercise of power relations that connect the author with the addressed audience. Both Butler (1997a) and Smaill (2010) use Shoshana Felman's (2002) notion of the body as 'an excess' of what is said in order to think about how the performance of illocutionary acts implicates the body, creating what Foucault denotes as bodily modifications. In this case, stating something like 'Lebanon is my birth place, where my roots are' situates Sam's body within a frame of reference for 'Lebaneseness' in Australia, but also performs what Butler describes as a redoubling: 'there is what is said, and then there is a kind of saying that the bodily "instrument" of the utterance performs' (Butler 1997a, p. 11). She explains:

> The illocutionary speech act performs its deed *at the moment* of the utterance, and yet to the extent that the moment is ritualized, it is never merely a single moment. The 'moment' in ritual is a condensed historicity: it exceeds itself in past and future directions, an effect of prior and future invocations that constitute and escape the instance of utterance. (p. 3)

In other words, what is said can only make sense in terms of the frames of the excess that support it. The viewer meets the digital story with a particular and pre-existing understanding of what it means to be multicultural or an ethnic Australia. The performance is then directed in certain ways and, as Smaill (2010, p. 138) writes, 'establishes the presence of the performing subject by directing our attention to that subject'. This presence is bound up with certain fantasies of the self and the Other, and ultimately affects the ways in which the various bodies involved in the performance are articulated.

Sam's use of accented English and Fatma's use of Turkish (with English subtitles) intimate the narrators' otherness to the implied viewers. Sam's English is spoken with a Lebanese (read: 'foreign') accent, and he often stumbles over words or phrases. Thus, even as we witness Sam doing Australianness – singing the national anthem, signing documents that prove his Australian citizenship – there remains a shortfall in his performance.

That being said, there is also a disruption involved with the use of different Englishes that can be particularly troubling for whiteness. Sam's English carries a strong Lebanese accent. However, the narration is clear, concise and full of colloquial Australian words.

This combination creates a performative glitch between the whiteness associated with English speaking and the unhomely or 'not-quite right' (not-quite white) sound of Sam's spoken English. The performativity of whiteness is passed on by speaking English, but Sam's accent means it is not passed on in the expected manner – it is producing something else, something other than, or in excess to, whiteness.[8]

This disturbance is exacerbated in Fatma's digital story, which is spoken entirely in Turkish with English subtitles. Her story emphasises that she is a happy Australian woman; however, the subtitles suggest she does not speak fluent English, or at least, she does not speak it confidently. In short, it suggests she has not properly assimilated into Australia. After all, these two adjectives – Australian and non-English speaking – are not considered synonymous by the public imagination of the nation.[9]

Conclusion

LLAA and *NLNC* draw on pre-existing notions of ethnicity in ways that move beyond the digital story and reconstitute notions of 'culturally diverse Australia'. To begin with, we can see that Sam's and Fatma's stories are presented within a framework of multicultural harmony and celebration-of-diversity, one that defines multicultural life in Australia as happy and enriching. Both stories perform the attainment of 'inclusiveness within Australia', which is presented as a performative accomplishment in their respective conclusions. As per Smaill's (2010, p. 97) discussion of documentaries pertaining to Asian Americans, what we see in most of ACMI's 'culturally diverse' digital stories is a framing of the authors as agents who use the particular characteristics of the genre to position Australia's multicultural society as the viewer's 'object of care'. The constitution of Australia as a collective – the who and what make up the Australian nation – is a continual becoming, (re)animated by stories like this.

Paying attention to what bodies are saying, or doing, placed the emphasis of this analysis on the mundane but material effects of culturally diverse storytelling for subjects of multiculturalism. Navarro's (2012, p. 142) examination of digital media argues that the genre's performances have 'concrete effects', noting that they illustrate not only the various possibilities available in exchange, but also the realisation of particular possibilities. Whether the presence of a particular audience is imagined or otherwise, the performance is acted out on its behalf and because of this it remains limited; only a certain amount of possibilities or norms are available for dramatisation and this does (as previously discussed) create effects that are implicated in the material dimension.

How these material effects are shaped will change over time and across contexts and so Sam's and Fatma's performances can never be static. (Indeed, in the conclusion of this

---

8. See Gunew's (2003, 2004) examination of how the spoken stammer can act as a conduit for political resistance and change; also, Rey Chow's (2014) *Not Like a Native Speaker: On Languaging as a Postcolonial Experience*. The excess can also, as Homi Bhabha (1994) has convincingly shown, create a 'third space' of political possibility.
9. See Noble (2005, p. 118) and Gunew (2017).

book, I add to this reading of Sam and his 2003 story based on email correspondence I had with him in 2019.) It is crucial to consider how *LLAA* and *NLNC* act in ways that draw on pre-existing notions of ethnicity and how this moves beyond the digital story to reconstitute notions of culturally diverse Australia. I deepen this exploration in the following chapter by reading and cross-analysing a collaborative digital story.

Chapter Five

HARMONISING DIVERSE VOICES: ETHNIC PERFORMATIVITY IN COLLABORATIVE DIGITAL STORYTELLING

In December 2005 there was a riot in Cronulla, New South Wales. This put the Sutherland Shire on the international map, causing shock and heartache for Australians across the country. *JUNK THEORY* was a forward-looking response to the shock and hurt in the community that aimed to prove it's harder to hurt someone when you know their story.

– Promotional statement for *Junk Theory* (Big hART 2007)

This Sunday every fucking Aussie in the shire, get down to North Cronulla to help support Leb and wog bashing day [. . .] Bring your mates down and let's show them this is our beach and they're never welcome back.

– Text message sent to hundreds of mobile phones in the Shire region between 5 and 11 December 2005
(*Four Corners* 2006)

Created by the Australian arts-for-social-change company Big hART in response to the 2005 Cronulla race riots, *Junk Theory* (*JT*) provides an example of how a single digital story can be produced by a community and represent certain unexpected notions of multiculturalism and nationhood, in this case, Australianness. While *JT* is somewhat different from the conventional digital story, it fits within the medium because of key defining factors. These factors include: facilitation of digital skills' workshops, the collection and use of personal artefacts (e.g. photographs), audio narration and the use of certain kinds of timing, sequence and silence that have come to be recognised as digital storytelling techniques. Whereas digital storytelling projects commonly involve individuals producing their personal stories in isolation, this project merged the participants' individual creative outputs and stories together to form an overall digital story, approximately 60 minutes long, that became a centrepiece of a moving media installation. How these individual digital stories were collected and framed as an overarching text is a useful exercise that explores how notions of community and diversity are negotiated to coalesce in collaborative digital storytelling projects.

Most community-based arts projects set the stage for ethnic performativity quite clearly, driving the work with particular aims and outcomes. Although it is clear that the *JT* project wanted to tell the story *as told by community members* and empower different voices, it is important to consider how this storytelling process was mediated. At some point, the personal stories of community and diversity had to merge with the broader vision/understanding of these concepts for the group at large. Thus, the implicit goals of the project warrant exploration in terms of how they are embedded within the facilitation of this process.

This exploration is particularly important given that the project set out to address the dehumanisation of non-Anglo-Celtic community members in the Sutherland Shire following the 2005 Cronulla riots. Big hART hoped to accentuate the 'human element' of the people involved in the riots in order to promote acceptance, tolerance and social cohesion. The organisation maintains a belief that 'the creative process used in arts-based work helps draw out both people's stories and their ability to make connections with others' (Big hART 2011).

In this chapter, I follow Papastergiadis's (2006) interest in mapping out artistic interventions and their political impacts in a site-specific place. Importantly, I use the theory of performativity to:

> see how the interconnection of these actions is part of an ongoing attempt to grasp the emerging sense of identity and the complex forms of relations with others that occur in everyday life [. . .] It is an attempt to reflect on broad trajectories and imaginatively construct the sense of the world that is forged when art is placed in specific environments. (p. 7)

JT insists on art that does not peddle the 'must see' but rather recognises moments in artistic practice where meaning is 'captured, celebrated and escaped from, in daily life' (Rankin and Bakes 1996, p. 24). I examine the moments in which these daily expressions were produced, resisted and challenged, and study how the formation of these expressions related to the broader imaginary of Australia. I draw on material publicly available on the programmes and stories, including online press releases, descriptions and media coverage, as well as two interviews with the project director, Michelle Kotevski.

The *Junk Theory* project

Big hART came into being as an arts organisation in Tasmania in 1992. The catalyst for establishing the organisation was the economic crisis experienced by the Burnie community after the region's paper mill industries were significantly downsized. The region had long depended on this industry, and its demise led to a range of social problems. Big hART held a series of sessions designed to gain an understanding of the community and the key problems it faced. Based on the feedback, Big hART piloted long-term art projects that incorporated local members of the community, with the intention to support those most disadvantaged/at risk by the economic collapse. The theatre production *GIRL* (1992) was the largest artistic output of this project, casting at-risk youth in acting roles and production support. The production told the story of a young female's descent into the juvenile justice system and used paper from the local paper mills to construct the visual set. The production was picked up by the National Festival of Australian Theatre in Canberra and, according to Big hART (2011), helped restore pride in the community and change the behaviour and attitude of at-risk youth. Statistics showed that at the beginning of the project at least one person in the arts group was charged with a criminal offence each week; however, by the end of the project, there was only one offence in ten months (Big hART 2011).

The project's success led Big hART to showcase the work at crime prevention initiatives and plan further art interventions in communities across the country. In 1996, it developed its core goals, stating it wanted to:

- make sustained changes with disadvantaged communities
- take the issues faced by these communities and make them visible in the public sphere
- influence social policy
- create high quality cultural activity which drives personal, community, and regional development
- produce critically acclaimed, high quality art for local, national and international audiences. (Big hART 2011).

Since then, the organisation has worked in 32 communities across Australia, utilising a range of artistic media, including theatre, film, multimedia installation and digital storytelling. Today, the organisation consists of a handful of full-time staff, and various contracted staff that include community workers, researchers, artists and arts producers. The importance of the everyday is evident in the ethic of the organisation, notably, its aim to promote artistic practice among community members who do not usu-ally engage with the arts, or would not otherwise get the opportunity to do so. For example, Big hART usually works with regional communities, arguing that these are an 'untapped cultural resource', frequently overlooked by artists and arts organisations that favour urban or city environments. It explains: 'Experience and work produced [in city environments] can become homogenised, diminishing the impact of the top-ography, colours, stories, horizons and the materials found in regional areas. Big hART project work is located in regional areas because of the inspiration they offer' (Rankin and Bakes 1996, p. 17). Additionally, Big hART sees marginalised groups of people, especially youth, as key to creating progressive art forms. It argues these groups of people have unique experiences to contribute and 'because of their lack of adherence to social norms, may provide art with a new voice for the benefit of the whole com-munity' (p. 15). Big hART believes that harnessing these voices in creative ways also encourages re-engagement between dominant and marginalised groups in communi-ties, allowing marginalised people to 're-experience appropriate goal achievement, self-discipline, literacy, kinetic skills, applause, affirmation, and acceptance' (pp. 15–16). This encouragement is considered especially important for jobless youth who, because of their work status, are frequently discounted from contributions to local and national forums. Big hART summarises this as a form of self-expression that energises local culture (pp. 22–23).

The overarching model for Big hART is the creation of art with large groups of people over comparatively long periods of time. The finished art product is then placed in relevant national and international arts festivals. In enacting this model, the organisation hopes to create new opportunities for community participants, build community capacity and contribute to national social policy debate in a way that helps shape the nation.

In a similar fashion to ACMI, the organisation incorporates ordinary art within a framework of artistic quality, that is, it attempts to translate everyday life into a quality creative output. Although its work begins from a premise of helping communities grow and prosper, its inclusion in high-end festivals and constant reference to high-quality artistic product qualifies the organisation as a producer of art 'in its own right'. However, unlike ACMI, Big hART's political motivations are accentuated and prioritised, so that the community processes of engagement, political change and social movement inform its aesthetic values of innovation, materials and delivery, rather than the other way around. This concern translates to a range of practical differences in the art projects facilitated by Big hART, most notably in the length of time spent with each community. Although ACMI will spend some time prior to its digital storytelling workshops liaising with the community, this tends to happen via the trust figure in a way that keeps the soon-to-be storytellers removed from the programme set-up. Following that, there is the intensive three-day workshop and perhaps some follow-up correspondence during post-production. In contrast, participants of Big hART projects will work with at least two key facilitators – an arts mentor and an arts organiser/producer – for approximately six months, but sometimes longer. The mentor guides the participants through pathways of personal learning and skills development. In these ways, Big hART mirrors the digital storytelling genre's philosophy of media democratisation – only it expands this philosophy to include democratisation of artistic practice more broadly, to a philosophy of 'art created across cultures from and for everyday life' (Rankin and Bakes 1996, p. 24).

JT was conceived by Big hART in 2005, following the Cronulla riots in Sydney's/Eora's Southern suburbs in 2005. Following the riots, Cronulla and its surrounding suburbs – which together form the Sutherland Shire – received a lot of media attention, highlighting some of the tensions present in the region. Big hART, which had traditionally worked within a crime prevention agenda, picked up on the unsettled feeling emanating from the Sutherland Shire and initiated an art intervention that would address this sentiment of anger and fear. It also hoped the project would nullify an increase of negative media attention on Cronulla, anticipated for the anniversary of the riots in 2006.

The official aims of the project were to: (1) increase positive media about Cronulla and the Sutherland Shire; (2) increase positive dialogue between members of the community; and (3) reinforce community connections through art (Big hART 2007). The name of the project drew on the 'theory of junk', which explores the ways in which something new and valuable becomes redundant and then, over time, regains its value (Big hART 2011). The connection made to this theory was that Cronulla – a beautiful beachside town and home of many thousands of Australians – had undergone significant demographic changes, leading to the creation of 'anger, fear and retribution'. It was hoped that by engaging members of the Sutherland Shire, new values could be created, reinstating pride and worth into the 'iconic Australian beachside suburb' (Big hART 2011).

Before analysing *JT* and the ways it engages with everyday multiculturalism, it is important to contextualise the project. Some understanding of that which prompted the project, namely, the Cronulla riots, is required. Chapter One briefly described the riots and the ways in which the incident went on to impact the scholarship of everyday multiculturalism in Australia. The Cronulla riots were instigated at Cronulla beach, Australia, on 4 December 2005, when three lifeguards became involved in an altercation with a group of men identified as Lebanese. The following Sunday, approximately five thousand people took part in a violent stand-off that intended to proclaim ownership of Cronulla beach and the Sutherland Shire – the Southern Sydney/Eora district known to locals as 'the Shire'.

The severity of the event shocked the Australian public and led to a tumult of media reports that called into question Australian multiculturalism. Although the Liberal prime minister of the time, John Howard, denied a link between the riots and racism, the divide between white Australians and non-white Australians was acutely visible. How did this event link itself to notions of the everyday ethnic, not only at a conceptual level but also at a physical or bodily level? Taylor's (2006) paper 'Australian Bodies, Australian Sands' does an excellent job of outlining the ways in which entitlement and strangeness were embodied during the riots. To extend Taylor's work, and further illustrate the riots' material implications, I combine here Butler's work on performativity with Ahmed's work on strangeness.

During the riots, the body became a symbol of either 'belonging' or 'strangeness' in the Shire, as well as the site through which these attachments could be managed. Drawing on Ahmed's work in *Strange Encounters* (2000, p. 9, 40), it can be seen that the bodies of the Sutherland Shire were recognised as familiar or strange according to a set of possibilities pre-established for the body. These possibilities were then reinforced in the Shire by performativity. The dominant social discourse at play in the riots was one of whiteness which allowed the body of the Other to be simultaneously formed and regulated through the terms of 'non-white'. In the case of the riots, Althusser's (1970) argument that discourse speaks to a subject, 'Hey, you there!', translates exceptionally well. During the riots, Anglo-Australian bodies roamed the Cronulla beach and nearby streets identifying 'Middle-Eastern' people and subsequently chasing or attacking them.

While there are, as Kevin M. Dunn (2006), Taylor (2006) and Stratton (2011) illustrate, various crossovers of norms pertaining to gender, class and social-status undoubtedly at play here, the bodies involved materialised in accordance with an economy of recognition structured on racial categories – the person of 'Middle Eastern appearance' hailed into a subject position of 'stranger' and the person of 'Anglo appearance' recognised as 'familiar, familial [or] friendly' (Ahmed 2000, p. 9). The slogan 'we grew here; you flew here' that adorned the chests of Anglo men during the altercation further illustrates the way bodily recognition occurs according to an understanding of whiteness as the rightful proprietor of Australia (see Taylor 2006, p. 113). The white body is hailed as the 'true' Aussie while the person with a Middle Eastern phenotype is hailed into a subject position in which it is 'already out of place' (Ahmed 2000, p. 23) on the 'white' Australian beach. This hailing serves to reaffirm the hailer as the 'lawful' citizen of Cronulla and the nation.

Importantly, some of the bodies targeted as unlawful and Other in the public space retaliated in a way that maintained the citational performance of whiteness. After initial attacks, revenge was plotted by some of the non-white Australian victims. The evening following the first altercation, more than 40 vehicles drove together to Sydney's/Eora's Eastern suburbs as a sign of defiance. The coastal town of Maroubra was set upon: cars were wrecked, people of 'Anglo' appearance were assaulted and Australian flags were set alight (Dunn 2006, pp. 83–84). As Dunn notes, these performances – especially the target of the Australian flag – ultimately served to reaffirm 'hierarchies of citizenship that privilege Anglo-Australians' (p. 84). By detaching themselves from the icon of Australian identity, the retaliators were further situated as un-Australian.

Since the Others in question were violently hands-on in response to the first alterca-tion, a performance of several 'ethnic' acts took place in a choreography built around and through the performance of various 'Anglo' acts. In turn, the need to act violently against ethnic others 'taking over' the white Australian beach became a strategy of legitimisa-tion, where the (re)interpellation performance (re)confirmed the fiction of 'rightfulness' and whiteness. The reinterpellation thus produces 'citizens who feel entitled and com-pelled to act in particular ways, and citizens who are constructed as deserving recipients of such actions' (Noble and Poynting 2010, p. 500). In this manner, the Cronulla riots were given 'the authority not just of a credible performance but performativity' (Gunew 2004, p. 76).

From this performativity emerged not only an authorised body, but ultimately the authority of 'humanness'. In these encounters, the place (Cronulla beach and the Shire) and the targeted ethnic community are analytically distinct, and yet the formation of both is 'intimately woven together in daily life' (Noble and Poynting 2010, p. 491). To respond to Butler's question 'what counts as a livable life?' we can answer that those recognised as non-white Australians on the Cronulla beach were viewed as illegitimate lives; their restriction in public space installing unlivability for their daily movements and ultimately life itself. Butler (2006, p. 91) writes: 'It is not just that some humans are treated as humans, and others are dehumanized; it is rather that dehumanization becomes the condition for the production of the human to the extent that a "Western" civilization defines itself over and against a population understood as, by definition, illegitimate, if not dubiously human.' The *JT* project began in December 2005 and attempted to address the dehumanisation of the Shire's non-white community members. Employing the tagline 'it's harder to hurt someone when you know their story', the project aimed to accentuate the human, or universal, element of the subjects involved in the riots, so as to promote acceptance, tolerance and social cohesion. As the creator of the project, Scott Rankin (2007), noted, *JT* was aimed at being 'a little ship of reconciliation'. This aim is indicative of Big hART's overall philosophy, which believes that the collaborative cre-ative process allows people to share their stories and make meaningful connections with one another. Big hART held several workshops and meetings where digital storytelling skills were taught and then worked with participants to help them gather anecdotes and objects and present a collective digital story of the people of Cronulla.

The collaboration occurred over approximately 18 months, allowing all participants time to settle into the project, learn about each other at a steady pace and grow comfort-able with the directors. This site-specificity acted as an affective investment in the place of Cronulla, allowing Big hART to become part of the local landscape and productively foster connectivity and deeper relations with the participants and the community at large. Big hART ran a series of focus groups with people in the Shire to brainstorm ideas for the project. In the following months, a variety of artistic and production workshops were held on such things as photography, editing, mapping, song recordings, media training and technical production (Big hART 2007, p. 5).

The collaboration's final product was a floating multimedia installation constructed on a 37-foot Chinese junk, featured at the 2007 Sydney Festival. Projected onto the junk's sails were 'films, portraits, messages, maps and animations' created from the workshops (p. 6). Artist Wei Zen Ho performed live on the deck during contained shows, and musical compositions created during the workshops were played while the junk was sailing. The first live performance was held at Manly Beach in Sydney/Eora on 25 January 2007, and went on for approximately 40 minutes. The installation was held in various places thereafter, sometimes moving along water, at other times docked. In 2008, for example, Big hART presented the work at the Adelaide Bank *Festival of Arts*, and in 2009, at the *10 Days on the Island* festival in Hobart/nipaluna.

Narrative structure

The narrative of the *JT* digital story differs in a few key ways from the conventional digital storytelling narrative seen in ACMI's stories. First, and most obviously, the narrative is not individualised like the conventional digital story. Since *JT*'s digital narrative was developed to represent a range of voices in the Sutherland Shire, the final story is much more layered and multifaceted. Indeed, the narrative does not 'tell' a sequential tale, but rather presents snippets of various speakers, written languages and sound effects that allow the story to unfold in an open and even disjointed manner. The diversity of the voices is signalled early in the narrative with the inclusion of Syrian proverbs and Chinese symbols presented alongside English people speaking. The voice in *JT* is neither singular nor coherent, so the viewer gets the sense that this is a story about people of the Shire developing their identities, rather than having bounded identities. The production is not a conventional or discrete digital story either – rather, it incorporates several individual outcomes/stories produced across the course of the year that utilise photographs, videos, songs, interviews and dance. The variety of mediums illustrates that different people with different skills and interests were involved.

Early in the digital story written text appears that quotes Nicholas N., presumably a participant: 'The future is not what older people think but what younger people do.' The notion of *doing* is intrinsic to Big hART's intervention into communities. The organisation encourages the community to actively *redo* its stories, and therefore its stereotypes. Although the project incorporated people from different generations, Nicholas's quotation speaks to youth in particular, perhaps responding to stereotypes about Western-Sydney/ Eora youth and the aggression demonstrated at the riots. The quotation encourages the community to 'be the change' for the Shire – and the process of making *JT* was clearly part of this change.

What becomes clear from viewing the *JT* film is that the creators and participants are reflecting on their own subjectivities in a way that has made these subjectivities complicated, even confusing. There are a range of techniques used in the digital story to indicate a type of subject in motion. Silhouettes are frequently used across the narrative, both in the film and in the live performance by the dance movements of Wei Zen Ho in front of the projector. These shadowy bodies often touch one another, forming new bodies or blurring into other shapes, colours and scenes. At one point, two people blend into one person, and it becomes impossible to work out who the 'new' person is.

The importance of getting together to share experiences of different identities is highlighted early on by the use of the proverb: 'Even paradise is no fun without people.' This statement points to the implicit tension in the Sutherland Shire – its beaches and associated beach culture are well known in Australia; however, the environmental beauty and relaxed culture of this place is constantly perturbed by issues of localism, cross-cultural clashes and, especially following the riots, aggression and violence. After the riots, many Shire locals retreated from the public space, and Big hART reports that tourism also suffered.

The narrative in *JT* begins by alluding to the idea that the public space of the Shire has become a peopleless paradise. The rest of the narrative attempts to rebuild the Shire and achieve closure on this rift, while at the same time allowing for the differences and contradictions inherent in the community to ripple through. Thus, despite the absence of the single-voiced monologue, and the incorporation of multiple cultural codes and languages, what does seem to carry through in the narrative is the sense of moving through the three stages present in the ACMI stories: a calm beginning which is soon disrupted, a middle section where chaos and confusion ensue and an ending in which the calm beginning is reinstated.

The viewer is guided through these stages mostly by visual and sound cues that allow the structure to retain a level of fluidity and abstractness. The closing scene of the digital story nonetheless looks and feels a lot like what we might expect from a project centred on community cohesion. The dancer performing atop the junk waves to those watching the performance on the beach/jetty while the film shows children hugging and a large black face smiles back at us. The sound of birds chirping completes this hopeful and determined digital ending.

Aesthetic techniques

Like all digital stories, *JT*'s digital story relies on photographs and the use of video footage. However, due to the time and resources allocated to the project, the incorporation of these elements is more sophisticated and creative than the ACMI stories discussed earlier. The images used are what the genre defines as implicit – the meaning is not obvious, the viewer needs to infer meaning. For example, images of fire are frequently used, seemingly from stock footage. The fire often appears in the middle section of the story when chaos and confusion are portrayed. Fire is symbolic of the riots in many ways, since, as noted earlier, many Australians burned the flag during the altercation to represent their detachment from white Australia. Water is a common aspect of *JT*'s visual narrative, contrasting with the fire and working to move the narrative to and from disorder/destruction and order/calmness. There are also photographs of streets and houses blended with scenes from the riots, pictures of lifeguards and portraits of ordinary people. This visual imagery allows the viewer to conceptualise a sense of the Shire neighbourhood and begin to weave a story around these sites and characters.

Colour is used more than black and white, differentiating it from most of the ACMI stories, which all tend to utilise black and white quite generously, especially when alluding to the past. Black and white is used in *JT* in a different way – at the end of the film a human figure wearing a white dress walks through green grass, an image that is contrasted with a human figure wearing all black, including a black veil, traditional for mourning or funeral attendances. The use of black and white here is not to signal past and present, as in the ACMI stories, but points instead to a rift between a sense of hope and peace on one hand, and death and despair on the other.

Sound techniques

Since *JT* does not centre on the personal narrative or individual voice-over, music and sound effects play a particularly pertinent role. The soundtrack increases and decreases in intensity, changing in accordance with the common storytelling trajectory: beginning, middle, conclusion. The music begins softly and serene; shifts into an eerie, suspenseful sequence of sounds (and correlating images); then into frantic, quick-paced music and sounds; and finally brings the story back to a calmer setting with softer music and the sounds of chirping birds. The sound sequence has the effect of mapping out a type of adventure narrative, with the viewer taken through a challenging liminal space and then returned to a quieter place of closure and reflection.

Another important audio aspect of *JT's* digital story is the use of people's voices, including what sounds like quotations from newsreels. The sound bites are often distorted or layered so that the spoken words echo. The use of ordinary people's voices is important for Big hART, which works to give voice to marginalised people or those in the community not normally heard or in a position to share. Used in conjunction with the newsreel snippets, the viewer becomes aware of a tension that most everyday multiculturalism scholarship alludes to: a tension between the public or official view of the Shire and the riots, and the ordinary experiences of them. The Cronulla riots were, as noted, one of the 'spotlight' moments for Australia, indicating that Australian multiculturalism was not necessarily the warm and welcoming space it is so often promoted as being. The careful placement of these sound bites gives the story a depth and pluralism that is not always present in individual digital stories.

Sailing on the winds of whiteness: Deconstructing or reinstating racialised bodies in the Shire?

The project adds to a growing number of community-based art projects in Australia that engage with cultural diversity and attempt to reconstitute the terms of Australian citizenship, community and nationhood. *JT* was conceptualised as a broad social project that was not specifically related to multiculturalism or marginalised ethnic communities. However, the artistic process and final product itself was developed in direct response to the 'shock and hurt' (Big hART 2011) caused by the Cronulla riots, an incident which came to be centred on notions of ethnicity and race in Australia. Although *JT* did not set out with multiculturalism as an objective, it nonetheless engaged with it and, in some senses, enacted it along the way.

A close analysis of the collaborative process of *JT*, as well as its final aesthetic outcome, begins to reveal where some of the key performative moments exist, in particular, how projects like *JT* can counter and/or reproduce the production of racialised bodies via a performativity of cultural diversity. When pitching the project, Big hART worked hard to accentuate the internal diversity of the Shire, which was not recognised in the imagined community, Cronulla. Big hART was also avidly against a project premised on putting Anglo-Australians and Arab-Australians together and 'getting them to play nice' (Kotevski 2012). This kind of project was common in the area, particularly following the riots. Pointing to the irony of such work, creative producer Michelle Kotevski states: 'They'd [the Arab-Australian community] been consulted to death.'

In an attempt to avoid a binary dynamic that, in Kotevski's term, 'quarantined' cultural encounters and multiculturalism, Big hART drew on a cross-section of people from the community. The working group was diverse in ethnicity, gender, age, occupation, locale and other demographic indices. The project was not prescriptive in the people it chose to engage with, nor did it require people to commit to involvement – participants were able to come and go over the weeks depending on their personal schedules, interests and wishes. Kotevski describes a sense of discomfort from Cronulla stakeholders when they realised this type of diversity (especially 'ethnic' diversity) existed *within* the Shire. She explains that many people saw ethnic diversity as existing *outside* the Shire, in peripheral towns such as Bankstown, so 'it was probably more subversive to be doing this [project] in the Shire' (Kotevski 2012). Locating the project here helped *JT* to illustrate that diversity constituted Cronulla itself, rather than being something that existed on the borders, as that which trespassed into the white national space.

The *JT* project performed a hybrid identity for the Shire – it was instigated by the persistent and authoritative presence of whiteness, but it attempted to disrupt this normative discourse by making internal diversity visible and implicit to the project. The use of the silhouettes in the digital story, especially the blending of one silhouette into another, allows us to think about what Michelle Aung Thin (2013, p. 75) terms 'border skin' and consider how skins act as political borders. In other words, it prompts us to ask how bodies in Australia are bordered by skins that have become deeply racialised.

Since the project focused on the community as a whole, it becomes easy for individual difference to be subsumed by a notion of the ideal community. The formation of a community acts to bind many and various members together; however, it can never be fully inclusive. As Khan (2011, p. 55) argues, there is a tension in these kinds of community-based art projects, which promote, on one hand, an acceptance of pluralisation, but continue to be informed, on the other, 'by communitarian notions of "community"' that 'attempt to govern through a specific and singular moral order'. It thus becomes easy for some bodies to be overlooked or misplaced in the formation of a community. For this reason, the topographical remapping carried out in *JT* is striking. As mentioned, the digital story frequently shows pictures of the public space – including streets and houses in the local area, as well as images of the sky, the sun shining through clouds, bodies walking on the street, a weather map and lots of images of water – sometimes waves crashing against rocks, other times a still sea below a blue sky. The water aesthetic is strengthened by the fact that the art takes place on either a moored or moving junk, so it involves an element of ever-moving water. The images are often manipulated digitally, for example, the edges are blurred or animated marks appear across them. As viewers, we get a sense of the community as three-dimensional and involving more than just individuals represented by a project like *JT*. During the digital story, we see images of people fold into the street and then into the sea, and so forth. The technique merges the place 'Cronulla' with the bodies that inhabit it and manipulates ideas of both. Since the riots were so much about the inscription of whiteness on the Cronulla beach and its surrounding space, this spatial remapping becomes politically important. As Noble and Poynting (2010, p. 499) argue, racism and white nationalism involve a 'complex interweaving of space and national belonging', and the weaving together of space and white ownership has been ongoing in Australia since colonial invasion.

JT seems to be attempting a deregulation of the space encapsulated by the Shire; to imagine it as something other than the white space it enacted during the riots. The use of spatial imagery perhaps was not intended to do this directly, but the project did explore how it could bring people, especially non-white Australians, back into the public space. The project's evaluation report argues this was successful, noting that the presence of the project in the community brought NESB (non-English speaking background) families back into the Shire for picnics and other social gatherings: 'We did it – we showed everyone it's safe and that we don't hate each other' (*JT* participant cited in Big hART 2007, p. 15). It is not clear from available data whether or not this sentiment is reflected across the community, but it does seem that *JT* offered an opening to at least reimagine a different kind of space, an opening which can be summarised by a line from the digital story itself: 'At the edge of the bay you will get a new vision.'

The particular aesthetic used in the project can also be seen to be a tactic for unsettling the performativity of whiteness operating in the Shire. The use of the Chinese junk as the digital story canvas encouraged counter-normativity. Boats – especially those resembling junks – carry the connotation of 'boat people' in contemporary Australia, referring to those people who arrive in Australia by boat seeking asylum, but who are relegated beyond the limits of humanness and thus denied protection.[1] *JT* attempted to thwart the negative image of the junk boat by interrogating the stereotype associated with it in

---

1. As briefly touched on in Chapter One, the abjection of asylum seekers has intensified since this project and following the most recent Australian election. One of the key election promises made in 2013 by the new prime minister Tony Abbott was to 'stop the boats', and since coming into office, his government and its Liberal successors have further increased the ferocity of Australia's asylum-seeker policy. The policy includes a military-led strategy, 'Operation Sovereign Borders', which involves offshore processing of asylum seekers at detention centres in Nauru and Papua New Guinea, and no Australian resettlement options. The government has requested all its officials and refugee workers to refer to the asylum seekers arriving by boat as 'illegal maritime arrivals', further denigrating the so-called boat people.

Australia: to make the junk a symbol that is at once strange and friendly. Furthermore, Kotevski argues that projecting portraits of ethnically diverse faces from the Shire on the sails of the junk was a direct attempt to unsettle dominant understandings of who constituted Cronulla. She states: 'Black face from Cronulla up on that sail . . . if you were seeing portraits of the Shire, that wasn't what you were going to expect' (Kotevski 2012). She extends: 'There's something about at that scale, portraiture, it's quite confronting but also just so . . . like each face is beautiful . . . at that scale and that proximity.' Together with the floating aspect of the work, these projections had the capacity to surprise or intrigue viewers and subsequently encourage them to reflect on themselves and the Shire as a community. As the junk sailed past it caught the eye of many people who then further investigated the project by sending messages via the website, or researching the project online (Big hART 2007, p. 6). Kotevski (2012) explains:

> The lovely thing about it was that if anybody did chase up about it the next day . . . they'd go: 'oh my god, it's this thing from Cronulla' . . . [the beauty of the piece] put people in a situation where they wouldn't have expected that to come from them [this segment of the Shire community] . . . the ideas are incongruous.

The remarks made by Kotevski can be linked to Ahmed's (2000) interest in how meeting others always has the capacity to surprise or intervene in normative discourses. Ahmed uses the word 'encounters' to describe meetings between people, arguing that it more clearly indicates how the act of meeting is determined, but only to a certain extent: 'The term encounter suggests a meeting, but a meeting which involves surprise and conflict' (p. 6). Ahmed's point is similar to Butler's argument that although the social stage is always normatively set, and thus predetermined to some degree, the actual performance or lived moment can never by fully determined. Ahmed asks: 'How does identity itself become instituted through encounters with others that surprise, that shift the boundaries of the familiar, of what we assume that we know?' (p. 7). In relation to *JT*, it does seem as if previous assumptions carried by some participants about others – especially about 'ethnic others' – were challenged and perhaps even shifted: 'I've come to see other's point of view and I try to stop and think what people are thinking. What people are thinking of what you're saying, and how you're saying it' (Big hART 2007, p. 15). A small shift, perhaps, but it illustrates that *JT* acted as an opening for self-reflexivity and prompted participants to consider the effect of everyday discourse.

JT worked to create ordinary interactions and relations that allowed for new ways of animating the body and helped to unravel the material production of Othered bodies. The project created a space where those bodies normally termed Other or strange could, in the words of Ahmed (2013, p. 119), 'take a break' from the daily ontological pressure of whiteness, and express themselves through alternative forms. The creation of a safe space is demonstrated by the ability of some participants to discuss and utilise their cultural practices and traditions in *JT* in ways they felt unable to do outside of the project space. For example, a young Egyptian-Australian participant opened up to a couple she was working with when she discovered the couple was also non-Anglo-Celtic. According to Big hART (2007, p. 14), the girl usually kept her cultural heritage hidden from others, but chose to discuss it with the couple: 'The participant felt she could reveal this because she felt safe with this couple.' Moreover, the project encouraged the deconstruction of certain stereotypes and roles. For example, in one workshop, youths were responsible for taking portraits of police officers. This activity inverted the usual relationship of authority: the youths, often well known to police due to crime history, performed the position of power by dictating the camera surveillance and documenting a narrative for the officer.

These stories indicate how the project renegotiated the terms of the 'ethnic' and Anglo-Australian performative chains so that the bodies that began as strange became familiar, or even familial. Kotevski (2012) notes that, at the end of the project, one of the participants said to her: 'you're like our Mum!' This comment is particularly poignant because, at the beginning of the project, Kotevski was often identified by some of the Anglo-Australian participants as an abject ethnic Other. She recalls a scenario in which another aggressive participant yelled: 'fucking wogs!' and then, turning to Kotevski, said, 'but not you; you're all right' (2012). By the end of the project, this participant had formed a respectful bond with Kotevski and proudly promoted the project to her friends, family and workmates. Similarly, Kotevski relates another anecdotal story in which a group of young Anglo-Australian girls revealed that, before *JT*, they did not know any-thing about the Somali-Australian girls in their school and community. After the pro-ject, they began to engage with news media about Somalia, and the two previously divided groups of teenage females intermingled in public places. Such stories are rife with problems, of course, but there are nonetheless significant intercultural interactions and shifts occurring here, even if, in Kotevski's (2012) words, these occur 'painstakingly, person by person'.

Despite the affirmative work enabled through *JT*, it is important to consider the dangers present in the project. Specifically: is there a risk that *JT* reinforces the performativity of whiteness, even as it tries to disrupt it? To what extent is the performativity of a cultur-ally diverse community tied to the normative narrative of whiteness and, in turn, a (re) production of racialised bodies? *JT* lists one of its main outcomes as the ability to build community harmony by exploring 'difficult issues such as racism, the riots and Shire Pride' (Big hART 2007, p. 15). This claim calls for an examination of how *JT* deployed the discourse of 'social cohesion', in particular, how it contributed to the normative assumption that cultural diversity is the cause of social disturbance and disharmony. The project indirectly suggests that diversity needs to be 'worked through' to alleviate issues of difference. This suggestion is a common theme of cultural diversity rhetoric which delimits essentialised notions of ethnic identity as 'sources' of community disruption. As Jupp (2007b, p. 18) explains, all multicultural policies/programmes that aim to build harmony imply a belief that ethnic diversity *causes* disharmony and friction. Therefore, art premised on 'cultural diversity' works like its own social technology, as a way to make 'sense of who and what ought to be held responsible for the successes and failures of these personal and national dreams' (Povinelli 2002, p. 7).

Such a sentiment is echoed by many Anglo-Celtic Australians living in the Shire, who, like 'Mark' and 'Sarah', two Shire locals involved in the riots, feel that the Muslim Australian community is responsible for causing disharmony in Cronulla. During an interview on *Four Corners*,[2] 'Mark' reflected the common sentiment towards Arab-Australians (see Poynting et al. 2004): 'They moved here and they brought their culture with them. And they've got to adapt to our culture' (*Four Corners* 2006). *JT* attempted to make all people responsible for harmony in Cronulla; however, underlying this attempt was the prevailing assumption that the onus of 'giving the Shire a good name again' rested on the ethnic Australian participants' ability to adapt to the dominant culture's agenda.

Given that *JT* was built as part of a 'pre-emptive strike', it further risked foreclosing the creative output before it had an opportunity to develop in a day-to-day way. It is troubling that the glue that held the project together was a desire to create a *positive* image of Cronulla and, indeed, encourage people to (re)visit the town. This strategy adds to many arts projects which attempt to paint a harmonious picture of cultural diversity but fail to delve deeper into the tensions, difficulties and negative reverberations that occur in daily encounters of a diverse community. Papastergiadis (2012b) notes that while culturally diverse arts projects might increase the visibility of cultural difference, this often remains transparent, that is, cultural difference is *seen* but not *engaged with*. As scholars like Claire Bishop (2006, 2012) have questioned, exactly how participatory or reflective of authentic community voices are participatory art projects? Who decides to take part in these projects and who gets excluded, and how well do the stories translate difference?[3]

Although *JT* was able to readdress some aspects of public exclusion, especially among its youth participants, it was not a project that directly interrogated the racist attitudes embedded within the Shire. Although the project facilitators wanted the project to be a 'little ship of reconciliation' that would 'show everyone the Shire's reunited', the extent to which it was able to do so remains limited (Rankin 2007; Big hART 2007).

The project can be meaningfully compared to Footscray Community Arts Centre's (FCAC) *The Go Show* (*TGS*, 2008), analysed by Khan (2011) as a site of artistic and cultural value. *TGS* was a community-based arts project designed to boost the pride of the Melbourne/Naarm suburb Footscray and the neighbouring towns that make up the West-Melbourne/Naarm area. Like the Sutherland Shire, the area is associated with high ethnic diversity and significant social and economic problems, including high crime and unemployment. *TGS* was a collaborative arts project between the FCAC and the local Western Bulldogs football club and, in much the same manner as *JT*, put an emphasis on including disadvantaged youth, ethnic minorities and people with disabilities. The art practice drew on collaborative notions of community, producing a hybrid-media project very similar to Big hART's *JT*. Indeed, both projects produced travelling/moving works – *TGS* used a travelling bus and *JT* a moving boat. Projects like this urge community

---

2. *Four Corners* is an Australian current affairs news programme that screens weekly on Australia's public broadcasting television station, ABC.
3. Stevenson (2004, cited in Khan 2011, p. 49) argues that social policy and programmes implemented for inclusion tend to 'seek to address the manifestations of exclusion, but not its causes'. See also Eva Fotiadi (2011) and the special edition of *Public* edited by Nina Möntmann (2009), entitled 'New Communities'.

members to participate in order to actively create what it means to not only be 'local' to an area, but to be 'an Australian citizen'.

The figure of the citizen is critical for Khan (2011, p. 4), who argues: ' "community" is aligned with the emergence of civil society as a significant site of political investment and struggle.' Stratton's (2011) critique of the Cronulla riots argues that in addition to the racist underpinnings of the Shire, there is also a growing sentiment of disenfranchisement among the Anglo-Celtic members of the area as a result of neoliberalism. He traces a shifting attitude towards citizenship in neoliberal Australia that increasingly associates social inclusion with civil activity, rather than moral equality.[4] In particular, Australian citizenship is no longer equated with the obligation of the nation-state to provide members of its society with certain rights (as it was previously); it is now something that must be earned through various actions (Stratton 2011). And, as Ahmed (2000, p. 108) explains, atypical (non-white) Australians must work extra hard to earn this citizenship, to 'fit in'. This 'work' can include the expression of difference, but only if a 'prior attachment and loyalty to "the future of the nation" ' has been demonstrated (ibid.).

TGS and *JT* called on all community members to actively create what it meant to be from the Shire, or from Melbourne's/Naarm's West. By creating a 'we the community', both projects feed into the Australian multiculturalism AoS and reassert the sneakily productive work of whiteness. As Ahmed argues, Australian multiculturalism suggests that anyone – including those who appear different or are not 'typically Australian' – can be a true Australian (p. 96). Like any formation of a community, Australian multiculturalism simultaneously imagines a neutral space devoid of difference (we are all the same underneath) while actively reproducing the figure of the stranger, or non-typical Australian. Ahmed explains: 'the stranger appears as a figure, as a way of containing that which the nation is not, and hence as a way of allowing the nation to be [. . .] The stranger appears as a figure through the marking out of the nation as dwelling, as a space of belonging in which some bodies are recognised as out of place' (p. 97). *TGS* and *JT* created art that also attempted to construct a diverse but cohesive community; however, in trying to include those culturally diverse subjects, it also worked to further mark them as non-typical Australians, non-typical citizens. I thus have reservations about the use of projected portraiture in *JT*'s digital story. As expanded upon in Chapter Seven, the face is commonly used in Australian multicultural programmes, a tactic seemingly designed to encourage communities to find the 'common humanity' in all people. The use of the portraiture aesthetic in *JT* was aimed at visually projecting the universality of people living in the Shire while representing diversity through facial expressions. The basic premise was that different faces make up Cronulla and surrounding suburbs and

---

4. Stratton (2011, p. 309) explains:

    The neo-liberal state, based on contract and not on shared rights, is not inclusive; it is exclusive and it does not consider others as moral equals but rather as entities in contractual relations. If the contract is not adhered to, or if there is not considered to be a contract, then those entities, those human beings, have the possibility of being reduced to bare life [an existence without protection from the sovereign or nation-state].

that recognising *the human* behind each face can make accepting one another's differences an easier task. Regarding the deployment of the face and body, Ahmed writes:

> Through strange encounters, the figure of the 'stranger' is produced, not as that which we fail to recognise, but as that which we have already recognised as 'a stranger'. In the gesture of recognising the one that we do not know, the one that is different from 'us', we flesh out the beyond, and give it a face and form. (p. 3)

By calling on culturally diverse people to 'face up to the community' through these portraits, there is a danger of maintaining the binary between the white 'underneath' and the culturally diverse person that must always remain strange and external. This problematic is reflected in some of the participant comments featured in *JT*'s evaluation report, which note the project's success in creating a better sense of belonging and tolerance among the participants. One participant is quoted as saying:

> We walked through Gunnamatta beach and took photos of a whole heap of different races and [...] religions and a whole group of different people, and just looking at it you can see that, oh, wow, that's a community [...] you could see that there might be an ethnic person, maybe, can I say a black person, and maybe a Chinese person and they all get along and they don't have the anger against each other. (Cited in Big hART 2007, p. 15)

While there can be no denying that there exists here some productive work towards cultural awareness, it is problematic that there is an underlying authoritative voice describing the 'ethnic situation' in the Sutherland community. The participant partakes in an ethnographic exercise: naming the Other and trying to assign an 'understandable' space for that Other. Referring to the migrant Australians of the project, one participant comments: 'You've just gotta know it, sit down and get to know them before you judge them, I'd judged them as a nobody [...] there've been a lot of great people working on [the project] and they've made it really interesting' (ibid.). The participant has clearly shifted their preconceived ideas about ethnic others – the participant began the project with the belief that these 'ethnic Australians' were 'nobody', an idea that explicitly reaffirms the earlier argument that some Australian bodies exist beyond the limits of humanness. In this case, the ethnic Other exists, but as a nobody. The participant comes to realise that the person is not 'a nobody', and is, in fact, 'worth knowing'. This is arguably a positive shift; however, it retains the problematic outlined by Hage (1998), namely, it involves a central, white 'we' that chooses to get to know these 'interesting' ethnic people on the periphery of Australian life. To arrive at the need for difference to be celebrated, there is first the need for that difference to be recognised, and as Povinelli (2002, p. 49) explains, the category of 'indigeneity' – and I would argue, 'the ethnic' – occurs through a 'passing through' of the white, colonial identity. The liberal pursuit of ethnic diversity comes to be constitutive of the white manager of this pursuit.

Conclusion

Literat et al. (2018, p. 264) argue that 'all participation is participation *in* something, and therefore has an implicit collective dimension, which can be more or less pronounced' (emphasis in the original). This implicit collective dimension is true for both individual digital stories (such as those produced by ACMI and previously discussed) and collaborative digital stories, such as *JT*. The latter exists on the collectivist end of the digital participation spectrum, involving a more deliberate 'mobilization of collective action around a shared agenda' (ibid.). In this chapter, I have illustrated how *JT* is mobilised around a shared agenda of community cohesiveness and belonging in the Shire, but implicit in this mobilisation is a collective performativity of certain ethnic norms. I examined Big hART's *JT* in relation to the previous chapter's analysis of ACMI's digital storytelling programme to consider how national storytelling takes place in digital storytelling as a personal/public relationship between ethnic authors and an implied white audience. Within both ACMI's and Big hART's projects, there is an underlying attempt to bring private stories of racism and related violence into the public realm. Inevitably, this public storying of ethnicity compresses the complicated characteristics of everyday cultural difference and encounters into an assimilatory narrative. This public narrative is edifying and also reinstates the power of the Australian nation-state. As such, typical digital storytelling on cultural diversity plays a role in ensuring that the AoS of Australian multiculturalism functions smoothly.

The analysis also suggests that in Australian digital stories pertaining to ethnicity, the outcome is a material one that produces white and non-white bodies in accordance with normative discourses of whiteness. The analysis illustrated that the longer, collaborative process enacted by Big hART produced a more complex narrative and aesthetic product than the individual digital stories generated by ACMI. The performativity of whiteness can be seen to be lingering at all times in *JT*, but the digital project never fully collapses into the norm in quite the same way as the individual stories seem to. Indeed, it offers several moments of performative departure. This is an interesting outcome, as one might imagine the highly personalised style of the ACMI stories – in particular, the invitation to tell a story of one's choosing – would create a more divergent film. Even across the films collected under 'cultural diversity', the type of ethnic performances carried out tend to conform to one another.

Nonetheless, *JT* also harbours manifestations of whiteness, especially in its formation of community, the underlying responsibility placed on 'ethnics' to enact social cohesiveness, and the reiteration of particular stereotypes and normative tropes about 'ethnic Australians' (even when trying to undo these). There is clearly a challenge facing Australian arts/media practice to continue in everyday settings but also remain attuned to how this practice might enact everyday forms of violence. The following chapter further explores this tension by examining how affective economies are regulated in migrant digital stories and to what outcome.

Chapter Six

IN PURSUIT OF THE PROMISE

'I didn't think it would turn out this way' is the secret epitaph of intimacy.

– Berlant (1998, p. 281)

How does will become a wall?

– Ahmed (2012a, p. 10)

The stage of ethnicity has been shown to be normatively predetermined in digital stories about cultural diversity. In this chapter, I consider how this stage is also affectively set, albeit always in relation to and embroiled with normative categories. Affect theory allows the analysis of the performative to be extended, helping to highlight the nuances of the digital story performance that might otherwise be overlooked. Adopting a 'micropolitics of the subliminal' (Thrift 2004, p. 71), I analyse how the racialised discourse of whiteness is influenced and conditioned by affect and manifests itself within the digital storytelling genre. In doing so, I add to the work carried out by Smaill, who highlights the importance of exploring the affective levels of non-fiction film. In *The Documentary: Politics, Emotion, Culture* (2010), Smaill emphasises the ways in which emotion fuses itself to the social agenda of the documentary, positioning and addressing the film's subjects and its audience. Understanding these forms of address involves taking notice of the patterning of stories and their sequential revelations, which 'figure and refigure' lifeworlds (Feld 1998, p. 446). It also means utilising a dynamic definition of affect, which, departing somewhat from Smaill (2010), considers affect as structures of energy that circulate in the non-discursive field, including – *but not limited to* – emotions. Grossberg (1987, p. 41) terms these structures 'affective economies'.

This chapter examines how affective economies operate according to whiteness in ACMI's migrant digital stories and Big hART's digital project *JT* and are ultimately deployed via the performative. I also introduce two new case studies co-produced by ACMI: Kenan Besiroglu's *Yeni Hayat = New Life* (*YHNL*, 2007) and Rita el-Khoury's *Where Do I Belong?* (*WDIB?*, 2007).[1] The analysis expands 'the envelope of what we call the political' beyond the discursive or representational elements that are more readily recognisable in these texts (Spinks 2001, p. 23; Thrift 2004, p. 64). As such, it also works towards Svetlana Boym's (1998) and Antwi et al.'s (2013) goal – to map diasporic or postcolonial

---

1. All efforts were made via ACMI to contact Besiroglu and el-Khoury regarding re-production of material from their respective digital stories herein, but unfortunately they were unsuccessful.

intimacies, that is, those intimacies that are created through the complex processes of migration.

When cross-comparing Big hART's *JT* with the ACMI-produced digital stories, particular affective patterns emerge, forming a map of affective structures and techniques. The map of intimacy in these digital stories involves three key aspects, or terrains, which I term here 'affective ethnic performativities'. The first uses affect to express the personal experience of ethnic difference in Australia, the affective terrain most often emphasised in digital storytelling methodologies and research. This affective ethnic performativity entails the voicing of a presence in the dominant culture and often describes the emotional duality of this presence. Second, and usually at the same time as the subjects of digital stories 'express' their ethnicity, there is an attempt to 'prove' the value of its presence to the viewers. In other words, there is an attempt to both highlight and validate the existence of 'ethnic Australians'.[2]

I consider here how digital stories work to create intimacy between the author and viewer so as to convince the implied white audience of ethnic worth. Part of my analysis concerns how the structure of affect works at the subjective and bodily level and, in particular, how the ethnic author attempts to consolidate discomfort and injury by willing an intimate connection with the audience. The act of witnessing carried out by the non-ethnic viewer becomes a form of validation, helping the ethnic subject to establish a self-assured subjectivity: to 'feel more comfortable in my skin'.

Third, and perhaps the subtlest of all ethnic affective performativities in these digital stories, is the perpetual longing for and the pursuit of the liberal 'good life'. The Australian good life is a phantasmagoric aspiration linked to the origins of migration and is continuously reinforced by the white imaginary; it is comparable to aspirations of 'upwards mobility' in the United Kingdom and North America. The good life for white Australia equates with success, happiness and equity – the last being the idea that the good life is attainable by all. In their digital life narratives, ethnic subjects can be seen to be trying to occupy the 'same psychic space' (Berlant 2011, p. 95) afforded to the dominant culture. Certainly, such a pursuit drives Australians at large; however, the following analysis will demonstrate that it takes a particular formation in the ethnic performances of this ambition. In particular, the pursuit of the good life creates a subjective tension for the ethnic author: the author is pushed close to the imaginary good life by the dominant culture, but never allowed to traverse into and inhabit this imaginary fully.

Expressing everyday ethnicity: 'What it feels like'

The first affective ethnic performativity emerging from the digital stories is organised around *what it feels like* to be an ethnic Australian. The digital storytelling genre

---

2. This is something that many scholars have addressed, including Hage (1998) who, as previously noted, carried out a close examination of how 'multicultural Australia' is promoted as an interesting, exciting product for the consumption and enjoyment of white Australia.

encourages the telling of an emotionally expressive story; it relies on individuals sharing highly personal stories in ways that others will emotionally connect with and respond. Expressing what it feels like to be a migrant in Australia frequently takes the form of straightforward description. Sam Haddad, for example, tells us, 'I felt anxious', and he also shares his affection for his old and new countries in the title of the film, *Loving Lebanon and Australia*. But the affective dimension of ethnicity is far more complex than verbal or even visual form, involving an intricate arrangement of objects that draw on both personal and public ideas of Australian multiculturalism. Furthermore, although the digital story genre works to create a succinct expression of identity and personal experience, those created by non-Anglo-Celtic Australians have a tendency to hover slightly above uncertain and unresolved moments. This uncertainty is not always obvious, with migrants moving the viewer of the digital story through a turbulent experience to a closed and finalised identity point in a quick and seemingly smooth fashion. However, when these stories are dissected more minutely, the ambiguities become more apparent.

An obvious starting point when examining the affective expression of personal experience in digital stories are the titles and narrative transcripts. These texts reveal the desire many migrant Australians have to share their experiences and, importantly, for these stories to be heard in a positive and relatable light. Of note is the frequency with which rhetorical questions appear in the transcripts or, in the case of Rita el-Khoury's digital story, in the title itself. These questions hint at how the process of telling the migrant narrative is, first, not an easy, quantifiable task and, second, seeks some form of answer or active response from the viewer. It also alludes to how so many migrants are forced to occupy a disposition of precarity, in which one is always waiting to 'fully land' in their new country. *Where Do I Belong?* reflects Rita's highly personal inquiry into her sense of self, an inquiry that relies heavily on the audience. 'Where *do* I belong?' Rita asks her audience, at the same time that she attempts to answer this problematic through storytelling. When these personal questions are delivered in conjunction with visual and sound techniques, an ambivalent subject position is portrayed, reflecting one of the key affective components of the physical act of migrating. The migration experience does, after all, cause a split in both time and space, disrupting the perceived linear formation of memory and history and creating complex attachments to both the origin country and the new country.

Kalpana Ram (2005, p. 134) argues that memories carry the same structure of affect into the present, so that when a memory from the past place occurs, the feeling is replicated. I propose, on the contrary, that the affective economy instigated when memories arise is altered to some degree by the new setting that summons it. As Ahmed (2010a, p. 49) argues:

> The concept of affective contagion tends to underestimate the extent to which affects are contingent (involving the hap of a happening): to be affected by another does not mean that an affect simply passes or 'leaps' from one body to another. The affect becomes an object only given the contingency of how we are affected, or only as an affect of how objects are given.

Similarly, the affective structure present in a memory cannot smoothly slide from one context to another and remain intact; it is morphed according to the present moment the memory transpires. Indeed, one of the key difficulties facing the migrant is the psycho-social disconnect present in memory recollection. When a memory is triggered, there is a familiarity about how it *feels*, echoing something like that which was once experienced. However, it is not exactly the same experience: the feeling is altered by the context it re-emerges within and this creates an affective split that is difficult to reconcile. Thus, the migrant tends to waver between fragmented and conflicting memories and the expression of a delimited identity.

Digital stories provide an opportunity for migrants to convey the difficulty of occupying a 'mixed' cultural identity, and several affective techniques are used to help them do this. One of the most common ways this difficulty is emphasised is through a focus on family separation. The family in the typical digital story represents a universally shared concept that holds universally shared attachments. Digital stories utilise old photographs of relatives from the homeland to depict the migrant's (dis)connection. For example, the photographs used by Fatma in *NLNC* when she describes leaving her family – her father in particular – are particularly emotionally laden. She uses a photo of her father holding a small girl, presumably a young Fatma, in such a way that prompts the viewer to consider their own familial relationships, especially the father-child relationship. The father-child relationship is conventionally structured as hierarchical – the father positioned at the apex of the hierarchy, providing security and reverence for the family members below. The fact that Fatma's father is so upset at her leaving both affirms this structure and destabilises it – the daughter leaves the family in pursuit of a life beyond the nuclear familial setting and her father, distraught by this rupture, weeps. The story constantly returns to her father as a signpost that marks the break between past and future, old identity and new identity.

The duality felt by migrants like Fatma is also expressed through a constant oscillation between the left behind and the 'kept alive'. The memory of Fatma's family (her father in particular) is kept alive in Australia through her own family, which at the end of the story includes several children and grandchildren in Australia. In *LLAA*, Sam also emphasises the family legacy in Australia, as well as the importance of his work with the Lebanese community. Photos of Sam surrounded by both the Australian and the Lebanese flag signal the importance of his homeland and his determination in sustaining this *past* as part of his Australian *present* – a theme common in migrant digital stories.

Interestingly, the films mostly avoid dwelling on the moments of change, or the sense of interstitiality, despite the constant to-and-fro movements. The difficulty negotiating memories and the affects they entail correlates to why we repeatedly witness hasty transitions in migrant digital stories between the old past origin and life in the new present destination. Opening up or dwelling on the past life is both emotionally trying and socially discouraged. It is also the case that the migrant is willed to move quickly into a 'new Australian' paradigm in everyday life. The digital story definition and methodology employed by ACMI incites this, encouraging authors to pinpoint a moment of change and then tracking the direction it subsequently takes. Thus, the moment of change or affective confusion is rarely explored; instead, the subjects are asked to tell us what happened *next*.

Authors are expected to learn the moving image skills and techniques within a short time frame; added to this is the fact that the digital storytelling genre itself requires the condensing of long, convoluted experiences (like migration) into snapshots. As a result, scenes in stories like *NLNC* and *LLAA* are ordered in particular ways, proposing a linear movement of time and space that leads to an understanding of history as cause and effect. The ordering simplifies the complexities and nuances of the migration experience that, due to its nature, creates a disjuncture leading to a constant oscillation between past and present/there and here/then and now.[3] Indeed, 'oscillation' is not sufficient for describing the complex affective economy that migrants embody. The embodiment is never fully of one or the other polarities, but a complicated mix of both.

Value, validation and comfort

The second affective terrain that emerges when viewing digital stories about cultural diversity moves beyond sharing what it is like to be 'ethnic' to an attempt to actively demonstrate the value or worth of this ethnicity. In the stories engaged with so far, there is an attempt to move the affective register associated with ethnic Australians from bad to good. *JT* and many of ACMI's migrant stories tend to shift characters and the narratives they occupy from a troubled place to a hopeful, happier one, though this is not immediately obvious in the ACMI-produced stories. Indeed, at first, it appears that the ACMI-produced stories begin on the opposite platform of the affective scale to *JT*. The ACMI-produced stories attempt to acknowledge and celebrate the successes of culturally diverse Australians, whereas *JT* is premised on the specific desire to remove a negative tarnish on the happy multicultural nation. The stories on migration emerged following appeals from ACMI via cultural organisations to work with communities to 'document diverse voices' (Simondson 2012a).

ACMI's migrant digital stories ultimately worked within Australia's multicultural framework of harmony and celebration-of-diversity. *JT*, on the other hand, was instigated in direct response to a specific, racialised incident, namely, the Cronulla riots.

---

3. It is also worth noting the difference between digital stories by older 'ethnic' Australians and younger 'ethnic' Australians. Sam's and Fatma's digital stories move very quickly from the past into the present, unlike stories by younger digital story authors who, when writing about migration, tend to make the narrative about the particular experience of inbetweeness and uncertainty. Rita's whole narrative is about establishing where she belongs as a person: is it in Australia, or in Lebanon? The narrative is quite different to Sam's and Fatma's, which work to demonstrate a pre-established *knowing* about belonging: for Fatma, Australia *is* her new country and her new life, this is her new identity; and for Sam, Australia and Lebanon are both homes that he loves equally, the title forming a statement and hiding doubt that inevitably surfaces in his narrative.

Nonetheless, all the stories perform, one way or another, the attainment of inclusive-ness within Australia, and thus set about redefining ethnic life in Australia as positive and enriching. It is also important to remember that there is already a series of pre-established notions about multicultural Australia that works to frame the projects in affective ways. As Ahmed (2004) argues, when we encounter objects we do so from a certain angle and we, in turn, are encountered by those objects from a certain angle. In encounters, we make an impression on others, and those others also press upon us (p. 6). Importantly, all subjects and objects have an emotional history, meaning the stage of the encounter is already affectively set. This stage acquires its structure over time, so that some objects become imbued with positive or negative affect and are thus positioned – often well before the encounter – as good or bad objects (Ahmed 2010a, p. 34). Ahmed writes: 'Objects are sticky because they are already attributed as being good or bad, as being the cause of happiness or unhappiness' (p. 35). To put it simplistically, if one is dreading a particular encounter, it is because 'bad feeling' has come to represent that future encounter. Likewise, a happy event might be looked forward to, so that 'good feeling' pre-empts the stage of the anticipated encounter.

The narrators of digital stories arrive at the story from a particular affective position, and we, as viewers, do as well. Non-white Australians are embedded within a history of negative Othering associated with particular stereotypes that gain meaning in rela-tion to the white Australian. The Australian digital stories examined so far were made in the early twenty-first century, a time at which anti-Muslim and anti-Arab sentiment was high in Australia, greatly influenced by a range of global and national events in the early 2000s. The Cronulla riots in Western Sydney/Eora were a climactic moment in this tense relationship and further exacerbated the negative sentiment towards Australia's Arab community. The riots involved a choreography of performative acts of whiteness and ethnicity which created certain kinds of emotion and ultimately reinstated bodies as either 'in' or 'out of bounds' in the Sutherland Shire. When the so-called Lebanese bodies performed their retaliation through violence, the bad feeling connected with the Arab community was reinstated in such a way that these bodies became identified as the cause of bad feeling in Australian race relations. Ahmed (2010a, p. 40) explains: 'Once an object is a feeling-cause, it can cause feeling, so that when we feel the feeling we expect to feel we are affirmed.'

Indeed, even when we do not encounter that object, but draw close(r) to an encounter with it, we pre-empt the feeling, so that 'some things more than others are encountered as "to be feared" in the event of proximity' (ibid.). The Cronulla riots were a violent manifestation of the daily racism that occurs in Australia towards its 'ethnic community' – the altercations reinstated the need to pre-empt bad feeling from encounters with Arab bodies, sending a sensationalised message of dread across the country. This dread is brought forward to the set of many migrant digital stories, and cultural workers and organisations like ACMI and Big hART seem to be aware of this baggage. The awareness is more obvious in a project like *JT*, which directly responded to the bad feeling surrounding the Cronulla riots. However, the riots compounded the pressure already on non-white Australians, implicating all 'ethnic Australians' to some degree. The central characters of the ACMI-produced digital stories are thus also tied to the negative ideas associated with non-white Australians that became explicit in the riots.

It is not surprising then that *JT* and so many community-based arts projects about 'cultural diversity' are contextualised negatively. The ethnic bodies that form the subjects of these digital stories – the culturally diverse Cronulla residents and the culturally diverse migrants of Victoria, Australia – already have a history of bad feeling attached to them in Australian public culture. The *JT* project made clear from the beginning that one of its main aims was to build community harmony by exploring 'difficult issues such as racism, the riots and Shire Pride' (Big hART 2007, p. 15). Big hART worked with the Sutherland Shire community to try to deconstruct the stereotypes performed in the riots, in particular, to humanise the community's ethnic members.

Stories such as *LLAA* and *NLNC* worked (albeit incidentally) to deconstruct the stereo-types of ethnic people in Australia more broadly, drawing heavily on the multicultural frameworks of harmony and celebration-of-diversity and indirectly pointing to the unease surrounding non-white Australians. Ultimately, both case studies exemplify Thrift's (2004, p. 70) concept of 'reparative knowing projects'. Similar to the self-confessional thematic of recent literature, these kinds of projects are 'becoming commonplace as means of producing affective orientations to knowledge which add another dimension to what knowing is' (ibid.). Both digital storytelling projects examined here work to shift the affective register associated with these bodies so that the dominant culture can 'know' the bodies in a different way, as objects associated with good feelings.

We see many examples, both direct and indirect, of the authors acting out different understandings of the subjectivities they have brought with them. Their performances create intimacy, which, although often regarded as being a highly personal connection, takes on a very public dimension. Berlant's (1998, p. 281) definition of intimacy elucidates this point: 'To intimate is to communicate with the sparest of signs and gestures, and at its root intimacy is the quality of eloquence and brevity. But intimacy also involves an aspir-ation for a narrative about something shared, a story about both oneself and others that will turn out in a particular way.' The stories rely on intimating experiences commonly understood as universally emotional or, at least, emotional to all Australians. Migrants in digital stories such as Sam and Fatma frequently allude to the hardship experienced in their homelands, compelling the viewers to understand their 'human' desire to seek a better life in their destination country, be it Australia, Canada, the United States or the United Kingdom. In the Australian examples of *LLAA* and *NLNC*, the authors empha-sise the invitation from the Australian government to migrants who could help Australia grow and they also stipulate their contribution to Australian society through work, family and active involvement in community and social life.

Similarly, *JT* places an emphasis on the commonality of all people in the culturally diverse Shire, most obviously through the incorporation of portraiture. The close-ups of people's faces, together with snippets of quotations from participants of the pro-ject, can be seen as a type of 'reaching out' to the Shire, a way to create an affective intimacy with the public. As the tagline of the Big hART project indicates, *JT* uses these techniques to draw people closer to the so-called Others of Cronulla: to listen, to under-stand and to *value* their contributions to Australian life. Boym (1998, p. 500) describes how intimacy is romanticised – constructed in the space between private and public and eventually 'adulterated' by the cultural specificities of that space. What is clear is that the intimacy created by Big hART and many of the ACMI digital stories is framed by norms associated with white Australia, norms that the dominant public culture can connect with and understand.

The creation of intimacy with the implied white Australia means that Sam's anger and melancholy about the conflict he experiences at work, or Fatma's anxiety about navigating the migration journey, are merged into the background of ethnic or Other experiences – no longer relevant in the dominant culture. There is a sense that the dis-comfort experienced by migrant Australians is not something that should be dwelled on; it existed at one time, but the focus should now be on the comfort of the present life. The resulting affective economy is very similar to that which Ahmed (2010a) describes in her critique of *Bend it Like Beckham (BILB)*. Here, Ahmed argues that migrants who refuse to let go of their suffering are represented as melancholic, 'as incorporating the very object of [their] own loss' (p. 48).

The father character in *BILB* is shown to be stubbornly attached to a previous injury, specifically, the hurt caused when the British cricket team rejected him because of his ethnicity. His daughter, now given the chance to play professional soccer in Britain, is 'held back' by her father because he does not want her to experience the same rejec-tion. But his injury is framed as being of the past, of the old Britain. By not letting his daughter play soccer the father is accused of 'not playing the game' of the contemporary nation. Thus, the father is seen to be actively enacting self-exclusion and self-suffering; in the process his actual suffering is publicly erased. Combining this analogy with Hage's (2009) work in *Waiting*, migrants who are melancholic, who are seen to be stuck in the past, are quickly labelled social problems. Hage describes the ways in which contem-porary Western life involves an overarching sense of *stuckedness* for its citizens, white or non-white. This stuckedness, or 'crisis', is a symptom of neoliberalism and is no longer seen as unusual, but as a normalcy. In order to be a good citizen, one is expected to endure the crisis, to put up with the discomfort of stuckedness: 'the more one is capable of enduring a crisis the more of a good citizen one is [. . .] the ones who do not know how to wait are the "lower classes", the uncivilized and racialised others' (p. 8). There is little space, therefore, for dwelling on the trying aspects of migration.

Kenan Besiroglu's *YHNL* further illustrates this predicament. The feel-good story is delivered in a rather sombre tone, and despite the happy ending, includes some distressing moments. Kenan migrated from Turkey to Australia with his wife and son in 1970. On the ACMI website, his digital story is described as 'a story of hard work, perseverance and the promise of a new life'. Like the other ACMI digital stories examined so far, his story describes migration and the early difficulties experienced in Australia, especially at work. Like Sam, Kenan did not know much English when he first arrived in Australia. Adding to the confusion, he worked alongside migrants from several other places who spoke a range of non-English languages. Kenan describes how the migrants supported each other and retells a distressing incident where he and another new migrant attempted to get home from work.

I was at General Motors in Port Melbourne. I had been here for a week. I took a train from Abbotsford to the city and then a bus. I was working at number 11. My workmates were from other countries. I was working the day shift. One day the boss came to me with someone who could speak Turkish. He asked me to do 4 hours overtime. I said to him I can stay but I wouldn't be able to get to the train station. The boss said, 'Don't worry about it. There's also a Greek guy from Richmond. The Italian leading hand will give you a lift to the train station.' I said OK. When we finished work the Italian guy gave us a lift to the city. But we couldn't find the train station. It was raining. We spent an hour trying to ask people but couldn't explain to them. We were not able to talk to each other either. He was new in Australia as well and couldn't speak English. I couldn't speak it either and we didn't understand each other's languages. We were communicating through signs. I could catch a taxi home but I did not want to leave my friend. I saw a Richmond sign on a tram. I tried to say to my friend, 'Take this one.' He too did not want to leave me. We were still communicating through signs. He took the tram and left me. I took a cab and explained my address with difficulty but managed to get home. It was 11 at night. My family was waiting outside the house for me. They were about to go to the police. But when they saw me they were very happy. I told them why I had been late and we had a laugh.

The experience relayed by Kenan is very distressing, highlighting the confusion, isolation and helplessness new migrants in Australia experience.[4] It also illustrates the way 'ethnic Australians' are continuously relegated to the margins of everyday life – so much so that instead of Kenan receiving help from a settled Australian, he receives it from another migrant, another 'outsider'. It is no coincidence that the migrants have to navigate their new home through their respective *difference*; it elucidates, once again, the way 'ethnic Australians' are amalgamated together as a homogenous entity distinct from white Australia. The amalgamation comes, first, through the active positioning of 'ethnic Australians' as abject, or on the margins of the dominant culture, and, second, through the active performance of this marginal position, as illustrated by Kenan, who is forced to 'join forces' with another migrant Other in order to survive the day. The two migrants are, in Ahmed's framework, 'sticky', and here must 'stick together'. The humour found at the end of the day, when the family 'has a laugh' about the situation, indicates another survival technique; at this moment Kenan and his family are so outside of the comfortable that it can only be humorous – a way of easing the discomfort, perhaps.

---

4. Much analysis has occurred on the cognitive aspect of this tension; however, as Noble (2005) stresses, this tension is regulated by a range of affects which have mostly been overlooked. Noble considers this regulation in terms of comfort, where comfort acts as a type of affective economy – it is not an affect in itself but a complex system of affects that constructs a feeling of being at home (or otherwise) in Australia. Exploring this at an affective level is important because, as Noble illustrates, comfort and discomfort are felt in material ways by the migrant. There is, for example, a visceral aspect to feeling uncomfortable: migrants who are exposed to racism regularly feel nauseous, nervous or reanimate their bodily movements to avoid certain sites, streets and areas (p. 110).

Despite the stress experienced by Kenan and his family, as well as the underlying tensions the experience alludes to, Kenan jolts the story along. In the same way that Sam and Fatma move us quickly through troubled territory, the next thing Kenan tells us after relaying the work incident is that he had his first Australian family photo in 1970. The two moments – the stress of the incident and the excitement of the photography – are dictated verbally as if they are part of the same event when in fact they are two very different experiences. The movement from bad old place to exciting new place is swift and seamless. Like several of the stories already discussed, Kenan's experiences are conflated into a successful migration story, even though the lived experience narrated does not necessarily reflect this.

Kenan's story, together with Fatma's and Sam's, sheds some light on why it is that representations and interpretations of migration and identity tend to fall into binary forms. The difficulty of negotiating the affective attachments to past and present is certainly accentuated by the fact that migration to Australia places a complex pressure upon the 'New Australian'. As Ram (2005, p. 134) explains, the migrant is charged with 'the crisis of appearing "modern" while maintaining a sense of cultural identity in a world where one is newly designated as an "ethnic minority".' While there is now a (small) space for culturally diverse expressions, the provision comes with a pressure to portray ethnicity in particular ways. A bind is created for 'ethnic Australians': on one hand they wish to move forward with their lives in Australia; on the other hand they are forced to manage the constant stream of personal memories alongside a bureaucratic desire for an 'ethnic' performativity:

> That which could once be left at the level of the taken for granted, as a set of assumptions sustained by the nature of social interaction itself, must now be made the object of conscious attention and deliberate effort if it is to be at all kept alive [. . .] Inevitably, this version of culture as explicit instruction is one which is more rigid, because it is more sharply defined and with more at stake in 'getting it right'. (p. 125)

In the real-life experience narrated by Kenan, he is pushed to the margins by his boss or the public culture; this recurs in the digital story structure, which, despite being designed to reveal and circulate individual stories, often pushes personal experiences of alienation to the public periphery. The desire of the dominant public culture is perspicuous: the ethnic Australian must be either this or that, here or there, comfortable or uncomfortable, and only by 'getting it right' can the ethnic Australian be deemed a legitimate Australian, an Australian whose difference is of worth and value.

Even when 'ethnic Australians' attempt to unravel themselves from binary positions of this or that, here or there, the interpretive tools and affective economies available to them act as apparatuses that shape this unravelling, so that, ultimately, they are undone and then redone according to a binary structure of us and them, white and non-white. Anti-racism theory, including everyday multiculturalism, continuously stresses the need for new ways to think cultural diversity in Australia. However, the common tropes and frameworks sneak in because of the force of performativity and the way ethnics come to assume their role on the periphery out of both a desire for homeliness and comfort, and a basic necessity for solidarity and survival.

Performing the multicultural promise

The work of Ahmed (2004, 2010a, 2010b) and Berlant (2011) allows the third aspect of affective ethnic performativity to be meaningfully explored. Ahmed's (2004, 2010b) work on 'happiness as a happening' intersects with Berlant's use of optimism in a way that assists the analysis of how it is that the subjects of digital stories are propelled across the narrative by a promise of multicultural happiness. Ahmed analyses how good and bad states of feeling, such as happiness or embarrassment, are produced in moments of power relations. For Ahmed (2004), happiness, like other emotions, is neither internal nor external to the body but is produced when the body encounters objects. Ahmed uses the word 'objects' to refer to certain kinds of bodies as well as clusters of subjects that become 'an object'. These objects get passed around the social unit and accumulate 'positive affective value', inevitably orienting subjects to certain ways of being (Ahmed 2010a, p. 29). In the stories analysed here, the objects are 'the assimilated migrant', 'the happy multicultural nation' and the like. Affect clusters the multicultural subjects of the ACMI-produced stories and directs the cluster in ways linked to the apparatus of security of multiculturalism. Assisting this process is happiness, which Ahmed defines as a promise that moves people in certain ways. The 'feel good' rhetoric of multiculturalism is (re)produced in public statements and migrant promotional work, setting up an expectation of reward for being an assimilated ethnic Other in Australia. This feel-good expectation is clearly evidenced in the most recent speech about formalising Australian multiculturalism in the twenty-first century.[5]

When considering promise in relation to the case studies, we can begin to see how certain aspects of multiculturalism have become objects of positive affective value, driving the digital story subjects towards them in certain ways. Two of the most obvious of these objects include the family and the notion of workplace success. Promoted as a stable and centralised unit of Australian life, the family becomes the epicentre of the good life – a good life that must be sustained by normative rituals like marriage and economic pursuit. As Ahmed (2010a, pp. 45–46) notes in her analysis of *BILB*, marriage is frequently conflated with the good life in feel-good films and stories about migration.[6]

Inherent in migrant narratives is the lure of a better life, one that offers more opportunities to better oneself. Hage's (2009) work on waiting describes this dynamic and shows how well-being is frequently associated with a sense of mobility. Language illustrates the importance of this, as seen in one of the most commonly asked questions in everyday life (in numerous languages): 'How are you going?' Hage argues that 'such language of

---

5. Bowen (2011) states: 'Multiculturalism is about inviting every individual member of society to be everything they can be, and supporting each new arrival in overcoming whatever obstacles they face as they adjust to a new country and society and allowing them to flourish as individuals.' This flourishing is supposedly enabled by committing to Australian society and values, including the formal pledge: 'loyalty to Australia and its people [. . .] whose democratic beliefs I share.'
6. The paradox regarding the wedding in *BILB* is that it concerns the older daughter and displays the fact that she is mired in the past (and, like her father, holding on too tightly to outdated cultural traditions). See Ahmed (2010a).

movement is not simply metaphoric but conveys a sense in which when a person feels well, they actually imagine and feel that they are moving well' (p. 2). He goes further to show that people who migrate do so because they seek a space that better constitutes a 'launching pad for their social and existential self. They are looking for a space and a life where they feel they are going somewhere.'

The compulsion to move forward onto something else, something better, is frequently seen in migrant digital stories, and is especially pronounced in the ACMI-produced case studies. When Fatma describes the risk of being sent back to Turkey, she expresses panic: 'How could we go back!' To go backwards would be even worse than never having left. Further, Sam and Kenan talk about their migration to Australia as one motivated by new possibilities, a new sense of self. This search is visually represented by technologies of flight – airplanes, airports and passports almost always appear in these stories and, as Ahmed (2010a, p. 47) asserts, 'happiness [. . .] is promised by what goes "up and away".' The desire to travel is validated by Australia's multiculturalism AoS, which promises 'a better return' for migrants than that of their homeland (ibid.). Thus, Australian multiculturalism feeds the quest for existential mobility, promoting migration to Australia as a rewarding experience. The reward only arrives, however, if the migrant behaves in an appropriate, self-motivating manner. In other words, happiness is promised to migrants so long as they orient themselves to everyday life in Australia in a particular way.

There are two other key aspects to this affective orientation: the pressure on ethnics to repair or make up for the losses caused by cultural difference, as well as biopolitics' own ability to override these losses by a focus on the future. These aspects are an example of what Thrift (2004, p. 69) terms 'affective utopianisms'. As discussed, migrants in the typical digital stories draw on certain affective registers to facilitate the reparation of a bad multicultural past to a good multicultural future. The digital story is created with a viewer in mind – a witness – who is taken on an emotive journey in the hope of shifting them from a place of bad feeling, shame and anger to one of good feeling, pride and happiness. The digital stories thus involve creating an optimistic attachment between creator and viewer, which is implied as an attachment between migrant and white Australian. Berlant (2011, pp. 1–2) describes the optimism driving these kinds of attachments as '[the energy] that moves you out of yourself and into the world in order to bring closer the satisfying something that you cannot generate on your own but sense in the wake of a person, a way of life, an object, project, concept, or scene.' Adding to this, we have seen in the past two decades a certain kind of positioning about the past, where Australia 'the nation' is shown to not only welcome diversity, but acknowledge former wrongdoings against cultural difference. However, as highlighted in Chapter One, the embrace of cultural difference is still premised on a white ontological foundation. Povinelli (1998, 2002) argues this when writing about an Indigenous land claim in Northern Australia. She contends that Australia presented itself as a nation striving for 'the Good', showing an emotional, redemptive side. For Povinelli, the issue was that the act of being redemptive, of acknowledging the past wrongs, allowed the contemporary nation to push forward into the future without properly addressing the injuries it caused in the past, injuries that recur in the present, albeit in different forms. She writes, 'Instead the court decision and the public discourse surrounding it urged dominant society on a journey to its own redemption, leaning heavily on the unarguable rightness of striving for the Good and for a national reparation and reconciliation' (Povinelli 1998, p. 587). A complex affective economy forms, whereby both private and public discourses propel migrant subjects towards the happiness of the nation. In the ACMI stories discussed so far, the authors form optimistic attachments to the idea of Australian belonging and acceptance, implied as needing to come from white Australia. The same is true for the culturally diverse participants in *JT*. The project's message, 'It's harder to hurt someone when you know their story', indicates its optimistic attempt to create an empathetic bond, hoping for acceptance from the audience that is implicitly understood to be white. This willing is what Berlant (2011, p. 27) terms a 'cruel optimism', that which incites the migrant to 'track the affective attachment to what we call "the good life", which nonetheless, and at the same time, find[s] their conditions of possibility within it'. The culturally diverse subjects of the digital stories are encouraged to inhabit the Australian good life in a cruel optimism; cruel because the terms of this good life are defined by normative whiteness and, therefore, unattainable to these subjects. In other words, an optimistic attachment is formed to the notion of achieving success and happiness in Australia, but the terms of these achievements are driven by the mainstream white culture, which ultimately stops short of the migrant Other.[7]

The migrant digital stories typically perform what Poynting et al. (2004) describe as the collapse of difference. Even spaces supposedly supportive of difference tend to dissolve into spaces of 'we the people', allowing ethnic otherness to be reinstated by whiteness under a guise of 'good and equal' liberalist principles (Poynting et al. 2004). The attainment of Sam's 'good life' seems to be compromised by the frame of whiteness driving it. The multicultural community and person representing it are cleverly deferred – a deferral that is hidden by shifting the emotive registers from bad to good. This process is summarised by Berlant's (2011, p. 95) argument that cruel optimism 'permits subjects to suspend themselves in the optimism of a potential occupation of the same psychic space of others, the objects of desire who make you possible (by having promising qualities, but also by not being there)'. In short, 'the ethnics' of these stories are denied the moment they are confirmed.[8] The migrant is left to tussle with an affective minefield: they are

---

7. In all these ways, the works actually lead us towards Otherness rather than towards a notion of equal cultures (as the genre suggests). This outcome is also common in documentary, as Smaill (2010, p. 104) discusses.

8. Povinelli (1998, p. 581) summarises this dynamic as follows:

   Alterity is not seen as a threat or challenge to self– and national coherence but is seen, instead, as compatible with an incorporative project, an 'invitation to absorption' [. . .] in this liberal imaginary, the now recognized subaltern subjects would slough off their traumatic histories, ambivalences, incoherencies, and angst like so much outgrown skin rather than remain for themselves or for others the wounded testament to the nation's past bad faith. The nation would then be able to come out from under the pall of its failed history, betrayed best intentions, and discursive impasses. And normative citizens would be freed to pursue their profits and enjoy their families without guilty glances over their shoulders into history or at the slum across the block.

persistently pulled in by the promise of full inclusion, and persistently pushed back when they move too close to attaining it.[9]

'I wasn't talking to you. Piss off!': Affective precarity in national belonging

Rita el-Khoury's *WDIB?* illustrates the highly complex economy of affective attachments in which the ethnic Australian is pulled in and pushed out of the national story. Produced in 2007, as part of ACMI's *Stories from the Lebanese Community*, and thus part of the collection that Sam Haddad's *LLAA* features in, Rita's story begins with a shot of the Australian flagpole beside a Lebanese flag pole. It then moves to Rita hugging someone. They are both holding Lebanese flags, but Rita also has a bag adorned with the Australian flag strapped over her shoulder. The two women appear to be in an airport, preparing for a trip. Script then appears across the frame, posing the question: 'Am I Australian or Lebanese???'

The film goes on to describe Rita's annual holidays to her birthplace, Lebanon, which retains a lot of meaning and good feeling for her. She describes the beautiful beaches, and the partying and clubbing she enjoys with friends in downtown Beirut. Pictures of idyllic beachscapes appear one after the other, along with images and video footage of Rita swimming in a hotel pool and drinking at bars with friends. During this sequence, we are told that while on one of these holidays Rita's cousin provokes her about her identity, in particular, about her Lebaneseness. It is here that the story begins to get complicated. 'Then my cousin said, "How could you care about your country [Lebanon] while you barely know

---

9. The push/pull aspect of this affective economy creates what Ken Gelder and Jane Jacobs (1995) refer to as 'the uncanny Australian'. Gelder and Jacobs draw on the work of Sigmund Freud to describe a particular dynamic whereby Australians feel a sense of being 'wrongly constituted'. Although their work was first carried out in relation to white Australians and Indigenous populations, it can be effectively transferred to the dynamic between white Australians and migrant or ethnic Australians. Anglo-Celtic Australians frequently express a begrudging attitude towards Australia's migrant communities, especially towards the non-white and non-English-speaking communities, claiming to be 'sick' of their presence in Australian neighbourhoods, to the point that they feel like 'strangers' in their 'own country' (Noble 2005, p. 118). How this dominant group of Australians understand Australia and their epistemic attachment to it is consequently unsettled – they experience an uncanny feeling of not belonging in their 'own country'. The uncanny discomfort felt by Anglo-Australians is blamed on the migrants, who are deemed to be 'the thief' who robs their comfort (p. 119). What ensues is a transfer of the uncanny: the dominant Anglo-Australian population impresses negative feelings of strangeness and illegitimacy on Australia's migrants. Migrant Australians are further denied their claims to Australianness and relegated to the border zone of dominant life. This denial occurs even for migrants who have lived in Australia for most of their lives and, as will be seen in Chapter Six, sometimes even for second- or third-generation migrants born here – especially if they have a non-white phenotype (see Hage 1998). An intense atmosphere is created whereby the non-white Australian is Australian 'but not really' and the white Australian is Australian but – due to the migrant presence – occupies this identity claim 'on borrowed time'.

it? You are only Lebanese by name. You're simply another tourist."' Rita, shocked by this comment, is not sure what to say in reply, eventually only managing to tell her cousin: 'It might be difficult to understand that those of us who are outside do try to make a difference.'

Following this scenario, the story moves abruptly forward: 'That night, Israel bombed Beirut airport.' The bombing is a dramatic segue to the inquiry Rita commences into her subjectivity and what the genre would likely view as Rita's 'moment'. After the bombing, Rita is thrust forward into a chaotic few days trying to return to Australia.

It is productive to deliberate on the moment before the bombing, the moment when Rita's cousin questions her Lebaneseness. This questioning is casually placed in the script, but it is significant. Rita is taken aback by her cousin's accusation, rendered speechless, struggling to defend herself and the form her Lebaneseness has taken in Australia. Her Lebanese cousin does not recognise Rita's Lebaneseness; her sense of herself as belonging to Lebanon is not reciprocated by 'Lebanon'. And yet, we know, given the comments Rita makes about herself in relation to Australia, that her Australianness is also not complete – it is undermined by her Lebanese cultural heritage. Rita thus experiences an affective suspension that Hage would describe as a form of mis-interpellation.

Hage (2010) describes mis-interpellation when he embarks on a critique of Michael Hardt's and Antonio Negri's (2009) adoption of a 'Fanonian schema'. Hardt and Negri use this schema to map out a politics of alter-modernity. Hage's critique includes a compelling reading of Fanon's (2008) *Black Skin, White Masks*, looking at the affective dimension of the book and its political ramifications. Hage then uses Althusser's (1971) notion of interpellation to describe three forms of racialisation: non-interpellation, negative interpellation and mis-interpellation. Non-interpellation refers to the type of racism associated with 'the experience of invisibility, where the racialised feel ignored and non-existent' (Hage 2010, p. 121). Negative interpellation, as Hage notes, is a form of racialisation most commonly associated with racism. 'Here the racialised is definitely noticed and made visible [. . .] the symbolic structure of society has a place for them, but it is a place defined by negative characteristics.'

As discussed earlier in relation to the ethnic authors of the ACMI case studies and Big hART's *JT*, the negative interpellated ethnic authors might already have visibility, but must also fight for valorisation (p. 122). The third form of racialisation, mis-interpellation, is for Hage 'a drama of two acts'. In the first act, the racialised person is interpellated as belonging to a collective, 'hailed by the cultural group or the nation or even by modernity which claims to be addressing "everyone"'. The person responds to this call, believing in the liberalist notion of a place for all. This response sets in motion the second act: 'no sooner do they answer the call and reclaim their spot that the symbolic order brutally reminds them that they are not part of everyone: no, I wasn't talking to you. Piss off (ibid.).

Rita is a good example of a mis-interpellated subject. In Australia, she is not fully Australian, but she attempts to fill the lacuna in her subjectivity by associating herself with Lebanon. However, in Lebanon, she is forced 'back onto the very domain that has been foreclosed' (p. 125), namely, white Australia.[10] The bombing that occurs in

---

10. As depicted in *Black Skin, White Masks*, Fanon (2008) is not able to exist as 'authentically black' but neither is he allowed to exist as anything *but* black in his new city and so-called cosmopolitan life.

Figure 6.1 (L-R) Screenshots from Rita el-Khoury's digital story *Where Do I Belong?* (2007), depicting her complex and disjointed experience of travelling to (and connecting with) her diasporic homelands.

Lebanon comes to represent something deeply affective for Rita. The blast symbolises the collapse of her sense of self as Lebanese. As her story describes the state of Beirut after the bombing, we come to understand that the Lebanese Rita is now also in ruins, the recognition from the 'authentic' Lebanese no longer extant. Rita then enters, like so many of the other migrants in these stories, an affective liminality: 'The roads were deserted. Time stood still. Unable to close my eyes for the whole nine hour drive. I'll never forget that image on the Lebanese-Syrian borders. Tourists waiting for their visas. Buses blocking the road. Kids selling drinks and people just randomly staring at each other.' As Rita describes her anxiety about how to leave Lebanon, an image of a building with bars barricading its entrance is shown. Rita pays a taxi driver one thousand dollars to drive her and her friend to Damascus Airport, where a flight back to Australia awaits them. The material and subjective barriers to her identity are visually represented by images of road blocks and traffic jams heavy with trucks – these objects get in her way on the path back to Australia and to Australian*ness*. Finally, the airport departure sign is shown. In the taxi, Rita turns to her friend and says, 'We are safe, and finally going back home.' She then tells us: 'At that moment, I had referred to Australia being home.

I had thought that Lebanon was my home – the place where I had spent eleven years growing up. After that, I realised that I have two homes. So my fear of never belonging disappeared on a taxi journey escaping the war.'

At the end of the story, Rita concludes that both Australia and Lebanon are her homes, and she no longer feels any tension about that. However, due to the particular combination of signs (music, visual, narrative), what affectively emanates is that this is not, in fact, the end of her anxiety about not belonging. The film's soundtrack begins with a traditional Lebanese beat, morphing into an upbeat club track as she describes her fun Lebanese holidays. The music stops sharply at a sound designed to represent the blast, and echoing sirens are then layered over the first visual shots of the Beirut ruins. From this point on, the backing music is a woman vocalist, her pitch getting higher as the story draws to a close. The woman's voice, unaccompanied by any other music, is highly emotive and somewhat eerie.

The story ends with Rita paying homage to her Lebanese roots while moving away from them (towards an Australian sense of belonging). At the close of the story, she shows us Australian family pictures, gives us the peace sign and then bold white script appears on a black screen: 'NEVER FORGET YOUR ROOTS.' This ending is complicated; Rita is seeking peace and safety in her Australian home following her escape from a violent moment in Lebanon, and we see this performed through the family photographs and her hand gesture of the peace sign. And yet, the digital story (produced in retrospect of the disturbed trip) still ends with a capitalised statement declaring her rootedness in Lebanon. The beautiful but ominous voice of the Lebanese folk singer makes this an emotional ending. It seems as if our emotion should be one of happiness and relief (that Rita has found her peace in Australia), but in my viewing of this film, I always feel a lingering sadness. In Lebanon, Rita experiences shock that she is not what she thought she was, that is, her Lebaneseness is not the same as the Lebaneseness of those living in Lebanon. However, this realisation comes via violence and destruction, and she is forced to abandon 'homeliness' in both a subjective and a literal sense.

What does it mean to be pushed out of a space that you have embodied as part of 'yourself'? How can it suddenly not be a part of your corporeality? As Hage (2014b) suggests, just because you are forced to forget or move on from a place does not mean you cease the desire associated with that place. Hage (2010, p. 124) explains the way this complicated desire manifests: 'mis-interpellated subjects develop an emotionally ambivalent relation to the source of their mis-interpellation. They continue to valorize it as the source of meaning in their life but they also have aggressive feelings towards it as the source of their rejection.' Rita is not aggressive towards the source of her mis-interpellation; however, as viewers we can sense the injury that this so-called holiday has caused and the glitch that has appeared in the performativity of her subjectivity. Antwi et al. (2013, p. 5) contend that this glitch in migrants is the result of inhabiting an 'anxious entanglement' of two conflicting narratives: 'the happy fictions of success and inclusion' that dominate accounts of multiculturalism and 'the various interruptive texts and textures that emerge from the accumulated everyday experience of various forms of structural violence'. This analysis indicates that in fact, this anxious entanglement involves more than dual narratives; it is an entanglement of many narratives, sometimes complementary, sometimes contradictory. Rita has several layers of affective tensions impressing upon her so that it is not simply about being Lebanese or Lebanese-Australian. She has adopted these dualities, but both have failed her to some degree. How this tension might be reconciled or harnessed by 'ethnic' Australians like Rita is discussed in Part Three. For now, it is evident that non-white migrants like Rita navigate an epistemological battleground where the attainment of the liberalist 'good life' is played off against persistent forms of everyday forms of racialised violence. And at stake in this play-off is always the body – how it moves, fits, exists.

Conclusion

Applying affect theory to the analysis of *JT* and ACMI's digital stories sheds further light on the ways in which whiteness becomes animated in new media forms. The relationship between the ethnic author of digital stories and an implied white audience is driven by certain attachments: an optimism for further connection and inclusion, and the promise of an accomplished universality. These attachments move within the digital story and between the screen and receiver in ways that accumulate a knowledge of the Anglo-settler nation as a place of successful multiculturalism, and, in the case of *JT* especially, as a place of ethnic redemption. A range of techniques allow for this movement, and all of them seek a particular kind of intimacy between the personal and the public. The use of personal photography, the timing of events in accordance with certain sounds or music and the statements and rhetorical questions about one's subjectivity all seek an exchange whereby the author of the digital story can be both recognised and valued.

What has also become clear is that although the digital stories are tightly organised – the ACMI ones in particular – there are highly complex economies of affects and norms at play in the stories from moment to moment. These economies of affect do not remain stagnant but rather move and stick and stick again, sometimes in surprising ways. This complexity is highlighted by the affective intricacies of Rita el-Khoury's story, particularly her experience of mis-interpellation.

Chapter Seven

THE HEART OF THE MATTER

The face speaks. It speaks, it is in this that it renders possible and begins all discourse [. . .] In discourse I have always distinguished, in fact, between the saying and the said. That the saying must bear a said is a necessity of the same order as that which imposes a society with laws, institutions and social relations. But the saying is the fact that before the face I do not simply remain there contemplating it, I respond to it.

— Levinas (1985, pp. 87–88)

In the UK when we ask: 'where are you from?' We want to know a lot more about you than just your place of birth.

— Daniel Meadows (2001), creator of BBC's *Capture Wales*
digital storytelling programme

In this chapter, I turn to the body more explicitly; specifically, I consider how affect operates via the force of performativity to shape bodies in certain ways. Certain techniques are used in digital storytelling to create a sense of intimacy between the author of the digital story and its viewers, techniques that frequently utilise the author's body. The author's body becomes a conduit for 'expressing' certain emotions, desires and ideals, positioned and moved in ways that connect this body to the audience. When we pay attention to the mundane practices of the body and the phenomenological experiences of embodying space, we begin to see the way affective economies call upon particular bodily practices that ultimately reproduce the borders of a certain kind of body. As Ahmed (2000, p. 42) argues, examining encounters with Others requires 'not only an analysis of body images or representations of bodily difference, but also an analysis of how bodily habits and gestures serve to constitute bodily matter and form'.

Following Ahmed (2000) and Nayak (2017), I investigate in this chapter how the bodies in digital stories become marked by differences; how the bodies 'come to be lived precisely through being differentiated from other bodies, whereby the differences in other bodies make a difference to such lived embodiment' (Ahmed 2000, p. 42). Examining the embodied practices of the authors in these digital stories also begins to reveal how agency is persistently activated through a complicated negotiation of affective encounters.

What repeatedly appears in the digital stories and community-based arts at large is the use of the face and the hands, especially in scenes with an emotive or serious tone. At times, the choreography of the hands and face appears obvious, or, to use the language of the digital storytelling genre, explicit; at other times, it appears much more subtle, even subconscious. These latter moments, which appear normal or natural, are most easily overlooked and, for this reason, I attempt to flesh them out here.

One of the main ways that the body – the face and hands particularly – are accentuated is via certain kinds of photography. In this chapter, I pause and consider the photographic image's ability to speak in two temporal modes in digital storytelling, that is, what has been and what will have been (Butler 2009, pp. 96–97). The stories can present what appear to be everyday photos – *honest* photos – of the author and the community the author represents. Like all photographs, those used in digital stories have the capacity to cast a particular life, face and body in the future tense. We have already seen the ways whiteness propels a future multicultural happiness that places the 'bad' racism of Australia in the past. It has also been illustrated that these works begin from a place of 'bad feeling', but these photographs choreograph affect to move implied viewers forward to a happy, white future. The multicultural subjects of migrant digital stories tend to enter the stage from a negative, marginal position. In that regard, they enter as Other than universal.

Common to both types of digital stories – individual and collaborative – is the prominent use of portraiture and a tendency to zoom in on the face of the portrait's subject. The use of the face raises several questions about the type of body the stories create/ hope to create, as well as how the public interacts with this body. How were the faces chosen and how did the audience perceive these faces? How did these faces work to produce notions of cultural diversity as linked, or not, to race? As Butler (2009, p. 131) asks in her analysis of war photography, how is it that 'others make moral claims upon us, address moral demands to us, ones that we do not ask for, ones that we are not free to refuse'?

These are pertinent questions because the use of portraiture in this manner is not only prominent in the digital story case studies discussed here but is a common trend in community-based artwork that engages with ethnicity. When carrying out the research, several Australian projects were found – both within the digital storytelling genre and beyond it – to use black-and-white portraiture, with a focus on the face in particular. For example, Ondru Arts, a Melbourne/Naarm-based arts initiative, utilised black-and-white portraiture as part of an ongoing community-based project called *Voiceless Journeys*. Ondru Arts is dedicated to art practice that explicitly explores cultural identity and diversity and nestles itself on the crux of the broader predicament facing diversity in arts, namely, how to forge belonging but allow for difference and impermanence? Like *JT*, *Voiceless Journeys* aims to tell stories about Australian residents that usually go unheard, and the means through which it does this simultaneously examines (and reaffirms) the bodies that shape the city of Melbourne/Naarm. The clearest demonstration of this is the organisation's use of black-and-white portraits of immigrants – printed and pasted on walls or digitally projected onto screens.

The director of this programme, Desh Balabsubramanium (2012), was very clear about the specificities of these portraits. During the photography shoots, the participants were asked to use their face and hands to express their experiences of migration. The photography component was carried out in conjunction with narrated stories that the participants were also asked to submit. The personal narrations could be as short or as long as the participants wanted but had to say something about the migration experience. The photographs and accompanying stories became part of a digital gallery, posted on Ondru's website and social media pages. The photographs were also blown up to billboard size or bigger and pasted or projected onto city walls.

The use of the immigrant face first invokes the subject of the portrait to be affected by the recalling of an experience and to perform this affectivity. Subsequently, it invokes *the viewer* to be affected by *the subject's* affective performance. There is something about the use of the face that aligns with the goals of art projects that centre on the recognition of cultural difference. As Gunew (2009, p. 19) has argued, the face can no longer be used innocently, so its prominence here must be subjected to a hermeneutics of suspicion. This chapter analyses how the body, in particular the face and the hands, is deployed in the digital story to regulate understandings of multiculturalism.

Intimating ethnicity through photography

The use of home photography is an innate aspect of the digital storytelling methodology, and when participants are given guidelines of things to bring to digital storytelling workshops, it is one of the first suggested items. The photographs act as narrative souvenirs; they usually feature the digital storyteller, their friends or loved ones and are threaded through the film to confirm the real existence of the narrator. Often, the photos are old and tattered, a condition that adds authenticity and intimacy to their materiality. In collaborative digital stories, photography workshops are sometimes built into the project, as was the case in *JT*.

The style used in these photographs – a style also found in many collaborative digital stories, including *JT* – combines deadpan and intimate photography techniques. Deadpan photography often uses an ethnographic lens, involving pictures of subjects in a seemingly detached manner. However, as Charlotte Cotton (2009, p. 81) explains, 'deadpan photography may be highly specific in its description of its subjects, but its seeming neutrality and totality of vision is of epic proportions'. Intimate photography also frames itself as natural and reflective of everyday happenings.

The use of personal photographs is not only about the connection to the personal or emotional but to the body attached to the personal or emotional, namely, the human. The ability to connect a story to a face, to a body, is considered to be an important element of the digital storytelling genre, and so it comes as no surprise that it is one of the most common aspects present in the case studies.

Indeed, a lack of photographs that feature the people spoken about in a digital story is generally viewed as a hurdle to narrative – and performative – completion. In the digital storytelling programme facilitated by Alexandra (2008) in Ireland, the participants were undocumented migrants. Consequently, some participants felt uncomfortable using personal photography because of the risk it posed to their respective visa applications. As the authors were dwelling temporarily – and often illegally – in the country, there was a range of concerns about showing their faces in the public stories. Similarly, some participants simply did not have photographs – a common issue for many migrants, especially those who have moved as refugees, leaving personal memorabilia behind or simply never having it in the first place. The project's facilitator was conflicted by the anomaly, believing that without the use of personal photography the intimacy between the story and the viewer would not be as intense or captivating:

> I trusted that the participants' own images would more powerfully elucidate their stories than a stock image downloaded from the Internet. Through a commitment to critical and participatory pedagogy I was acutely conscious of the creative tension between my vision of best practice and the artistic vision of each participant, as well as the tension between the process of creating the multi-mediated narrative and the end 'product'. (p. 104)

With these tensions in mind, Alexandra spent much time deliberating with the participants about the images that would best convey the personal aspects of their stories. One participant, Edwina, did not want to use images from her home for fear of being identified in public. She started thinking about using a graph to illustrate her migration story. Alexandra sensed that Edwina wanted to use imagery that verified her existence as a migrant:

> A graph could officially demonstrate Edwina's lived experiences as she spoke to a public that disbelieves. I asked Edwina if there were images from her daily life that could lend credibility and provide 'proof'. She said she would think about it and began making images. (p. 109).

When they wouldn't use 'face' photographs, or in cases where there were no photographs at all, the authors were encouraged to take photographs of their living environment, for example, of their kitchen, hallways, and so on. Edwina took a series of abstract photos of her body and eventually of her home environment (obscure images of her apartment). Similarly, Zaman's story about his father initially used stock images of fathers and sons from the internet; however, the white bodies depicted in the pictures sat uncomfortably in Zaman's story:

> We watched this version of the story together. The images of white, Northern European men and boys juxtaposed against Zaman's Bengali accented English created a jarring dissonance to his story. I asked Zaman what he thought. He explained that all the images of fathers and sons in domestic settings he had found on the Internet were of white faces. 'This is not me', he concluded (fieldnotes, 6 November, 2007). Zaman was indeed absent from the stock images; they were entirely un-representational. Based on this experience with stock images he decided to use his own photographs; images from the restaurant where he worked in North Dublin, his commute on the bus to and from work, and sites around Dublin. Zaman's presence surfaced in the images he created with his camera - photos from his everyday life. (p. 105)

Revealing spaces that the participants move through in their personal lives is seen to enable the creation of intimacy between them and their viewers. The intimacy created is shown to be defined by specific terms, including validity, seamlessness and a distinct ability to convey 'Otherness'. Both Edwina and Zaman are guided to choose images that prove their Otherness and do not disturb or confuse the narrative of migrant hardship that the stories tell. It might seem like the two participants only slightly shift their attitudes towards image use, but at the end of the digital story programme, Zaman illustrates the pressure underlying these kinds of shifts.

> Unlike the other digital stories, Zaman's story did not explicitly narrate circumstances of workplace discrimination. Perhaps based on this difference, he became concerned that his story did not represent 'the migrant experience'. 'I need to change my story', he told me; it needed to be 'more migrant' (fieldnotes, 4 December 2007). As a group we discussed Zaman's first edit and his concerns that the story wasn't 'migrant enough'. One of the workshop participants, Edwina, argued that Zaman's images were 'powerful'. Another workshop participant, Abdel, told the group that Zaman's story *was* a 'migrant' story; 'you are separate from your family, you were alone' (fieldnotes, 4 December 2007). After the discussion Zaman decided to change his story slightly by adding the following sentence in the postscript: 'At this moment my life in Ireland is so hard.' He explained that the sentence clarified his current position and situated him within the larger group context (fieldnotes, 11 December 2007). After this final edit Zaman seemed comfortable with his work portraying a different kind of story, not a stock migrant story, and perhaps not immediately identifiable as a migrant story at all, but a story that nevertheless intimately involved migration in ways both nuanced and generative. (p. 106; emphasis in the original)

This passage evinces the complex affective attachments that migrants negotiate when creating a private digital story for public consumption. Zaman chooses to produce a story about his father, but then feels it does not do justice to the 'larger group' of migrants, and so he compromises to match what he reads as an unstated expectation and responsibility. Yet, when it comes to speaking about the difficulty of being a migrant, he only gestures towards it, saying his life is 'so hard at the moment'. The hardship is an add-on to his story – thinly described and framed as momentary, even fleeting. Zaman thus ensures that the viewers will not be made to feel *too* uncomfortable with how difficult it actually is to be a migrant in Ireland. The intense morphing of these stories greatly contradicts the authenticity so often associated with the genre.

Facing up to the nation

In *JT*, participants were taught by professional photographers to take portraits. Then, as a way to document the faces of the Shire, the newly acquired photography skills were put to use – participants took photographic portraits of Big hART community workers, people on the street and at home, and each other. These portraits tended to take a particular form: black and white, shot from the chest up, and with a focus on the face. The portraits are frequently zoomed in so that the audience gets 'up-close' with the subject, in particular with the subject's face and eyes. These features frequently take up the entire span of the junk's sails, projected in conjunction with music and audio recordings.

The use of the face, hands and body in the ACMI case studies is underpinned by similar principles as those employed in *JT*; however, due to the more personalised nature of the stories, it adopts a slightly different aesthetic. *JT* involved photography workshops, where participants learned how to take portraits that would be used for the digital project. Given that the ACMI digital storytelling programme runs over a much shorter time

frame, there is no room for the workshopping of other creative skills beyond producing the digital story itself. Furthermore, as noted by Simondson (2012a), the fact that
participants could bring archival objects to the three-day workshop was a significant asset
to the digital storytelling programme. Thus, the portraiture used in the ACMI stories is
usually from the author's personal collections.

A relational connection between viewer and author is created, an excellent example
of Thrift's (2004) notion of the performative loop. The particular positioning and timing
of these portraits in the digital stories works to bring what are (often private) stories of
displacement, trauma and identity further into the public domain. In *JT*, the Sutherland
Shire is incited to witness the experiences of its ethnic members and – more importantly – *the human* at the centre of the experiences. At one stage during *JT*, we see the
script 'my family', followed by a close-up of a surf lifesaver's red-and-yellow flag. The
film then reverts to images of fire and smoke, previously seen in the story. Placed here,
the pictures create a friction between the preceding images of the happy family and fun
beach culture, and the chaotic, destructive feeling conveyed by the fire and smoke. What
accentuates this friction, however, is the subsequent close-up of a small black child's face
and the gradual zooming into their eyes. The child's eyes are designed to call on the
viewer, to demand something of us.

Ahmed (2004, p. 192) discusses the use of the child's face as the face of the inno-
cent: 'The threat of difference is transformed into the promise of hope or likeness. That
child *could be* mine; his pain is universalised through the imagined loss of *any* child as a loss
that could be my loss' (emphases in the original). The face points to a bodily presence,
someone real, intimating an identification with the ethnic Other, who has come to exist
in the Sutherland Shire as less-than-human. The use of the face in this way is thus an
aesthetic example of the project's overall theme: 'It's harder to hurt someone when you
know their story.' The theme implies that if white Australia can relate to the human
element of 'ethnic Australians' – to the human child occupying this boy's body – it will
become hard, if not impossible, to exclude them. As Ahmed writes: 'We can be "with
them" in the face of this pain' (ibid.).

Silvan Tomkins's (1995, p. 89) pioneering work in affect theory demonstrates how the
face is understood as the main site of affect. Tomkins came 'to regard the skin, in general,
and the skin of the face in particular, as of the greatest importance in producing the feel
of affect'. The face is seen to signify universal emotion, so the close-up of the eyes is an
attempt to humanise the photographic subject. As Cotton (2009, p. 172) describes in her
analysis of deadpan photography: 'We read their talks of injustice and are invited to map
this onto their faces and bodies.' In the case of *JT*, these tales of injustice are accentuated
with affective audio forms, such as snippets of narration, media grabs and emotive music,
so that the body becomes a mediated, affective source – a plea for acceptance and tolerance. In itself, the name *Big hART* demonstrates this intention, with the organisation
describing the meaning behind its name as relating to:

1. The geography of the continent. 2 The colloquial expression of core human values
expressed in the phrase 'big heart'. 3. A 'big', inclusive and equitable discussion of ideas
through the arts. 4 That the way we treat marginalised people reflects what is at the 'heart'

of our communities. 5. Art as a big resource, not a luxury or a side issue. (Rankin and Bakes 1996, p. 10)

Of all the body's organs, the heart is the one most commonly associated with emotion, in particular, with the deepest personal desires of a person. The image of the heart symbolises love, fear, shame and, above all, truth: 'follow your heart; not your head', we are often advised when we are unsure of the right or 'authentic' choice to make. However, the documentary style of the digital storytelling genre makes it difficult for authors to represent visually the emotionality of the human heart, and this is perhaps why the face and the eyes step in.

To explore the affective and discursive force of this strategy, Elsbeth Probyn's (2005) work on shame becomes useful, since, in a way, the implied white viewer is being called upon by the child's eyes to feel shame. Probyn positions the category of 'shame' at the centre of her work in affect, arguing that it needs to be rethought. Similar to Ahmed's insistence on the productive use of bad feeling, Probyn sees political potential for shame, arguing that if it is activated correctly it can create hope and allow for the positive recon-stitution of political campaigns and identity claims. She relies heavily on the work of Silvan Tomkins, in particular his argument that shame is invoked when 'interest' – or good feeling – is interrupted, that is, when we become interested in something, we will wish for that interest to continue, but if something or someone disturbs this climbing affective interest, we are hastily brought back to ourselves: 'The body wants to continue being interested, but something happens to "incompletely reduce" that interest' (p. 15).

Probyn uses this definition of shame for self-evaluation, asking why were we interested. This is a productive question to ask when analysing digital stories which, as described, have a tendency to will the multicultural subject, and those witnessing it, forwards, towards the multicultural promise, but rarely offering space for respite or reflection – space for what Tanja Dreher (2012, pp. 162–63) would call 'difficult listening'. But, if the eyes of a child interrupt this movement and create feelings of shame, then this interruption might lead us to question our 'interest' in the otherwise good-feeling of the story. Why were we invested in the forwards, upwards trajectory of this narrative? If we become uncomfortable, we can explore our own positions and investments – we can ask, in Probyn's terms, why were we interested?

Nonetheless, I find something disconcerting about the structure of this logic, specific-ally how shame is positioned within it as an essential or global experience. The dominant discourse surrounding shame, or in Big hART's ethos, 'heart feelings', ultimately positions love at one end of the affective spectrum and shame at the other, a structure that, when incited in certain ways, can become tied to a problematic concept of universality.

Grossberg (2010b) contends that there is a troubling tendency in contemporary affect analyses to collapse everything into the body or the somatic. I want to extend this conten-tion to consider how the concept of shame might be misused when we collapse affective analyses into a single body or framework; further, to ask: does this (mis)use of shame offer reprieve for the ethnic body but ultimately deny it enduring justice?

At a different stage during *JT*, a close-up of a person's face moves in to focus on the face's eyes. The eyes, as expressive of the heart, become a vessel for intimating universality; to initiate the reparation, or to 'unstick' the ethnic Australian from bad feeling. The eyes fill the entire frame, and after a slow-motion blink, a sequence of several eyes appears; these eyes fold into each other and eventually form a single body. Once again, the culturally diverse body collapses into a single, bounded shape. This technique seems to imply what Probyn (2005, p. 65) posits in *Blush*; namely, 'one thing we all share is a biological body [. . .] the body *is*' (emphasis in the original). Again, we arrive at this troubling notion of that which 'just is', as echoed in everyday multiculturalism scholarship and that continuously haunts the dominant discourse of race. This dominant discourse perpetuates the idea that race is an essential or biological given, that it 'just is'. A body that 'just is' fails to adequately acknowledge, as Grossberg (2010b) insists, that all affect has to come through machinic assemblages surrounding – and indeed, forming – the body. In this regard, the body never 'just is'.[1]

The affective impulse of Big hART and the digital storytelling genre at large is an optimistic one, driven by a yearning to understand different affective responses as universal ('we all *feel* the same way, so let's unite on that fact'). However, as discussed, feelings are highly productive and politicised tools, and their appearance and deployment cannot escape the social context within which they exist. By attempting to elucidate feelings deemed to be at 'the heart' of the matter (the heart *of* matter) as natural affective responses, the genre can also lead to moral judgements about what *is* heartfelt. The

---

1. The body as something that 'just is' is both a conflation and a delimiting concept, and in fact seems to go against the work Probyn seeks to do for the body – that is, to show that the body is a moving subject with fluid contours. After all, Probyn (2010, p. 74) argues that affect is too often discussed as an 'amorphous category' and intensities of emotion and affect are therefore frequently misrepresented. Yet, when asking what shame can tell us, there is a quick conflation by Probyn of Tomkins's work with Darwinism – and therefore biological innateness. Probyn introduces Darwin's argument that all human beings blush, regardless of their colour or race, and then moves to take this as a truth claim. Aside from the fact that Probyn assumes this to be correct without much to support its truth (she notes that she 'takes Darwin at his word'; 2005, p. 28), it resonates with a long-standing discourse of race which has tied itself to the biological body as a way to 'prove' the relevance and so-called reality of race and, ultimately, of racism. As shown in previous chapters: this argument continues to have force in Western societies, even though it has long been shown by geneticists that race is not linked to genetic composition as initially argued in scientific discourse. Collapsing the body and affective response into a seamless chain risks reproducing the biological discourse of racism in some instances. It also raises what Gunew (2009) signals as a persistent problem in the scholarship of affect, that is, the failure to critically consider the Eurocentric nature of affect theory and the category of experience. A reconsideration of how Western scientific discourse creates shame, and the shamed person in particular, is required.

A more productive view of the body is developed in 'Writing Shame', in which Probyn (2010) uses the Deleuzian concept of the body. The body exists not as a unified being or whole, but as a moving and differing totality of various parts 'whizzing around' (p. 76). Probyn also draws on the methodology pioneered by Foucault in *The Order of Things*, in particular, the understanding that words and things are related – the former creating the latter, and looping back again – a relationship that creates what it means to be human (p. 74). This methodology allows for important critiques of the way in which performative loops operate between discourse, bodies and things.

heartfelt response might be provoked by representations of shame (the viewer is shamed into responding, such as by the use of the black, big-eyed child) or love (the viewer is encouraged to see the ethnic Other as loving, such as by the use of their family photos). However, as Ahmed (2015) reminds us, 'the universal is a structure not an event. It is how those who are assembled are assembled. It is how assembly becomes a universe'. What kind of universe is assembled when the face and eyes of a racialised body are used to conjure happiness or shame? What bodies are already inside 'the universal' in order to assume this feeling of happiness or shame?

Again, I would argue that these seemingly innocuous uses of the body can inadvertently enable the racialised underpinnings of the AoS of multiculturalism. Posited as universal, these affective techniques and implied responses shift between private and public registers in an ostensibly seamless manner, indirectly morphing the ethnic individual into grand narratives about race and the body of 'the nation'. Povinelli speaks to this enabling when discussing the relationship between State institutions and their recognition of Indigenous peoples. Her analysis can be meaningfully understood in relation to digital stories, which, although private, operate within the AoS of multiculturalism. 'The law and state care deeply about subaltern bodies, desires, rhetorics, and words, seek to demonstrate their concern, to mirror these corporealities, to beckon them towards their remedial institutions. But [. . .], *intimacy, in the remedial hands of the law, advances national hegemonic projects rather than subaltern standards or dreaming*' (Povinelli 1998, p. 610; italics added). The intimacy invoked through community storytelling projects can advance viewers of digital stories towards a future in which the ethnic body comes into universality (and validation) via the authorised universal, namely, hegemonic whiteness. Whiteness receives the call of the face and eyes and whiteness chooses to deem human or otherwise.

Ethnic snaps

LLAA provides useful examples of the way the face, hands and ultimately the body act as a conduit for the affective performativity of ethnicity. It needs to be reasserted that referring to the body as a conduit does not mean to conceptualise the body as a naturally occurring entity waiting to become live through action. The body occurs only in its doing; it is material only to the extent that it is active, and so the body and the action cannot be split apart. Sam's body does certain things in his digital story, and this doing becomes *affectively* associated with ethnicity in Australia. Like the other stories, *LLAA* promotes a particular Australian feel, intimated through family pictures taken in the backyard, at the kitchen table, the local pub and the workplace.

Sam is also shown to be actively performing scenes of his story; breaking it down moment to moment through the use of bodily movements. When describing the violent altercation he has with a co-worker, he uses a sequence of images taken specifically for his digital story. His movements in this sequence are especially affective, the shots moving from his feet, to his hands, to his face. Sam's arm acts a form of resistance; first it is 'tied up in knots' behind his back, then it forms a fist and finally it punches out in anger.

Sam's arm becomes what Ahmed (2014) might call the arm of the wilful subject. At first, his arm is held back. It is held back because its will does not support the general will, the will of the social body. Sam is ridiculed for his attire, his language, his ethnicity: his body is, effectively, an irritation to the white bodies at the workplace. Then, one day, Sam loses his temper; he snaps. As Ahmed describes, the snap of a twig can feel like a sudden break – as if out of nowhere – but actually it is the result of what Berlant calls 'slow death'; it can no longer bear witness to the slow violence and ongoing pressure bearing upon it (cited in Ahmed 2014).

Ahmed (2014) discusses a 'feminist snap', but here we can consider an ethnic snap. Sam's arm punches out and, at that moment, it 'gets in the way of what is on the way', namely, the continued abjection of Sam's body in the workplace (ibid.). Something interesting then happens. The ethnic snap could have resulted in Sam's further expulsion from the white social body – as seen in the Cronulla riots, the violent retaliation by ethnic bodies reaffirmed the performative force of whiteness, and further legitimated the actions of the white bodies. In this instance, however, Sam's punch epitomises a likeness to the bodies that support the white social body. The other co-workers view Sam's action with respect, and so he becomes an honorary member of the white social body. The entrance into this body, or what Hage might call the white national space, is depicted by an image of Sam standing in front of a pub, his arm reaching out to the pub door, about to push it open and walk in. His arm now leads him forward into this space. Sam's wilful arm thus undergoes a transformation: it begins as the arm of resistance, but because of the way the form of resistance is shaped by and within the framework of whiteness, it morphs into the arm of the white masculine will. As Ahmed suggests, arms create but they are also shaped by that which they labour. Arms both exercise agencies and are exercised by agencies.

The re-enactment performed by Sam materialises Sam's body as one that is *becoming* white; one that has survived and is now on the way to 'the good life'. Bill Nichols (2008) argues that re-enactments not only reanimate the force of desire, but also enable desire to be brought into being. Re-enactments allow subjects to experience more vividly what it feels like to occupy a certain position: 'The authentic image becomes remote, an instigation for memory and identification, whereas the reenacted image [. . .] gratifies a personal desire, it makes possible the enjoyment of going through the motions' (p. 77). Sam goes through the motions of survival, even though the specific moment of defence is lodged in the past. He becomes caught up in the re-enactment of his moment of workplace agency, accentuating each movement so that each one becomes distinct. As Nichols suggests, this is especially important for film-makers who have no 'authentic image' of a past event. Sam 'transports himself back to that which now functions as a lost object through the social gests he puts into motion. It allows him to own his past in a corporeal but fantasmatic form' (p. 83).

The re-enactment is also a form of appeal – to Sam himself, who wishes to 'own' this action, but also to the audience, who Sam is 'winning over'. Re-enactments can gratify the force of desire, 'intensify[ing] the degree to which a given argument or perspective appears compelling, contributing to the work's emotional appeal, or convincing, contrib-uting to its rational appeal by means of real or apparent proof' (p. 88).[2] Sam is able to

---

2. There is also a relationship between the bodily sense of scale of nationalist practices (Hage 1998) and the body itself. Hage takes an interest in the metaphor of the hand ripping off

use his body to activate a particular subjectivity, a particular way of being a multicultural Australian.

Conclusion

A common way migrant digital stories attempt to prove value is to draw the viewer continuously back to the human at the 'heart' of the matter; to the 'bodies that matter' (Butler 1993). To accentuate the human, the stories are prone to focusing on the face, eyes and hands of the subjects, those parts of the body that have come to represent essentialised emotion and the authentic self. The tendency to deploy these body parts in digital stories carries a danger of reinforcing binary modes of thinking, whereby the idea of the universal comes only via the idea of cultural difference as contrastable to norma-tive whiteness.

Similarly, the body that experiences comfort is one that experiences homeliness in whiteness – any discomfort in that space is not only positioned as a marginal, irrelevant part of life in Australia, it is actively ignored or 'disappeared'. In that regard, constraint is frequently built into the attachments that orient these stories so that the good and bad feeling produced further perpetuates the performativity of whiteness and reassures the operation of multiculturalism as an AoS.

Nonetheless, these stories, as predictable and constrained as they might seem at first, are building archives of liberal multiculturalism that can be strange, surprising, even unsettling. The following chapter turns its attention to these unsettling components and asks whether they can be accentuated in digital storytelling as a mode of everyday politics.

---

the burqa in *White Nation* (1998), and in *Arab-Australians Today* (2002a, p. 198) becomes again interested in 'mutterings and bodily movements', including hand gestures and actions, as 'strat-egies of intensification'.

Chapter Eight

SLIPPING UP: PERFORMATIVE GLITCHES

The body feels pain
but the hand
keeps
reaching out.

– Deo (2017)

The body does not stay in its own place.

– Butler (2015, p. 212)

Temporal selves created in other circumstances intrude in unexpected ways.

– Gunew (2018)

Describing their migration from Quandong province, China, to Charlottetown, Canada, Theresa states in their digital story *What Is Meaningful Life*? (2012–13): 'We landed in Canada on June 21, 2010. Yet that moment as if just happened yesterday. Adapt to a new environment has never been easy, especially for adults. You feel like you suddenly fell on the floor from the sky.' This final sentence, presented casually among a series of other familiar statements about migration, leaps out at me. I realise that when I imagine migration – and not only the migrations of the authors I analyse in this book, but the migrations of my own family members – I tend to imagine, in the first instance, the thrilling moments of take-off or landing: the ship slowly pulling out of the dock, the plane wheels touching down. Both these imaginative poles, including the landings, are tied to the mobilising trajectory of migration, which involves moving up, up and away (Ahmed 2010a, p. 47). But migration as a fall-from-sky is a starkly different metaphor to the upwards moving description of migration typically repeated in digital stories. It sharply reminds me that migration also involves falling, moving downwards and sometimes crash landings. In this chapter I identify the ambiguities, tensions and the falls-from-the-skies in migrant digital stories. In doing so, I seek to demonstrate how these moments: (1) tell us something about the ways in which cultural diversity manifests itself/ is experienced in everyday life; and (2) can be digitally harnessed and channelled in ways that destabilise the discourse of whiteness.

    I have been building the argument that recent forms of culturally diverse art practice have a tendency to operate according to an either/or modality, despite committed and sincere attempts to open up understandings of difference by exploring its manifestations 'on the ground'. These types of practices can be seen to be operating mostly according to what Papastergiadis (2012a) describes as the first level of cultural transformation. For Papastergiadis, most analyses of cultural exchange start and stop at the first level, in such a way that cross-cultural creativity is rendered immobile or obsolete. He describes this first level as the 'visible effects of difference within identity as a consequence of the incorporation of foreign elements' (p. 117). Those carrying out studies of cultural diffe-rence at this level tend to either celebrate the positive effects the new cultural signs have had on a dominant culture, or criticise the way the dominant culture has contaminated or subsumed the new cultural signs (ibid.).[1]

In this chapter I pursue Papastergiadis's endeavour of 'rethinking cultural belonging and creative practice' in an Australian-based context (ibid.). In particular, I wish to engage with the third level of hybridity, or cultural translation. For Papastergiadis, the third level allows for both relational and transgressive practices, those 'unconscious and ambivalent forces' that the culturally diverse subject faces on a daily level – especially when produ-cing cultural works. This level is appropriate for the following analysis because of the performative and affective tensions shown to exist in the digital stories so far discussed, a tension seemingly driven by 'the simultaneous desire for both separation and connection' (p. 132). Papastergiadis argues: 'When driven by this husky desire, hybridity can exceed the boundaries of moral codes and political processes. The vivacious energy of hybridity leads it towards risky encounters' (ibid.).

The following analysis works to identify the 'husky desires' in ACMI's digital stories and consider them as moments of political potential, or pathways towards 'risky encounters'. To do so, it further combines performativity and affect theory and closely explores the spaces between authors and viewers of digital stories, that is, the spaces in which the performative is traversed.

I have been using the two theoretical frameworks of performativity and affect in order to bring another dimension to race critiques and avoid falling into the binary forms of analyses that plague many of the rhetorical claims about multiculturalism. As seen in the digital stories themselves, the discursive structure of 'ethnic telling' often necessitates a dichotomous understanding of good and bad feeling, comfort and discomfort, inside and outside. Nonetheless, the performative does not invest the body with essential elements, even though it does create material outcomes. Similarly, affect does not work in a linear, cause-and-effect manner. For this reason, the analysis carried out so far has mapped cultural difference as a precarious terrain, one that is highly complex, paradoxical and implicated in Australia's dominant script of whiteness. This chapter extends the analysis by examining how the precariousness of this map might reveal aspects of everyday multi-cultural life that are currently obscured.

---

1. Prominent examples of this include Taylor's (1994) work on recognition and Jonathan Friedman's (1999) exploration of cultural hybridity. See Papastergiadis (2012a) for further reading.

Prompting this move is the observation that in migrant digital stories, slightly out of place moments often arise; these moments can be irritating and disrupt the overall narrative. These moments often appear in digital stories that are less polished and in accordance with the genre's criteria for 'good' digital storytelling would likely be deemed poor quality. This chapter considers how the odd moments represent what Butler (1993, p. 219) refers to as 'performative slippages'. Butler uses this term to refer to slight moments of instability that ripple the surface of bodies as norms are being passed along the performative chain, from one person or object to another.

I begin by focusing on the odd moments of Huseyin Duman's (2007) *Ithal Damat = Imported Groom* (*IDIG*), an ACMI-produced digital story seemingly typical of the genre. I will consider how the peculiarities irritate not only the narrative and aesthetic structure commonly employed in migrant digital stories, but the normative context of whiteness within which these stories take place. These moments are perhaps not immediately obvious if approached within the critical framework of identity and subjectivity, which, as Grossberg (1997) argues, is precisely the framework that tends to be utilised in critiques of racialised representations. It is, after all, easy to read a certain narrative in digital stories like *IDIG*, and discount some of the awkward moments as poor storytelling and/or digital literacy. Instead, this chapter explores how these tense moments might impart new understandings of everyday multicultural life in Australia.

Husky desires and risky encounters

Ithal Damat = Imported Groom describes Huseyin Duman's migration experience from Turkey to Australia as a young adult. The narrative structure of the story resembles that of other migration stories so far discussed, beginning at a moment of change in Huseyin's usual life and thus accompanied by feelings of excitement and anxiety. Huseyin's moment of change is his departure from his hometown, Ankara; specifically the moment he says goodbye to his mother and family. It is an emotional moment for the characters; however, as seen in Kenan's digital story, Huseyin attempts to lighten the sadness with humour, somewhat downplaying the intensity of the farewell. Huseyin's narrative then moves us through a liminal space, represented (as it commonly is) through flight. On the plane, Huseyin feels a heaviness in his stomach, and when he arrives at the crowded airport with his sister-in-law, he is unable to locate the woman he is due to marry. These uncertain movements are quickly surpassed by the third, or closing, section of the story, which sees Huseyin enter the Australian workforce, marry and have children. The three-and-a-half minute story finishes with photos of Huseyin as an older man on holiday, back-dropped by the words: 'I now try to visit Australian cities. Thank you.' *IDIG* thus ends as many migrant digital stories tend to – with a positive reflection on life in Australia, usually associated with the good life. As we've seen previously, we are shown signposts along the way that indicate Huseyin's successful migration experience and immersion into Australian life. No signpost is more poignant than Huseyin's change of citizenship and later, his name change. Huseyin becomes an Australian citizen in

1988 and tells us: 'a couple of years later, because I love Australia, I changed my name to Jimmy Domain.'[2]

The photos that he shares with us work to mirror the migration success he verbally expresses. The images used are mostly explicit in form, for example, photographs of himself and his wife on their wedding day when he mentions his marriage. Due to the nature of collecting and documenting history using the scrapbook method, it is not surprising that the digital story begins with black-and-white photographs of Huseyin's family, in particular, his mother and father. These fade in and out and gradually move to coloured images of his fiancée, his children and his workmates. Like the digital stories previously discussed, the selection of photographs matches the conventional movement through time – from past to present, home country to new country, youth to maturity and so on. To close, Huseyin uses photographs of himself holidaying, standing in front of iconic Australian landscapes, such as the Gold Coast skyscraper cityscape. He is wearing iconic Australian clothing as well: boardshorts and a white singlet, often associated with white Australian masculinity. These final images of Huseyin point to his immersion in Australian culture: his name has changed to something 'more Australian' and his clothing and actions now fit this name.

Reading Huseyin's story from one level shows the narrative to be linear, conforming to a familiar trajectory that starts with rupture, moves to confusion and settles on a resolution. However, there are elements of *IDIG* that slightly perturb this trajectory, somewhat disjointing the movements through each of the conventional stages. As noted, the story begins with the intense emotionality of Huseyin's moment of farewell. However, it is not until the middle of the digital story that we discover he is moving to Australia for an arranged marriage. In fact, the opening of the story, aimed to set the narrative context, does not mention anything about migration, or Australia. Instead, it provides clues, by telling us:

It was 1977. It was a cold winter month. My sister-in-law and I were happily packing our suitcases with summer clothes. When I was about to leave Ankara I could hear my mother's sobbing, which made me lose my excitement and feel emotional. I had tears in my eyes, I said to my mother, 'Don't be sorry Mum, I will go and come back in a couple of months.'

The weight of the emotion that comes across in this opening sequence does not match the supposed casualness of the planned adventure – Huseyin assures his mother (and the viewers) that this is a short trip; however, his mother's response, and subtle clues provided in Huseyin's own actions, suggest otherwise. As Huseyin and his sister-in-law drive away, his mother and friends pour a bucket of water over the road, in accordance with local tradition. It is explained that the ritual is carried out to ensure that the person leaving will return quickly, or 'before the water dries'. Huseyin describes:

After several meters I said to the taxi driver, 'Go back, go back, I want to see my mother again.' I saw my mother sitting on the steps crying. There were people around her who were

---

2. Although his name is changed to Jimmy Domain, the short film is authored in the credits under his original name, Huseyin Duman. The book thus continues to use Huseyin Duman.

accompanying her. When they saw me they were shocked. They were very happy and all smiled. I said to them, 'See! I came back before the water dried.' They all stopped crying and started laughing. I said to them, 'This is how I always want to see you.'

The intimacy of this moment conveys deep love and concern for family, and there is an evident desire, if not intention, to return to it soon. This part of the narrative takes up a significant section of the story, so it comes as a bit of a shock when we discover halfway, when Huseyin is on the plane, that he is going to Australia to get married. The institutional commitment and implied permanence of marriage seems at odds with what has been described until now as a temporary trip to an unknown place – although it does go some way towards explaining the gravity of emotion present in the opening scenes.

Huseyin's movement into the liminal space quickly overshadows the emotionality of the departure, which, once again, is casually narrated despite an underlying sense that this is a significantly intense experience. Huseyin states: 'That was the first time I had flown. I was excited and also a little bit scared. I felt something moving inside me. Later on I found out that I was travelling with pop music group ABBA. I myself was excited because I was going to see my fiancée for the first time.' A separate visual frame accompanies each sentence, however, the frames move quickly, and we do not have much time to take them in. What is worth noting is the disparateness between each sentence, in terms of the conveyed mood. Each sentence seems to sit in awkward juxtaposition with the one just before and the one just after. For example, 'I felt something moving inside me' suggests a significant affective shift in Huseyin, but the next sentence describes something external to this personal experience, namely, the internationally famous pop group, ABBA. Huseyin then tells us he is personally excited because he is due to meet his fiancée, but this does not sit comfortably with what he has told us just three sentences earlier: 'I was excited but also a little bit scared.' The aspect of fear seems to have vanished. Upon arrival, we get the sense that Huseyin and his travelling companion are overwhelmed by the crowded airport – there are people everywhere and Huseyin cannot distinguish his fiancée, whom he has come to know via photos and letters. He tells us: 'My fiancée had seen us at the gate but did not recognise us. My sister-in-law pointed out her sister to me. Then I confirmed, yes, yes, it's her.' His new, extended family greets him with hugs, and they leave the airport.

Although these scenes are brushed over quickly, some elements of them disturb the linear narrative and hence the viewer's affective involvement. First, it is interesting to note the sentences chosen by Huseyin to describe his arrival, in particular, the awkwardness of finding his fiancée in the crowd. He has just finished telling us about his excitement. However, the actual meeting is somewhat of an anticlimax: she does not recognise him, and he relies on his sister-in-law to connect them. The meeting comes across as rather solemn, and no further comments are made about it by Huseyin. After greeting his fiancée and her family, he moves us to the drive home. Second, it is easy to miss the family connection information translated in these sentences: his sister-in-law points out her own sister, who turns out to be his fiancée. Here, we are given a little more information about this arranged marriage: he is marrying his travel companion's sister. What is not clear is whether the sister-in-law is married to one of his siblings or whether, in fact, he already refers to her as his sister-in-law because it is pre-empted that he will marry her sister. Ultimately, it is not important, but it forms a small distraction and undermines the genre's attempt to provide succinct stories of closure. Tying these awkward liminal moments up is the commentary provided immediately after the airport encounter: 'We drove home. The first thing I noticed was the difference in the traffic. In Turkey the steering is on the left but in Australia it is on the right. A couple of months later we had our wedding reception. In Coburg Town Hall. I've been married for thirty years. I have both good and bad memories.' It becomes clear that we are not going to be given any further insight into his personal interactions. The car becomes our symbol of movement, of moving *on*. The narrative is now moving us towards the end of this liminal space and we are heading to the resolution.

I became frustrated watching the story – drawn into the emotional at times, but quickly pushed out again. After the meeting in the airport, his partner/wife is never again discussed, except to record the date of their marriage. We do not know her name, and we are not given any indication of her personality. We are only told that they are married soon after Huseyin's arrival, they have children together and this provides both good and bad memories for Huseyin. Similarly, his mother and other family members that are so prominent in the opening section of the digital story are never again mentioned. It is almost as if the opening of the story belongs to a different digital story, to someone else's history. This split is compounded by the fact that, although explicit imagery is used to reinforce Huseyin's successful integration into Australia, *IDIG* sometimes includes imagery that offsets the narrative. When he mentions his Australian naturalisation and name change, he shows what appears to be a professional photograph of himself, sitting in front of a blue photographic screen. His expression in this photograph does not match the sentiment that he is describing, that is, his pride and joy in becoming Australian. As a viewer, it is hard to share or believe his happiness, although the fact that this photograph looks recognisable as what used to be known as a 'Pixie Photo' does invite a sense of endearment and connection. The final picture shown is of a dog, sitting happily beside his food bowl as if smiling. It is a happy image, but no mention of this furry character is given. The moving, misty borders surrounding several of the images are significant – sometimes the hazy layer is so prominent that it is difficult to make out the picture. The use of this technique hints at the opacity of his memories and the characters of his past – which, as the story moves forward – we understand include himself, as a *past character*.

The persistent resistance of the personal becomes a provocative aspect of *IDIG*. The many openings that arise in the story but that are never returned to or closed can unsettle the viewer. There is, clearly, a significant aspect of Huseyin attempting to move forward with his life in Australia, and yet, because he dedicates so much of his story to the day he left Ankara, it is also clear that this past life traipses over his present one. As he describes the departure, his humour hints at the difficulty he is having negotiating the mixed feelings, and this difficulty is repeated throughout the story. Huseyin frequently slips into emotionally 'tricky' territory, but promptly pulls himself back by diverting his (and our) attention to something non-personal/emotional, usually

Figure 8.1 Screenshots from Jimmy Domain's digital story *Ithal Damat* = *Imported Groom* (2007) at key moments of the story's plot, for example, the family photo appears as he discusses his feelings of displacement at the airport upon arriving in Australia. The hazy portraits at the beginning of the story contrast with the final portrait of Jimmy standing on a beach on holiday, adding to the sense of Huysein as the *past, migrant character* and Jimmy as the *present, Australian character.* Courtesy of the author.

something external to himself, such as ABBA and the traffic. In these ways, what is presented as a completed success story actually becomes a disjointed narrative that always remains unresolved.

What is seen in *IDIG* are small blips in an otherwise typical looking digital story about migration to Australia. Cumulatively, these blips create speculation for the viewer that lead to an alternative story, an alternative reality. The creation of these questions does not appear to be a deliberate technique designed by Huseyin to confuse the representation of cultural translation. The roughness of the story can easily be read as poor quality digital storytelling. However, as flagged at the outset, the book is not interested in whether these are 'good' or 'bad' stories, rather, in what they produce and how these productivities relate to cultural diversity in Australia. The everyday aspects of these stories remain the focus.

The odd moments in *IDIG* seem to be incidental, and because of this, they begin to form what Boym describes as a diasporic intimacy.[3] Diasporic intimacies are those unsuspecting affects that sneak into everyday situations and restructure the moment of experience for migrants and those around them. This concept proposes a subtle but rigorous understanding of intimacy that goes beyond that which the digital storytelling genre and other forms of community-based projects try to package and represent. Boym (1998, p. 501) describes:

> The diasporic intimacy that interests me is neither the touchy-feely imperative of the fresh breath commercial nor the fraternal/sororial warmth of a minority group. Diasporic intimacy does not promise a comforting recovery of identity through shared nostalgia for the lost home and homeland. In fact, it's the opposite. It might be seen as the mutual enchantment of two immigrants from different parts of the world or as the sense of the fragile coziness of a foreign home. *Just as one learns to live with alienation and reconciles oneself to the uncanniness of the world around and to the strangeness of the human touch, there comes a surprise, a pang of intimate recognition, a hope that sneaks in through the back door, punctuating the habitual estrangement of everyday life abroad.* (Italics added)

These 'pangs' have been shown to sneak into *IDIG* quite regularly, but they are also seen in the other, more polished stories examined so far. In *LLAA*, Sam ventures from his old world of pain and abjection into his new world of happiness and belonging. As described in Chapters Three and Five, this is visually represented by a picture of Sam standing before a pub door, about to enter. However, just before this scene, and immediately following the reperformance of the work altercation, there is a fleeting scene of Sam walking onto a streetscape. The colour of the photograph is intensely contrasted making it glary and blurry. The accompanying sound emphasises the 'white noise' of the street, culminating in a sense of confusion and distress. It is a brief moment of disruption – the frames before and after fit the neat movement from bad past to good future, but in this window something does not 'add up' (see picture on left, Figure 8.2).

---

3. They also resemble a type of 'phantom limb' – a concept of phenomenologist Maurice Merleau-Ponty (c.1962) and used in postcolonial studies by scholars such as Ram (2005). Merleau-Ponty took interest in people with amputated limbs who continue to experience the lost limb, even when a prosthetic limb is received. Ram (2005, p. 123) outlines the two situations that Merleau-Ponty describes: in some people, the new limb holds the same position the real limb was in at the moment of injury. For others, a particular circumstance or emotion can trigger a memory about how the wound was received, creating a 'phantom limb', that is, the feeling that the limb is still there. The phantom limb is not physically present, and a lot of rehabilitation can take place to help the amputee adapt to the new or missing limb. And yet, because the old limb has been routinely exercised 'as second-nature' for so long – has been subconsciously connected to the person's identity and subjective performance – it does not take much for something to bring it back to life, to disrupt the new body and all its efforts to perform in a new way. When considering migration, we can think about how embodiment of ethnicity, of the past place, gets re-experienced in the present place, even when much 'rehabilitation' has taken place. In *IDIG*, the niggling appearance of the 'phantom limb' creates an affective economy that does not performatively loop smoothly or in the 'desired' fashion.

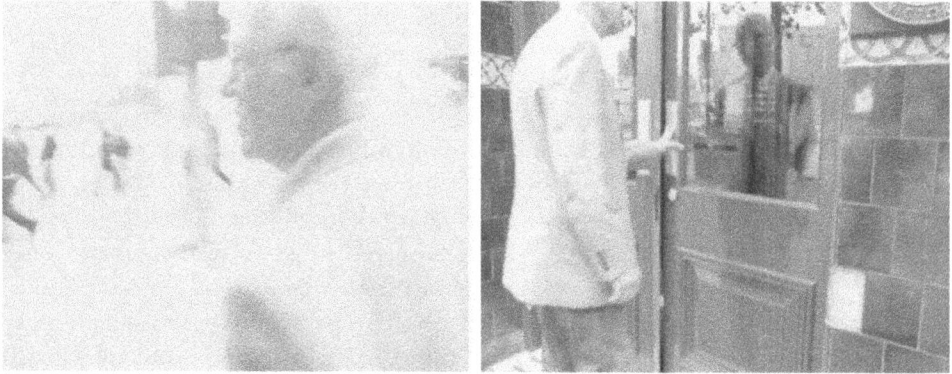

Figure 8.2 (L-R) Screenshots from Sam Haddad's digital story *Loving Lebanon and Australia* (2007). This bright, blurry picture of Sam on a busy street appears right before he enters his new Aussie social life, represented by him being seen before the pub door, arm outstretched. Courtesy of the author.

The pauses or pangs create an opening – a performative blip, or, in Butler's (1993, p. 219) terms, a performative slippage. Sam is moving forward, but despite the confidence with which he enacts this movement, the stressful, apprehensive frame here 'sneaks in through the backdoor' (Boym 1998, p. 501). What this illustrates is that even when we have memorised an identity script and reperform it continuously, we can never be fully contained by the performance or the script. A script materialises in relation to everything that comes before it and everything that might come after it, but it is only ever materialising in the moment, and kinetic moments cannot be fully predicted or foreclosed. The emotions evinced in the digital stories are once again shown to be something produced in encounters, rather than something that the author and viewer 'has': 'it is through emotions or how we respond to objects and others, that surfaces or boundaries are made: the "I" and the "we" are shaped by, and even take the shape of, contact with others' (Ahmed 2004, p. 10).

The digital stories are producers of intimacy, constructed as emotive sites where understanding and compassion for Others is acquired. However, since the body always has the capacity to affect and be affected, affect can be seen to be constantly creating possibilities for both the body in question and those bodies it engages with. These possibilities appear at unexpected moments and threaten to destabilise the promises made in the digital storytelling exchange. Indeed, the twinges of diasporic intimacy are frequent enough in *IDIG* that it is difficult to experience the feeling the digital story genre intends to give the viewer. The pangs create suspicion, unease or 'more to the story'. This aspect unexpectedly affects the viewer and the perception of Huseyin, even if the viewer is unable to pinpoint why. The same is certainly true for Kenan's *YHNL*, discussed in Chapter Six. As detailed, Kenan's story promotes successful migration, designed to leave the viewer confident about multicultural Australia and its capacity to provide happiness to Others. But it does not provide this satisfaction – the happiness is agitated by the harsh and almost desperate dimensions of Kenan's experience as a New Australian. In fact, if we reconsider all the stories examined so far, we find such slippages in all of them.

Migrant digital storytelling projects typically promise to offer happiness and social inclusion by acting as a sign that can be given to others, what Ahmed (2004, p. 196) describes as the 'right kind of feeling' and providing 'the right kind of subject'. After an analysis of *IDIG*, we can now consider what is produced when a digital story does not give us the right kind of feeling. What is produced when the promise made is not fulfilled? The straightforward response might be that the digital story's gift of compassion or good feeling has not been given or received properly, and thus the digital story has failed in some way. However, as both Ahmed (2004, 2010a,b) and Cvetkovich (2003) demonstrate, bad feeling works in productive, powerful ways and requires our close attention. Indeed, it seems as if it is precisely when the promise of multicultural happiness is unfulfilled (for either the author or the viewer) that the possibility for effective ethnic politics arises. In the case of digital stories about cultural diversity, the collapse of the promise creates a slippage in the normative chain of whiteness, willing us to acknowledge our very relationality to these norms. Although categories such as 'ethnic', 'multicultural' and 'culturally diverse' act as promises to signify discrete subjects in relation to the 'non-ethnic', the 'monocultural' and the 'non-diverse', constraint is built into their formations. This constraint guarantees the failure of such terms to fully enact or fulfil their promises and intrudes at the edges of performative whiteness.

In *IDIG*, this failed outcome is most clearly seen in the use of the author's name. Despite the proud proclamation of the author's name change to Jimmy Domain, the film itself is introduced and officially listed under his original name, Huseyin Duman. (Adding further confusion, when the Culture Victoria website introduces the film, it lists the author as Jimmy Damat, blending the author and the title.) Did Jimmy Domain decide to use his original name as a way of paying homage to his past? Or did the producers use his 'ethnic name' in order to match his 'ethnic story'? Ultimately, the impact is the same: the viewer cannot name him as one or the other, and any attempt to label him as such will fail. The fact that such limits to recognition exist for people like Huseyin creates the possibility of a third space of livability. The performative chain of whiteness is not passed over smoothly – Huseyin's body is being constructed in a particular way, but the slippage suggests it could be done in a different way. Huseyin is unable to exist outside the norm of whiteness here; but whiteness is also unable to concretely bind his body to a discrete and defined category.

We are thus reminded that the subject of multiculturalism, the 'I' that forms the subject of these digital stories, is tenuous and always historically located. Our ethnic liveability is clearly dependent on the boundaries of ethnicity that racialised norms construct and deploy. However, when Foucault outlined that what one can 'be' is governed by norms, it did not follow that this being is governed in the sense that it is decided and without possibility (Butler 2008, p. 30). As Butler (2004, p. 32) writes,

Our lives, our very persistence, depend upon such norms or, at least, on the possibility that we will be able to negotiate within them, derive our agency from the field of their operation. In our very ability to persist, we are dependent on what is outside of us, on a broader sociality, and survivability. When we assert our 'right', as we do and we must, we are not carving out a place for our autonomy [. . .] I am outside myself from the outset, and must be, in order to survive, and in order to enter into the realm of the possible.

Conclusion

This chapter has proposed that Butler's notion of performative slippage be integrated with affective economies in studies of cultural diversity. It has argued that doing so can illuminate the tensions of cultural difference and subsequently provide a tactic for harnessing the tensions as a reperformance of multicultural Australia, a performance that is not tied to 'race'.

Huseyin Duman's *IDIG* illustrates how performative slippages surface in digital stories, how the performative accomplishment always involves a tenuous relationship to norms – norms are passed on under duress, pleasure and conflicting needs. The story can be read as a typical migrant narrative that, due to technological inefficiency, is less smooth or convincing. However, a close examination of its disjointed elements reveals that odd or confusing aspects can disclose something else about everyday multiculturalism that is very different from the typical multicultural narrative. This alternative narrative – illuminated by what can be described as pangs of diasporic intimacy – troubles the binary structures embedded within multicultural discourse. In particular, the binaries between public and private, external and internal, home and away. A persistent tension is always extant, threatening to disrupt the racialised outcome. As such, there is always room for disruption – even within the most rigid, normatively organised digital stories.

When we tell our stories, we stake a claim, or name ourselves, in order to become possible as human subjects. However, because doing so requires an undoing, a giving over to norms, it also allows the realm of the impossible to surface, or shimmer in the distance. To refer back to Papastergiadis's three models of cultural translation – 'the impossible' is activated when we engage with it in a considered manner, allowing us to venture into a third space, a space in which other life-worlds and identity scripts can be imagined. Unlike the contemporary art practice that Papastergiadis (2012a) analyses, digital stories are not conventional or deliberate ways of exploring these other worlds. Nonetheless, the genre is unable to fully represent whiteness and ethnicity, moving beyond mere representation and illustrating, ever so subtly, that it has the capacity to manipulate the borders of imagined corporeality. In other words, the genre can activate a reimagining of cultural difference, towards 'risky encounters'.

Part Three

FUTURE DIGITAL MULTICULTURALISMS

This final section focuses on instances in which digital storytelling produces counter-normative moments. I argue that these instances or performative slippages resist racialisation by unexpectedly disrupting the performative chain of whiteness. I introduce some atypical individual migrant digital stories found in ACMI's digital storytelling collection, which resist a linear structure and the affective resolution associated with State-based 'successful' multiculturalism. Digital stories produced by the Sydney-/Eora-based organisation Curious Works are used as an example of reflexive community-based art practice. Together, these case studies illustrate how the digital storytelling genre can be reimagined to productively engage with the dynamism of lived cultural difference. I close this section by arguing that a critical, cosmopolitanism framework for community-based work can open the parameters of multiculturalism and, ultimately, resist the racialised binary conventionally embedded within.

Chapter Nine

DIASPORIC DISTURBANCES: ALTERNATIVE DIGITAL STORYTELLING TECHNIQUES

We must get beyond the rhetoric of continuance and inheritance in which the articulation of past and present is effected; we must resist what Walter Benjamin describes as the historicist (not historical) causality represented in 'a sequence like the beads of a rosary'.

– Bhabha (1996, p. 191)

If the relations that have had to be denied emerge to floor us, the competent and useful subject unravels a little.

– Bell (2007)

A closer reading of digital stories that combines elements of performativity and affect has revealed moments of political possibility. The question remains: can these moments of tension be harnessed to create a noticeable friction on normative whiteness and enable new, more inclusive ways of being multicultural? Although typical migrant digital stories collapse difference into racialised binaries, some are adept at locating moments of instability and channelling them elsewhere.

In this chapter, I examine a small collection of films created in ACMI's digital storytelling programme that are able to carefully exploit slippages in the performative chain of whiteness. These stories, which include Ximena Silberman's *Second Life* (*SL*, 2007), Carla Pascoe's *The Spaces In Between* (*SIB*, 2007), Raymond Nashar's *el ajnabi* (*EA*, 2007) and Adam Nudelman's *The Shoemaker* (*TS*, 2007), utilise a few key tactics. Ximena's and Carla's stories not only refuse to fulfil the promise of multicultural Australia, but thwart the terms the promise is built upon, highlighting the violence that the multi-cultural promise silences and conceals. Raymond's and Adam's stories demonstrate a restless reanimation of the 'ethnic Australian', interrogating cultural memory, identity and – importantly – the material manifestations of whiteness in both themselves and their surroundings.

Failed multicultural feelings

SL describes Ximena's migration from Buenos Aires to Australia following her graduation as an architect. The story reminisces on Ximena's student life and expresses a yearning for the company of her student friends. There is sadness present when Ximena talks of this past. When she turns to talking about her present life in Australia, she describes discovering her Jewish heritage in Melbourne/Naarm and forming a new connection with it. Today, she feels settled and happy in Australia and, as such, the trajectory seems to mirror the typical migrant digital story examined so far.

Despite the familiar trajectory, Ximena's story is able to create moments of tension and ultimately resist a reperformance of the stereotypical 'happy migrant' story. This resistance is enacted in the ownership she takes of her name. When she first moves to Australia, she discovers that most Australians have difficulty pronouncing Ximena – the 'X' having an English 'h' sound. As a result, she begins to use a different first name. Ximena opens her story with the event of this name change, saying: 'My name is Ximena, a bit hard to pronounce for the Aussies, so when I arrived in Melbourne/Naarm in 2003, I started using my second name, Paula.'

Name changes are a common occurrence for migrants in Australia, as mentioned in the discussion of *IDIG* in Chapter Eight. Ximena goes on to tell us that she *hates* her new name and asserts: 'I am not Paula. I am Ximena!' Her use of the word 'hate' is almost shocking in this context. Most of the ACMI-based digital stories about cultural diversity are saturated in positive terminology (e.g. words like happiness, success and love). Furthermore, when the stories do describe discomfort, the language is relatively neutral and delivered in an even tone. Ximena's use of the word 'hate' is still delivered relatively flaccidly, but it grabs our attention and offsets the happy migrant story we have become accustomed to. Adding to this, Ximena openly describes the difficulty of migrating: 'To migrate is like being born again. Nobody knows you and you don't know anyone. For us, we at least had family.' This statement has resonances with Theresa's (2012–13) story, mentioned at the beginning of Chapter Eight, who after describing her migration as a fall from the sky says: 'You feel you are shrinking, you can't find your position.' When Paula begins to transition into contentment, the transition feels steady-paced, rather than enthusiastically or desperately embraced, as seen in some other stories. Just after she finishes telling us that she likes it here, she states: 'Paula needs to go.'

Paula reclaims her name and, almost as a gesture of the hybrid identity she assumes, changes the first letter to *H* so that Australians reading her name will pronounce it properly. It could be argued that this is another example of having to compromise with the discursive force of whiteness, which assumes English as its language. However, it comes across as an active negotiation for Himena, a way for her to integrate plurality into her life, a life in which she is not fully South American, not fully Australian and now – not fully Jewish. This pluralism is not finite but constantly reconstituting, illustrating that cultural translation is not finished at the moment one arrives at a destination or even when contentment is acquired. Indeed, it is only through the estrangement from the site of her Jewish roots that she discovers a connection with these roots, which translates to a new kind of Australian locatedness. To summarise this evolving journey through culture, *SL* uses an image of a spiral staircase, the shot looking down at the spiral from above. The image effectively symbolises the way Ximena is moving through her Australian life, travelling in circular motions and cumulatively learning along the way. To conclude the story, the name Himena appears, written in white on a black screen. Himena is employing the force of discourse to inscribe ownership of her name, to 'be' that which she names.

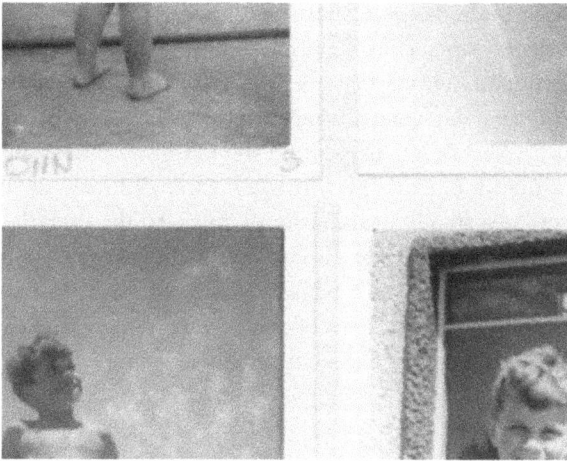

Figure 9.1 Screenshot from Carla Pascoe's digital story *The Spaces In Between* (2007). Courtesy of the author.

In a similar fashion to *SL*, Carla Pascoe's *SIB* resists the happy multicultural narrative discussed in the earlier chapters. Carla resists even though her family has a tendency to romanticise its cultural past. She tells us the sparse stories she has of her family, but states they are rarely shared and very little is known about her family history. She is troubled by the pieces of information she does have about the migration history – simultaneously intrigued and frustrated by them: 'I know only the bare facts of my family history, not the longings and desires of these people whose blood I share.' *SIB* thus becomes an inquiry into the lack of information about her shared family past. Carla is suspicious of the ways in which the stories of her family's culture and migration do not align with the signs that represent these experiences. For example, she closely examines the few photographs her family have of the past and suggests they tell only a certain kind of story/history. These typical signs feature smiling faces; however, the happy migrant performance captured in the photographs is troubled by whispers of suicide, family rifts, sexism and gaps in knowledge. After retelling her grandfather's success in establishing himself as an Australian businessman, she states: 'These are the proud triumphs of our past. But as I grew older, I began to realise that there were some details unmentioned ... Behind many of my family photos depicting success and happiness, are whole albums of photos that were never taken. Photos of loneliness, rejection and grief; images so blurred I can only guess at their contents.' It would be easy for Carla to fall into a romanticised depiction of her family heritage, as we have seen so often, and as the material representations of her migration history cajole her to do. Instead, Carla fleshes out the fissures – literally zooming in on the gaps between old Polaroid pictures throughout her film (see Figure 9.1).

Carla is unable to gain closure for her history and expresses a deep melancholy about this, and yet, gaining the closure does not seem to be the main point, or at least the only point, of her story. The most productive aspect of *SIB* is its capacity to give life to the shadows of her cultural identity and share the frustrations about her cultural lacunae. By doing this, the digital story considers how bodies are formed in Othered space, at the edges of the dominant culture. Carla fears terrible things happened to some of her ancestors and by exploring this using abstract imagery, the story provokes us to ask if these ancestors, these particular bodies, are beyond the margins of Australian grievability. By deliberating on this question, Carla performs a meaningful form of grief or mourning. Her digital story acts as a small but important witness to the everyday traumas that, as Cvetkovich (2003, 2007) stresses, are easily buried in everyday life, particularly when they occur as non-white traumas in a white sociality. In short, Carla is able to reclaim the borders, manipulating the boundary of the 'ethnic' subject that the broader AoS of multiculturalism attempts to contain. A similar 'failed feeling' of multiculturalism is present in Giovanni Sgro's *Australia: per forze e per amore* (2003), as I have discussed elsewhere (see Trimboli 2019).

Performing plurality

Complementing the work carried out by Ximena and Carla, Raymond Nashar's *EA* and Adam Nudelman's *TS* creatively perform different aspects of 'the multicultural person' and further explore the nuances of cultural difference in Australia. *EA* begins as many digital stories do, with self-reflection or self-identification: 'I used to be Lebanese.' In a similar fashion to Rita's identification in *WDIB?*, Lebanon 'makes sense' as home for Raymond. He explains: 'I used to be Lebanese. At least, I always knew I wasn't Australian. From a very young age the mean kids would often tell me to go back to where I came from. Even though I had never been there, it still made sense that I belonged there, and that one day I would go back.' Raymond then moves to describe a five-month family trip to Lebanon in 1994. Again, in a similar fashion to Rita, he is made to feel out of place in Lebanon: 'For the first three days I stayed in my room, on my grandfather's deathbed. People thought I was just jetlagged. For the next week or so I wandered the village of my forefathers with my headphones on, wondering what was happening back home; back where I came from. It was like another planet and I was an alien.' The trip prompts him to think about Australia as the place where 'he comes from'. When Raymond returns, he alters the way he performs his identity: dressing differently and listening to more American-style music, and incorporating more English into his at-home use of Lebanese. He feels he is different 'to the [Australian-]Lebanese kids', a difference that seems to be a way for Raymond to deal with the mis-interpellation that occurs in Lebanon. However, he explains that after a few years he once again warms to his Lebanese heritage, to 'these strangers who are my blood'.[1] And so begins what becomes a persistent exploration of his cultural identity.

---

1. It is worthwhile noting the recurring theme of 'bloodlines' in some of these migrant digital stories and the perpetual tension it creates between cultural hybridity and essentialised understandings of identity in Australia.

The discovery of his plurality is illustrated by his narrative and use of visuals. The digital story begins as many do with photographs of Raymond when he is young. It then shows Raymond moving through the streets of Lebanon, walking them for the first time and attempting to map the space. He shows various photographs and video snippets of himself at different ages, illustrating the active role-playing he assumes at certain times. At the appearance of a picture of Raymond in army uniform, he describes that this is him in Lebanon, 'trying to hang out with the boys'. The story finishes with home-movie footage of Raymond on a tower: 'This is me with my Lebo haircut', he narrates, 'and my Lebo jeans, and my Lebo beach shoes.' Raymond is slyly poking fun at what Butler terms the corporeal project, acknowledging how his body adjusts itself according to the norms of ethnicity operating in each context. His subjective journey is affirmed by his use of sound throughout the film. The story opens with traditional music – a group of people chanting – which then disappears so that we can hear only Raymond's voice. This technique singles him out and highlights his sense of isolation and loneliness. The music turns to the hip-hop he experiments with during his early teens, before returning to the traditional chanting. The background music alludes to the way Raymond keeps returning to his cultural roots – he is bounded to them in ways he cannot fully understand or explain, even though they create distress for him at regular intervals.

Raymond's identity experiment might not be a deliberate act and it certainly isn't an example of pure agency – as Butler (1997b, 2004) reminds us: one does not wake up and decide which 'I' they will wear that day, or which performance they will 'put on'. However, the negotiation of norms and expectations that Raymond carries out in his everyday life allows his 'I' to be continuously reshaped. His performance of 'Australianness' or 'Lebaneseness' happens in a back-and-forth motion that ultimately prevents the normativity of whiteness to fully control his corporeality. He reflects upon the way he has changed over the years, and how terrifying it was when he first went to Lebanon and 'lost his identity'. Despite this terror, and the several ways he attempts to deal with it, in the end he seems to understand himself as a type of shape-shifter.

There is a sense of power and possibility that comes with this understanding of himself as doubled or multiplied. The resolution for Raymond contrasts with the other stories examined, which describe a distinct tension between one place and another. As we have seen, in these stories the authors tend to conclude (although not always convincingly) that they belong to both places equally. For Raymond, the meaning of his attachment to Lebanon is not to find the answer to his 'true self', or his whole being, but to give himself more flexibility as a person. He concludes by saying: 'I thought I'd discover who I was in Lebanon. Instead, I discovered two lands that I love completely, but no place that I completely belong to.' With this conclusion, he does not try to align himself with one or the other, or split himself evenly across two – he estranges himself a little from them both, with an understanding that he will be drawn towards each place at different times and for different reasons.

In a similar manner, Adam Nudelman's digital story also reflects on his cultural heritage in a way that productively destabilises the common assumptions of non-white Australia. As a visual artist, Adam uses his own paintings in *TS* to think through the conflicts, longings and mysteries of his cultural upbringing. He is interested in exploring how traumas impacted his ethnic ancestors and how these traumas have been pressed upon him – and, now, are carried forth by him in new ways. In an interview with Adam about his digital story, he explains that when painting the works featured in *TS*, he was not consciously trying to explore this aspect of himself. Upon reflection, he can see how the works were shaped by the process of learning about his Jewish ancestry and, more importantly, by the process of asking questions and exploring different possibilities of cultural life in Australia.

> They're portraits of me, basically [...] And [...] they operate [...] from that level of questioning who I am, and also questioning those ideas about when you're little and you think you can be anyone: you can be a sports star, you can be a doctor [...] So there's all that conversation going on. But you are also the influence of the Pinocchio story of the boy whose fashioned by a father and he just made him, not so much in his image, but made to be something and given all this stuff and ends up being something different anyway. (Nudelman 2012)

Throughout his digital story, Adam explores how norms constrain us, but mobilise us too. *TS* reflects on how Adam previously understood himself as growing into a person of his own choosing, but over time began to realise that he was being unavoidably shaped by his historical-cultural context. Adam paints himself as a wooden doll reminiscent of the folktale character Pinocchio – the puppet carved from wood by toolmaker Geppetto. Pinocchio's body is physically reshaped by his actions and requires other people to direct its movements. When Pinocchio is given a spirit, he can move and explore independently. This independence eventually leads him to rebel against his father and venture away from home. His bad behaviour – in particular, his lying – causes his nose to grow, and because his actions do not comply with social expectations, the change is seen as a deformity. Eventually, Pinocchio readjusts his behaviour and is transformed into a human boy: his good behaviour makes him a '*real* boy', a legitimate subject. By comparing himself to Pinocchio, Adam is considering how he is shaped by his family and his cultural history. He experiments with his sense of self, venturing away from his family and particular cultural belongings. However, he is led back to them, almost mimetically, so that a positive back-and-forth occurs in every encounter, as a constant iteration of self-production. This process is similar to the way Raymond is persistently drawn to his Lebaneseness, even when fervently trying to disavow it. He eventually realises that this attachment is a deeply material one, but not an all-encompassing, or controlling aspect of himself.

Another key likeness between the two stories is the way they both perform a remapping of public space through their private performances. There is a poignant moment in *EA* when Raymond is strolling through the streets of Lebanon, soon after his family arrived for their 1994 holiday. He describes: 'For the next week or so I wandered the village of my forefathers with my headphones on ... The buildings wore the scars of war and poverty. The streets weren't like Australian streets – they were just spaces between the buildings. It was beautiful, but it wasn't me.' The act of walking through what Raymond sees as 'just spaces' becomes a useful metaphor for thinking about his on-the-ground multicultural experience. In particular, it demonstrates the doing of everyday multiculturalism, that is, the ways in which the walking and talking of multiculturalism is 'experienced in the development of subjectivities in concrete places' (Noble and Poynting 2010, p. 502). The way Raymond viscerally responds to walking the streets of Lebanon in comparison to walking Australia provides a useful example of how belonging is grounded in movement. Raymond finds Lebanon's 'unmapped' spaces beautiful but confronting, and they prompt him to long for Australia. In suburban Australia, where Raymond resides, streets have a carefully mapped and uniform aesthetic: demarcated footpaths organise pedestrians' movements, often into buildings, and the footpaths run adjacent to clearly marked roads. Upon his arrival in Lebanon, Raymond suddenly longs for the structure of Australian streets. The performativity of ethnicity materialises a certain kind of human subject and, here, the performance is clearly shown to be relational to space. As Noble and Poynting illustrate, spaces are sites for 'the regulation of national belonging [. . .] invested with meanings around national belonging, freedom, citizenship, community, democracy' (p. 495).

The performativity of Australianness or Lebaneseness is what Noble and Poynting describe as a pedagogical process, impacting how migrants *learn* to act in public spaces and thus how to *be* in space. Institutionalised forms of mobility regulation entail 'systematic and procedurally entrenched discrimination' and always occur alongside 'informal modes of the regulation of movement' (p. 493). Walking through the streets of Lebanon, Raymond begins to re-experience himself, and actively engages 'the peculiar politics of perambulation that we might identify as "walking while Leb"' (p. 491). The ending of *EA* reinforces this political assemblage. To close, the film cuts to home-video footage of Raymond atop a high tower in Lebanon. After showing us his 'Lebo' attire and hairstyle, he points to something beyond the camera frame and says: 'That's Lebanon.' The camera shot slides down to the dry landscape of Lebanon, and from this height people and objects are small and impossible to distinguish. Raymond's Lebaneseness is impacted by the regulations of identity inscribed in the spatial dimensions of his home country; however, this scene represents the way Raymond creates a reflective distance from the various identity regulations. By the end of the film, we see Raymond's ability to resist these regulations. He continues to walk the spaces in-between: committing himself to being 'space between the buildings'. He is active in his exploration of his cultural attachments, moving through different cultural spaces in an attempt to understand himself. But, much like the streets of Lebanon, he does not map himself out definitively, or according to the rules of Australian streetscapes.

In *TS*, Adam shows pictures of his paintings, the subjects of which engage with space in clever, albeit subtle ways. The paintings feature wooden dolls, shoes and boxes. Adam places these objects in shadowy or in-between spaces on the canvases. One doll stands in the shadow of a slightly open door crack, the darkness of the room beyond looming ominously; another stands before a pair of large, empty shoes; yet another in front of wooden boxes. The paintings create a sense of spatial disproportion and contrast, magnifying the unknown or 'beyond the entrance' spaces. This physical perspective is exaggerated by pictures featuring piles of everyday items. Adam makes links between these tall piles of artefacts and the cultural weight he and his family have borne. In the interview, he explains how, as a child, he could sense a pressure but was unable to make sense of it (Figure 9.2).

Figure 9.2 Four individual screenshots taken from Adam Nudelman's digital story *The Shoemaker* (2007). Courtesy of the author.

The cultural 'weight' he describes here produces different formations of Adam and his everyday experiences as an Australian. This dynamic is something Adam begins to understand through his art practice, reflecting on how images, stories and snippets of childhood memories construct a particular reality for him as a child, but acquire new meaning when he recalls them as an adult. *TS* deliberately invokes this reflection, examining how Adam's body fits into the Jewish-Australian cultural space, and how it

Figure 9.3 (L-R) Adam Nudelman's *Mania's Shoes*, oil on canvas (2002), featured in *The Shoemaker* (2007); and *Diaspora*, oil on canvas (2002). Image courtesy of Adam Nudelman.

can be adjusted to fit within broader Australian culture at large. When visiting Adam at his studio, a painting of a wooden doll wearing half a Jewish concentration camp jumper and half a Collingwood guernsey (a Melbourne/Naarm-based AFL football team) was viewed. The uniform mixes Adam's traumatic heritage with his present Australian lifestyle and points to his complicated becoming. It seems that Adam views himself as growing into the person he might become, an iterative growing that occurs on the border between cultural trauma and the Australian 'good life'. Again, we see the way affective performativity is passed from one body to another but impresses upon each in various ways. The affective economy carried by Adam's grandparents is restructured when Adam engages with it, and it continues to be restructured as he grows older.

The connection Adam makes between his materiality and the cultural regulations of Australia is further illustrated by his paintings of people-less landscapes. In the interview, Adam describes his inclination to do these kinds of works:

> Some [of the landscapes] have structures and towers, and so, some people read them as states of decay, other people read them as states of rebuilding . . . and it's sort of that conversation about the landscape itself . . . my family, or part of my family doesn't exist in that landscape and it's taken away in that landscape but it's also . . . these works, the later works, they sort of also have the, the reference to immigrants and placing immigrants into camps and there's that . . . they're multilayered in that whole political argument thing, those works you know, with my coming here on a boat, they could have well been treated the way we treat the immigrants coming to this country now.

The landscape paintings attempt to capture the severe sense of isolation that many migrant Australians, including Adam's family, experience. The presence of these Australians is not recognised as part of the national landscape, the national imaginary.

In that sense, they have 'disappeared' from the script of Australian whiteness. This disappearance materially manifests itself in the everyday life of Adam and his extended family. Adam describes how strange it used to be to visit his grandparents and his Great Aunt in their Melbourne/Naarm home – the house was always dark, and many of its rooms were closed off and he was not allowed to enter them. As a child, he would imagine what existed beyond the closed doors: 'I used to imagine that she [my Great Aunt] lived in that room and she'd have ... books of poetry ... books she'd loved reading, she'd write, she must draw in there.' When his last remaining grandparent passes away, he returns to the house as an adult, to help his father clean and prepare the property for sale. He is shocked to discover that the formerly hidden rooms are small, with piles of rags and rubbish: 'When we ... opened the door to clean that room it was just floor to ceiling full of rags ... and there was just this little goat track to this little corner where she slept on this pile of stuff and there's nothing to identify her existence whatsoever, there's nothing that she looked at, did.' Adam begins to comprehend the trauma experienced by his ancestors and their desire to be isolated once they were safe in Australia. He finds an eerie connection between the debris that his relatives surround themselves with at home in Australia, and the debris of the Holocaust aftermath:

> Those sorts of images which ... really impregnated themselves on my visual memory ... and then at a very deep core I realised that sort of imagery is imagery I'd seen time and time again and associated with the Holocaust – and not just with the Jewish Holocaust but also with pilgrims against all sorts of genocide and, you know, the piling of shoes, the piling of clothes.

In that sense, he sees his ancestors reperforming their disappearance in accordance with the script of Australian whiteness – they retreat to the darkness of their home, their rooms. This multicultural life is very different from the other multicultural lives we have so far seen in digital stories: most of the stories have suggested boundlessness and a sense of having a legitimate space within the Australian good life. Through his artwork, Adam gently shows us the claustrophobic, almost non-existence, which some migrants experience in Australia.

Like Raymond, Adam comes to a realisation that it is fine to be culturally confused, and also to be indulgent in particular ethnic spaces. He gives himself permission to feel safe and comfortable in his cultural traditions and practices. Adam feels his Jewishness is somehow imbued in him, perhaps even biologically, as he describes feeling 'at home' in the synagogue or at Jewish dinners:

> The interesting thing was when I started – because I'd never had anything to do with the Jewish community whatsoever until I started working at the Jewish Museum ... and I suddenly found myself with not so much *like-minded* [emphasises word] people because it's, obviously there's diversity in any community, but there was a sense of, I can't even really articulate it, there was a sense of belonging.

Whether or not his Jewishness is innate or culturally acquired is not a major concern for Adam. He is interested, rather, in being open to the animation of his history in new ways, of honouring it in ways his ancestors could not. He is, in short, finding comfort in the discomfort of ambiguity. As he describes: 'It took me a long time to allow that, to feel comfortable and to accept that it was actually . . . it wasn't just an invention of my own imagination, it was actually something that was there.'

Conclusion

Combining performativity theory with affect theory can both illuminate and produce instances of political resistance in digital storytelling analysis. Carla Pascoe's *SIB*, Ximena Silberman's *SL*, Raymond Nashar's *EA* and Adam Nudelman's *TS* are all able to actively manipulate the chain of performativity that enforces whiteness in Australia. The stories challenge the affective economies that normally circulate in migration narratives, resisting the urge to move seamlessly from a sad, difficult past to a happy, successful present. The troubling aspects of cultural ancestry are given time and care, providing a space for the 'disappeared' persons and experiences of multicultural Australia to be both recognised and grieved in public space. The stories do not end resolutely but remain powerful because they draw attention to the edges of Australian cultural difference that seclude and seduce some Australian bodies and ultimately attempt to reinforce the material white body.

The digital stories discussed here also point to ways that migrants embody memories that are discursively inaccessible. The invocations are beginning to take on an alternative formation, reminiscent of what Hage (2014b) denotes the 'diasporic condition'.[2] In his most recent work, Hage examines how migration and diaspora do not act as events or additions to the lives of Lebanese people. He argues, instead, that those born in Lebanon are born with a diasporic subjectivity – migration pervades their social environment so that culture and migration are inseparable. Hage argues it is impossible for people born in Lebanon to think about the act of migration as something that *could* happen; it already defines all aspects of their lives, even if they have not physically migrated. Migration is, for those who live with the diasporic condition, like a 'bug', affecting people in different ways; however, 'everyone catches it the moment they breathe' (Hage 2014b).

The conception of the diasporic condition takes a range of formations in various locations, but it is a useful way to end the analysis carried out in this chapter. Raymond and Carla fall into the diasporic condition outlined by Hage quite seamlessly, having been born and raised within the Lebanese diaspora. It seems relevant for Adam and Ximena as well, given their Jewish heritage and the similarities that exist in the construction of Jewish identity via its particular diaspora. The Jewish population carries with it an association of 'movement and displacement' (Hage 2014b), so that the diasporic condition becomes constitutive of its subjectivity. This association is present even for those diasporic subjects that have not migrated themselves: being a migrant subject who has experienced or wants to experience migration is only one mode of being a diasporic subject; there are, as Hage (2014b) describes, a number of ways one becomes constituted as

---

2. Gunew uses the term 'diasporic condition' (1998, p. 101) and 'migrant condition' (2017), respectively, in a similar fashion to Hage.

a diasporic subject. Thus, even though Adam has not migrated in the conventional way, the diasporic condition penetrates his body. Migration and its associated effects are a part of his milieu, acting as an intermediary between his body and the bodies of others. As Hage (2014b) denotes, the diasporic condition is the 'culture of a fragmented geographically non-continuous space that *includes* the space of emigration' (italics added).

This concept is useful because understandings of cultural diversity are so often formulated on the basis of a gulf between two (or more) distinct cultures. Binary thinking permeates the narrative of liberal multiculturalism. The binary structure is constructed despite the fact that the experience of multiculturalism is complicated; as the digital storytelling analysis has shown, living cultural difference involves criss-crossing the social landscape, rather than existing as one identity or another. Australia most certainly has a long way to go before it could be considered a place that embraces a diasporic condition. However, this chapter indicates that such a possibility is not completely out of reach. The following chapter adapts the tactics employed by these stories to propose a model for digital interventions and everyday multiculturalism engagements – one that makes the most of this diasporic condition.

Chapter Ten

THE COSMOS IN THE EVERYDAY

We are engaged in modes of being that are in turn also modes of constituting the habitats in which other entities (concepts, organisms, objects) survive or disappear. To partake in these environments or assemblages, then, is to partake in the actualization of the present's potential, the composition of tomorrow.

– Bell (2007, p. 124)

A past [...] is never sealed off because traces of it retain into the present, but equally important, from the perspective of the past-as-present (the past when it was present), it also protends some futural horizon. Each past imagines, if you will, certain possibilities [...] the past [...] is always anticipating possible futures.

– Ngo (2019, p. 243)

Even though the digital storytelling model is understood to be a humble and genuine form of sharing personal experience, digital stories about multicultural life are not necessarily telling us what we think they are or hope they might be. Their representations of ethnicity are significantly impacted by the performative force of whiteness, and the broader apparatus of security of multiculturalism. Nonetheless, there are always excesses that thwart the translation and ultimately provide clues to other migrant realities and possibilities. These clues are more frequent and easier to trace in digital stories that practice a greater degree of 'genre bending', swerving from the conventional digital storytelling methodology. Exemplifying this swerving is the digital storytelling work of Curious Works, which, alongside Big hART, has been instrumental in the development of collaborative digital storytelling formats in Australia. Their blending of the two dominant digital storytelling methodologies (individual and collaborative) robustly situates ethnicity, helping the ethnic body to become disentangled from race.

Curious Works is a not-for-profit organisation that works with Australian communities on art projects about 'diverse Australia'. Like Big hART, Curious Works establishes itself within communities for months at a time, working with community members on a range of media arts projects. The organisation predominantly works in the Australian capital cities of Sydney/Eora, Melbourne/Naarm and Hobart/nipaluna, though it has more recently expanded into regional Australian towns. Under the direction of Shakthi Sivanathan, Curious Works began with broader arts media in its scope, most prominently, theatre and dance. However, since its inception, it has become increasingly associated with digital media platforms. The organisation has been active in developing best practice models of digital storytelling, frequently delivering workshops with government and other community-based organisations on how to facilitate their own digital storytelling workshops. It has thus assisted organisations like ACMI and Big hART in spreading digital storytelling across Australia.

Unlike many other community-based organisations, Curious Works does not begin from an assumed position of neutrality. Indeed, it distinguishes itself from ACMI and Big hART through its commitment to analysing its discursive framework. Sivanathan (the then director) was acutely aware of the complexity of cultural diversity and built an acknowledgement of the organisation's own set of power relations into the fabric of Curious Works. The organisation is particularly mindful of the power it produces when it intervenes in communities, as well as its own impact on constructions of 'community' and 'cultural diversity'. Many of Curious Works' digital storytelling workshops spend time critically reflecting on what the term 'community' means for the participants. As the organisation specifies: 'A lot of people talk about producing "community media", without pausing to get clarity on what is meant by "community"' (Curious Works 2013).

One of the organisation's aims is to enable political power to be exercised by those who have limited opportunities to do so. Achieving this goal involves subtly adjusting dominant stories and the assumptions they carry. At first glance, such an approach does not seem very different from Big hART's philosophy, or from the philosophy of the digital storytelling genre at large. However, as illustrated earlier in this book, this kind of 'talk back to the centre' philosophy comes with its own sets of problems. Curious Works is aware of these sets of problems, identifying the potential for its own assumptions to become normative at its sites of social practice, 'whether a school, an individual or a country' (Sivanathan 2014a). Given this risk, the organisation is constantly considering how 'we' as a diverse and often contradictory term is constructed in its work, and endeavours to keep the term open and malleable. Its objectives thus involve more than attempts to shift assumptions; they also involve consistently reinterpreting the shifts they instigate and produce (Sivanathan 2014a).[1]

Curious Works illustrates a commitment to tracking and interpreting both micro and macro cultural discourses. The organisation attributes stories with the power to inform and embed cultural assumptions, acting as a means through which cultural fictions are normalised in Australian society. It recognises that this occurs at many different scales, from the institutional to the everyday. Due to this, Curious Works is interested in the relationship between the various levels of cultural translation. This approach is contrastable to the handling of stories by the digital storytelling genre, as formulated by the StoryCenter. The StoryCenter tends to privilege ordinary stories as 'truth' crusaders against grand narratives and institutional practices, reluctant to acknowledge, let alone engage with, formal institutions.

One way Curious Works engages the relationship between micro and macro is by working strategically in both formal and informal spheres. For example, Sivanathan

---

1.   This strategy resembles Tania Bruguera's use of 'aesth-ethics', which describes an active reflec-
     tion of 'ethics' and our reactions (including emotional) to it. Bruguera (2014) argues that aes-
     thetics should be put to work for ethics – where 'ethics' is not normative, but is itself a critical
     practice of redefining and reproposing (via artistic practice).

(2014a) notes that the organisation has significant goals pertaining to the way cultural difference is understood, describing these goals as the ones 'you string your sleep in'. However, he also notes that there is a 'game to be played'. For Curious Works, this means having to negotiate its aspirations with the goals of its institutional patrons and funding bodies. The aims of organisational bodies external to Curious Works need to be achieved for its own internal goals to become possible. Consequently, proposing projects to government and other funding bodies involves the strategic use of language – a need to couch the politicised and critical goals of Curious Works in 'conservative speak' (Sivanathan 2014a). Like Big hART – and so many other artists and organisations who fall beneath the 'multicultural banner' – Curious Works has to invert the speech so that the external body is exposed as being outdated or harmful. 'Why is equality of voices a radical idea?' Sivanathan quips, 'To be *against that* is radical!' Curious Works pitches potential work in such a way that the external body is positioned as the 'radical' body, coming to view Curious Works, even for just a moment, as the rational party. This brief moment of inversion enables the entry point and from here the work is opened up.

Based on a philosophy of cultural openness and change, Curious Works has been able to create an eclectic collection of digital stories produced by ordinary Australians. This collection includes conventional digital stories, short films and online comedy sketches, creating plural and multilayered representations of Australianness. Often, such as in *The Stories Project* (*TSP*), the works are iterative so that initial digital stories are further developed. A group of young people involved in the two digital storytelling projects *Urban Stories* (2010) and *Desert Stories* (2010) were selected to participate in *TSP* (2010–12). The participants were mentored by the staff at Curious Works on media and film production over a two-year period. While several of the stories were single-authored, there were also many collaborative stories, with two or more writers/directors.

Each story in these collections looks and feels different. Morika Blijabu's and Curtis Taylor's *OJ on Broadway* (2010), for example, is told through song, with Owen Gibbs performing a desert song on a train platform at Sydney's/Eora's Central Railway Station. The short film is designed to convey the homesickness and disconnect that authors Gibbs, Blijabu and Taylor experience in Sydney/Eora while working with *TSP* crew. Inspired by Sydney's/Eora's buskers, OJ is filmed sitting on the platform, singing and playing guitar, as hundreds of commuters rush past. The commuters' walking pace is sped up and down, their bodily figures faded in and out. The contrast between the stationary OJ and the hurried commuters, together with the use of song, creates an abstract but powerful impression of movement and the vast reach of cultural identity in Australia. It also puts an emphasis on the spatial dimension of cultural difference.

Cultural identity becomes an intersecting point in *Ama and Chan's Kitchen Rescue* (2012) – an ongoing series of short films that parody Australian cooking shows and the stereotypes applied to 'ethnic Australians'. In the 'Fluffy White Rice' episode, Ama and Chan respond to a 'question' posed by a 'viewer', namely: 'How do you cook your rice?' They proclaim sarcastically, 'If there's one thing Asians and Africans know, it's rice.' This sentiment is further exaggerated by certain aspects of the performance, including Chan's attire – a traditional silk kimono that connotes his 'Asianness'. A small tweet-like snippet appears at the bottom of the screen: 'White people don't know how to cook white rice, ironic.' The two hosts spend the next few minutes taking the audience step-by-step through the making of 'fluffy white rice for fluffy white people'.

Also featured in the *TSP* collection is *Villawood Mums* (2010), a conventional-looking digital story by Guido Gonzalez and Saif Jari that focuses on two different experiences of Villawood Centre in the suburbs of Victoria. First, the centre acts as a place of refuge for asylum seekers; second as a place of detention for asylum seekers. Guido begins narrating the story, telling us that his mother, Maria, migrated to Australia as a refugee following political unrest in her home country, Chile. Maria then describes the deeply upsetting experience of her migration in 1985. She missed her friends and family immensely and 'cried and cried' for them. She explains that her sadness was subdued somewhat by the care she received at the Villawood refuge centre. Here, Maria was welcomed by kind and gentle workers, who were active and passionate about helping her settle into the new country.

Like other characters in digital stories seen so far, Maria explains her settlement into Australian life and expresses her affection for her new home. However, the usual trajectory from sad to happy is disrupted, as the second half of the story shifts to the rejection Zahoor experiences as a refugee in Australia. Arriving in 1995, Zahoor also spends time at Villawood; however, unlike Maria, she is deported to the centre as an illegal immigrant, discursively positioned as abject and made to wait for a long time to have her application processed. Some reflection is then carried out by the two main characters, and Maria tells us: 'For Australia to become like this – to have Villawood transformed into that is painful.' The digital story thus provides a tension that we do not often see in the digital story archive of multicultural Australia. Indeed, the entire affective economy that normally operates to move the viewer from sad to happy is inverted: the past becomes the happier place and the present or future Australia is the place of sadness and despair.

Cumulatively, the stories give rise to alternative patterns and rhythms that cannot be easily traced or categorised. A cultural landscape is created that shifts the way place is mapped and understood in Australia. The stories collated across the three programmes give 'cultural diversity' an engaging but rather unexpected three-dimensional texture – conveying a sense of the complex, non-linear formations of Australian subjectivities. Importantly, the stories in this collection are not always about cultural diversity per se; cultural diversity emerges as part of place and how that place connects to other places and people. Due to this, the stories often indirectly engage with notions of cultural difference, as something to be reflected on 'along the way', rather than being treated as a subject that needs to be totalised.

The Afro and the white Australians: Chronicling everyday multiculturalism via Liam's Hair

The digital story *The Chronicles of Liam's Hair* (*COLH*, 2010) is particularly good at illustrating an 'incidental critique' of cultural difference. Created by a group of Newman youth, self-titled the Newman Film Group, the short film combines aspects of both individual and collaborative digital storytelling in a more discrete manner than usually seen. Forming a story within the broader project *Newman Stories*, *COLH* turns an ordinary part of life – the body (in particular, hair) – into something extraordinary. In doing so, the digital story indirectly produces a critical reflection on how cultural difference is encountered and racialised in everyday Australia.

Liam's afro becomes the subject of the highly satirical digital story *COLH*. The four-and-a-half-minute film takes place in what appears to be Liam's classroom. Liam opens the digital story by telling the camera: 'I used to be a normal kid ... until I was about thirteen. And then I noticed that I grew *hair* [emphasises word]. Lots of hair.' In a mockumentary style, *COLH* presents a 'non-fiction' account of Liam's afro, cutting together snippets of interviews and re-enactments. The interviewees dramatise their 'risky encounters' (Papastergiadis 2012a, p. 132) with Liam's hair, emphasising their emotive reactions with exaggerated facial expressions and bodily movements. In this way, the characters parody a documentary-style news show, in the vein of *A Current Affair*, or *Today Tonight*.[2] The interviewees talk to the camera sincerely and seemingly in response to questions that have been asked by an off-camera interviewer. Towards the end of the film, this style is confirmed, as a voice-over explicitly asks one of the interviewees a series of questions.

In the process of parodying non-fiction film formats, and having a laugh at the expense of Liam's comparatively 'strange' hair, *COLH* makes a number of highly reflexive and critical moves. The speech acts of the 'witnesses' turn Liam's afro into a world of its own, described in detail by one interviewee as a parallel universe, one that exists in another place, beyond the realm of the normal and the human. While it seems unlikely that the authors set about making *COLH* with the intention of critique, their film effectively speaks to the ways whiteness situates non-whiteness as other-worldly. Viewers implicitly understand that Liam's afro is a subject of conversation because it is unlike everyone else's hair, where 'everyone else' in the classroom is implied to be Anglo-Celtic Australian. The other people interviewed about Liam's hair have a white phenotype: fair skin and hair.

Significantly, Liam's afro materialises as Other according to (extra)ordinary encounters and is verified as such by 'science'. An older man, later revealed as the students' science teacher, assumes the role of 'afro expert'. He begins by explaining:

Yes, well, most people have hair that just sort of grows normally, a little bit like your fingernails. Liam's hair is a bit different. And if you look at the broad spectrum of his hair ... what you see is just hair, but on the inside you have a whole solar system, a whole complex ecosystem happening in there.

He struggles to explicate the nature of the afro's force to Liam and others:

I mean, I put it simply, and I talked about the black hole or the worm in outer space [frame goes to close up of Liam, who raises his eyebrows in playful manner, then camera zooms into

Figure 10.1 Screenshots from Newman Film Group's digital story *The Chronicles of Liam's Hair* (2010) featuring the 'afro expert' (Liam's teacher), eyewitnesses (Liam's classmates) and Liam's infamous afro. Courtesy of the author.

his hair] . . . and on the technical side of that, it's got sciences baffled on how this sort of takes place. But if you look at the synthetic vortex of the curriculum, you'll be very . . . you'll be very surprised at how difficult it can be to understand.

The role-playing here purposively exaggerates science and becomes a playful account of Liam's afro. The expert's gestures are emphasised as he explains the ecosystem that is Liam's hair, informally lecturing us on the 'facts' of Liam's hair. The badge on his shirt further connotes his prestige and authority.

Within this playful parody of science, one can read a very fitting critique of the way ethnicity continues to be framed according to long-standing forms of biological racism. Liam's non-white hair materialises as wild and Other in accordance with scientific notions of nature and racial purity. Science verifies his afro as a complex system that can pull people into it. During the film we hear first-hand accounts from people who have been unexpectedly hauled into Liam's hair, resulting in injury and suffering: 'There was a sharp bone in there as I went in', describes one of the interviewees, 'and it got me, right there.' The boy taps his chest to indicate that the sharp bone in Liam's hair stabbed him in the heart region. But, it is not only people who get sucked into the hair maelstrom – we learn that all manner of objects falls prey to its force, such as pens and bedding. Approximately halfway in, Liam tells us he keeps waking up with no pillows, but he has no idea where the pillows are going, or who is taking them. His comments alert us to the fact that Liam is oblivious to the danger his own body carries. This set-up impersonates the way non-white Australians have been discursively positioned as dangerous and destructive, but unaware of this aspect of themselves. As such, the white

authority has to manage the 'problem' that is blackness or ethnicity. When the interviewer asks the teacher what people should do if they find themselves stuck in the vortex
of Liam's hair, the teacher advises people to keep their distance. It seems that once you
are in the vortex, there is no telling what will happen, so it is best to avoid Liam and
his hair altogether: 'if you get in close proximity to his hairdo you . . . you're asking for
trouble', the 'expert' warns.

A significant performative slippage is harnessed towards the end of the short film.
It comes in a moment of error, in which 'the expert' mis-performs his lines. This mis-
performance, or what could be read as a type of 'bloopers reel', is added to the end of
the film, in between the credit frames. Following a frame featuring a classic sci-fi galaxy
image (also shown at the start of the film and thus signalling the film's official end), an
off-camera voice asks the expert if he has coined a scientific name for Liam's 'disorder'.
The expert replies, 'yes', but his face is beginning to show faint signs of laughter. He is
further prompted by the interviewer to tell the viewers the term. Halfway through the
expert's reply, his voice falters, and he warbles out the words: 'The Liam.' He then fully
gives into his amusement and, turning from the camera, shouts, 'Cut!' A wave of rau-
cous laughter is then heard off-camera. While there are preceding moments that suggest
the characters are on the edge of breaking character, this is the first time that the 'serious' tone of the film is clearly broken. The teacher finds his rehearsed lines comical
and cannot keep a straight face. His laugh causes me, the viewer, to laugh, though his
inability to keep a straight face is hardly surprising to me. What he is saying is, in this
instance, ridiculous.

Although the case of Liam's hair seems preposterous, it is actually not too far removed
from how cultural difference emerges as a subject of contention in Australian society.
Liam's hair has been thoroughly described, analysed and reported on, so much so that it
is no longer just hair: it is a force unto itself, 'The Liam'. In the same way that colonial
Australia's First Nations became 'the Aborigines', or today's diverse Arab-Australians
have become 'the Muslims', the cumulative discourse about Liam's hair turns it into its
own separate entity. When the teacher is shown laughing at the silliness of this process, it
exposes the process of racialization as absurd and completely unstable – it is laughable.
The laughter allows for a movement in perspective, what Homi Bhabha (1996) might
term a 'parallaxal shift'.[3] At first, it seems as if *COLH* has taken us to a different place –
giving something normal an absurd narrative. But, upon reflection, we can see that it is,
in fact, a place – and a narrative – that we are familiar with, and this can surprise us.
When the teacher laughs, a performative slippage ensues: the strangeness of what is comfortable (the discourse of science, a person's hair) is exposed. In this exposure glimmers

---

3. Bhabha (1996) develops his notion of the parallaxal shift in a reading of Adrienne Rich's
    poetry. Bhabha argues that Rich's work displaces the speaking 'I', so that 'its place of enunci-
    ation . . . is iteratively and interrogatively staged' (1996, p. 97). Together with a deliberate use
    of repetition, this interrogative staging places moments of experience alongside one other,
    but provides no way of ordering these moments historically, nor a way of drawing parallels
    between them. What ensues is 'a parallaxal shift in the subject of the event as the enunciating
    I shifts its geopolitical location and rhetorical locution' (1996, p. 97, original italics).

an alternative possibility – not only might Liam's hair be pretty normal after all, but *the way we create cultural difference* might be the abnormal, or peculiar, aspect.

COLH is not the product of professional contemporary art; it is a film created by young people in an everyday Australian setting – a high school classroom. The characters are not professional actors, and the moving image involves no fancy camera work, sliding frames or animations. Yet, the performativity of cultural difference enabled in *COLH* is more edifying than the happy multicultural performances we have become habituated to in these kinds of digital stories. It creates what Papastergiadis (2012a) envisions in the hybrid work of diasporic contemporary artists. Hybrid works that enter a third space of cultural translation can manipulate the discursive and affective borders between subjects and objects in new and surprising ways. As Papastergiadis illustrates, diasporic artists 'neither celebrate the cultural differences in their own identity nor valorize border cultures. They are hybrid in the way that they examine the complex psychic responses to political structures and the diverse layers that are enfolded within historical symbols' (p. 118). Liam certainly exemplifies this. He makes fun of his different hair at the same time that he illustrates how silly it is to make fun of his hair. Papastergiadis (2012a) joins Vince Marotta (2008) in explaining how this kind of irony is often indicative of hybrid artwork. Diasporic artists borrow and blend cultural signs and practices, mimicking public symbols in a personalised manner. The binary that haunts cultural difference and the myriad of ways it is represented and managed becomes increasingly delicate – it is no longer clear where the borders between public and personal, self and Other, dominant and marginalised begin and end.

The digital story about Liam's hair thus undertakes an interrogation of the ethnic body and its limitations in white society, a tactic often seen in the work of diasporic artists. Migrants often create a fusion of bodily acts that consists of the gestures and movements they have become accustomed to performing in their home countries, as well as the corporeal practices they are compelled to perform in order to 'fit' into their new countries. In other words, they (re)produce their bodies according to what Foucault (1977) terms a disciplinary practice. The contribution of affect theory to the notion of disciplinary power is the insight that affect engages limits which include skin or bodily borders: 'a literal border, as well as the ideas, myths and metaphors, and affects that inform subjectivity' (Aung Thin 2013, p. 69).

Exploring the affective aspects of stories like *COLH* provides an understanding of the ways in which racist materialities are produced in colonial nations such as Australia and reorganised by hybrid artists. This digital story performs a subtle interrogation of what Aung Thin terms 'border skin' (p. 75), a deliberate play on bodily characteristics such as hair and skin that in turn question how these characteristics act as political borders. As Ahmed (2013) describes, skin both orders and is ordered. In Australia, white skin constantly alludes to the skin of the non-white, the Other. In this way, white skin acts as an ironic intimacy (Aung Thin 2013, p. 75). The same can be said for the hair of Liam's (white) classmates. Liam and his co-creators construct his hair as fuzzy, black and dangerous and then help us to find humour in the construction. The act of laughter chafes against what we know exists in contrast to his 'outrageous' hair: 'normal' hair, or the hair of the white classmate. The first interviewee explains, 'Being near Liam's hair was absolutely terrifying. There were giant lice and I had to fight them off with my pen that I lost. It was *so scary*, I couldn't bear it . . . I just had to get out [looks at camera, shaking head in disbelief. Very troubled expression].' The other interviewees also describe the risks involved in getting too close to Liam's hair, one describing: 'I decided to have some fun one day in class, so I started throwing my pens in Liam's hair [frame is of him and another boy sitting behind Liam in class; Liam is smiling, unaware of their bullying]. I needed my pen, so I went to grab it and then some unknown force pulled me in.' The boy then shudders, physically repelled by the act of retelling this experience. These testimonies push us away from the black body towards the white body, creating a confusing reaction that is both funny and troubling.

In all of these ways, the simple digital story performs what Paul Gilroy (2005, 2006) also sees in the comic work of Sascha Baron Cohen. One of Baron Cohen's characters, Ali G, created a great deal of controversy, as people wondered whether he was 'a white Jew pretending to be black, a white Jew pretending to be a white pretending to be black, a white Jew pretending to be an Asian pretending to be black, and so on' (Gilroy 2006, p. 79). Much of this controversy was, however, because those who watched him knew that what it meant to be English, indeed, what it meant to be a human in postcolonial England, was at stake: 'every notion of culture as property is broken and dispersed by the swirling, vertiginous motion of the postcolonial world for which Ali was an unwitting spokesman' (ibid.). No subject is safe from Ali's critique, and no one is fully able to determine the place from which Ali's critique launches. As Gilroy points out, Baron Cohen's actual political alliances were shielded from the public by his commitment to remaining in-character throughout all public appearances and interviews. In doing so, he practiced an active form of disloyalty to his own locality, something key to our understanding of our positions of power and in order to 'interact equitably with others formed elsewhere' (ibid.).

Liam can be seen to be utilising a similar strategy in *COLH*. In the film, he maintains his performance of the unassuming ethnic Australian. He is seemingly oblivious to the danger his hair carries, acting as a naïve bystander whom others talk about at length, unbeknownst to him. The same is true for the supporting characters in *COLH*, who perform the shocked and fearful 'victims' of Liam's hair. All characters distance themselves somewhat from their own usual localities, acting out an identity exaggerated as Other to themselves. For Gilroy (2006, p. 75), performing a carefully cultivated 'degree of estrangement' puts in motion an effective form of cosmopolitanism. *COLH* enacts this kind of estrangement in a clever, but subtle manner. As viewers, we know that Liam's hair is connected to Liam – to his person – but when watching the digital story, we begin to view the hair as separate from Liam, as existing somewhere else. His hair is flung into the biosphere, and we are then positioned as historical witnesses, observing the nature of this 'entity'. A few minutes later, we are back, but we are no longer facing the same way. Liam has caught the audience off-guard by showing it the bloopers reel – he has exposed white colonialism to itself. In this way, he has enacted a form of cosmopolitanism from below, providing the audience with an opportunity to better think through ways to 'invent conceptions of humanity' (ibid.). As Gilroy argues, 'imagining oneself as a stranger in a limited and creative sense might instructively be linked to actually becoming estranged from the cultural habits one is born to' (p. 78).

Conclusion

If more digital stories can rouse the self-reflexive function found in *COLH*, both from the point of view of the creator and the consumer, new forms of embodiment can arise. It is for this reason that Gilroy sees Ali G as enabling an effective cosmopolitanism: his own origin, especially that which is constructed as nationalistic, can be reintroduced to itself. This kind of cosmopolitanism is aligned with a critical multiculturalism, one that refuses state-centeredness by taking place at local sites but always shifting inwards and outwards: '[it] finds civic and ethical value in the process of exposure to otherness. It glories in the ordinary virtues and ironies – listening, looking, discretion, friendship – that can be cultivated when mundane encounters with difference become rewarding. The self-knowledge that can be acquired through the proximity to strangers is certainly precious but is no longer the primary issue' (Gilroy 2006, p. 75). The 'primary issue' is now how to act ethically and justly, not only in the mundane encounters with others, but in extreme instances where violence and xenophobia attempt to 'engulf, purify, or erase' cultural difference (ibid.). By displacing the speaking 'I', Liam's story practices a form of critical cosmopolitanism, which also moves the viewers to a place of cultural estrangement. In turn, the racist fictions embedded in common deployments of 'cultural diversity' are illuminated. For a few moments, the digital story is also able to bring different groups 'into the same present . . . fusing their horizons so that the possibility of a common future becomes conceivable' (p. 74).

The capacity to undo our own identities and the identities of others can be powerfully cultivated within mundane, everyday interactions – such as Liam's classroom. *COLH* carries out a form of undoing, providing a space where one can glimpse an alternative translation of cultural difference. It is a small gesture, but if fervently channelled, the possibilities for interrupting larger, more obvious moments of racist violence expand (p. 75). How might this gesture be harnessed in multicultural studies at large?

Chapter Eleven

DIGITAL COSMOPOLITANISMS, DIASPORIC INTIMACIES

The other is what can only be imagined – as a coming community, as a planetary humanity, or even as 'the earth' – in its 'absence', while its presence can only be embraced in its concrete embodiment in every particular instance (in every individual or community). We engage with power for the sake of the other, an other that is always unknown but knowable, always abstract and yet concretized. This is the obligation to imagine an other world, and to an imagination that can only be produced through the concrete effort to bring it about, to embody it in the concrete practice of relationship as belonging together. It is there that ethics and politics, practice and desire, meet. And that, for me at least, is the driving force of cultural studies.

— Grossberg (2010a, p. 100)

During a panel discussion at a 2014 arts conference, Shakthi Sivanathan, director of Curious Works, argued that cultural diversity is a revolution. For Sivanathan, the revolution will occur when cultural diversity becomes redundant. In this final chapter, I linger on Sivanathan's claim that cultural diversity acts as both potential revolution *and* future redundancy, an idea which gets to the core of the dilemma plaguing migrant digital storytelling and multicultural work more broadly.

As I have been arguing throughout the book, there remains within contemporary multiculturalism and culturally diverse work a persistent tension, namely, the need to acknowledge cultural difference, on the one hand, and the realisation, on the other, that persistent acknowledgement of cultural difference reinforces the border between dominant cultures and Others. As Gunew (2005, p. 365) succinctly summarises: 'In the long run, all such activities to change power relations amount to an all-or-nothing paralysis that ultimately serves to shore up binarism, that is, the assertion of any kinds of difference runs the risk of being relegated to abject liminality.' This contradictory dilemma is not a new problem and race and ethnic scholars have explored it routinely in the twentieth century. However, the problem has resurfaced in the twenty-first century in new, more exaggerated ways, exacerbated by increased mobility, transient migration patterns and multifarious points of identity.

By bringing a critical cosmopolitanism model into dialogue with diasporic intimacy, I propose in this chapter an alternative approach of migrant digital storytelling and cultural work at large. Using the digital story *Khaled vs. Khaled*, co-produced by Curious Works, I illustrate how this approach can allow migrant narratives to be opened up and ultimately help unbind everyday multiculturalism from its enduring paradox. I argue that cultural work requires ongoing critical attention – it should be driven by a future-to-come, but the arrival of this future should be perpetually delayed.

Cultural difference: Revolution or redundancy?

Shakthi Sivanathan (2014a) identifies two axes of power in contemporary Australia: institutional power and grassroots or activist power. He argues that many political possibilities are closed off for ordinary people by institutional power, which is able to guide normative cultural assumptions. Curious Works thus positions itself as an activist power or a grass-roots intermediary that seeks to give ordinary people the skills to connect using everyday storytelling. This position is not dissimilar to that of organisations such as the StoryCenter and ACMI that occupy intermediary positions and that hope to fill the Australian landscape with everyday stories that promote cultural difference. Indeed, the claim of Curious Works that cultural diversity is a *revolution* mirrors claims by the StoryCenter that telling and sharing stories of difference can radically alter the world. In 2014, Sivanathan went further, suggesting that the revolution will be realised once cultural diversity becomes *redundant.*

There is a great deal of merit to this claim and my intention is not to dismiss its worth outright. As Ahmed's (2012a,b) critiques of cultural diversity within universities and beyond have only too clearly illustrated, culturally diverse work is set up as a movement towards inclusivity; however, intrinsic to this set-up is often a set of obstacles which foreclose the possibility of inclusivity occurring, so 'true' culturally diverse environments are always 'just ahead', in view but perpetually out-of-reach. The same argument can be made about multiculturalism at large, and in many ways, this is the argument I have been making in this book. After all, as Mishra (2012) points out, there would be no need for multiculturalism if all cultures were already equal. Attempting to saturate or nullify cultural difference is thus not a 'bad' goal in and of itself. However, as the digital storytelling analysis in this book has indicated, attempting to eradicate a void runs the risk of 'filling in' the void prescriptively, rather than mapping the conjuncture as 'a place of organization' that needs to be, in Grossberg's (2010b, p. 315) words, de-territorialised and decoded.

The 'filling in' approach of digital storytelling and, indeed, everyday multiculturalism tends to treat the everyday and institutional power as opposites, overlooking how the everyday body becomes embodied in relation to the managerial aspects of the national body. Any space in between is, as Semi et al. (2009) note, full of tensions, overlaps and inconsistencies, so much so, in fact, that it is impossible to fully separate one from the other. In addition, the attempt to bridge the two spheres often involves appealing to the humanity of the dominant culture, which can accentuate the vastness perceived to exist between dominant and marginalised cultures.[1]

---

1. As Spivak has illustrated many times, the Master-Slave dialectic is reinstated when the dominant (white) culture is charged with the responsibility of bestowing tolerance and enacting liberal multiculturalism to marginalised non-white Others.

Nonetheless, the material ramifications of racism and its auxiliary systems, including some forms of multiculturalism, have not been adequately addressed. This fact has been made abundantly clear in the twenty-first century which has seen continued violence against people of colour and other cultural minorities, as well as the global rise of white nationalist parties. Cultural diversity must play a significant role in the re-storying of the Anglo-settler colonies this book has discussed, notably Australia, the United Kingdom, Canada and the United States.

In his recent book *We All Want to Change the World* (2015), Grossberg rightly argues that we need to tell better stories if we are to create a truly inclusive world. There can be no denying that digital storytelling is going to play a crucial, if not leading, role in this quest. Grossberg stresses that these stories should not privilege any single dimension – body, gender, race, environmentalism and so on – but he also argues that cultural work must resist becoming overwhelmed by the fragmented, mobile and hyper diversity of the particular or its accumulation (p. 489). Occupying this balance is, of course, an onerous task, and one that Grossberg acknowledges as such. While recognising that 'transforming the world depends upon understanding what one is transforming', he also recognises that all attempts to understand the conjuncture will fail: 'one's analyses are always provisional, always incomplete, offered without certainty and what Stuart Hall once called "the solace of closure"' (p. 501). A familiar predicament arises, and the tension created by Grossberg's two points permeates so much of his argument that the 'all-or-nothing paralysis' Gunew (2005) observes becomes difficult to shake off.

I propose that merging Gunew's critical cosmopolitan conception of 'acoustics' with Boym's 'diasporic intimacy' can enable the conjuncture of neocolonial contexts, including those that Grossberg and other cultural studies scholars' work takes place within, to be mapped and decoded more thoroughly and – significantly – in a more mobilising manner. Grossberg (2015, p. 475) argues that cultural studies can enable political possibility if it 'listens to the demands of the empirical world as a problem space and allows it to answer back to our efforts to describe it'.

Gunew's notion of acoustics not only acknowledges the multifarious voices – whispers, shouts, restraints, echoes and languages – of contemporary cultures but, significantly, it makes spaces to critically *listen* to them. Summarising the core thesis of her book *Post-multicultural Writers as Neo-cosmopolitanism Mediators* (2017, p. 3), Gunew writes:

> The neo-cosmopolitan debates have shown that while we are more aware of being connected than ever, this understanding is accompanied by a blindness concerning many groups, histories and geo-political areas that were overlooked in the past and that need to be brought to the centre of our cultural criticism so that we can engage more ethically and sustainably with global cultures and languages - including those at risk. The discussion also questions traditional ways of conceptualizing space and time by invoking the planetary to set against the ubiquitous use of the global and by referring to deep or geological time (often associated with Indigeneity) as distinct from a linear colonial time that undergirds most national histories.

Gunew's theory of a cosmopolitan acoustics enables both the spatialisations and the temporalities of cultural knowledge to be recognised and then harnessed for the

deconstruction of norms such as whiteness. She begins developing her conceptualisation of acoustics in her 2005 reading of Rey Chow's *The Protestant Ethnic and the Spirit of
Capitalism* (2002), in which she provides clues for how we might unbind cultural work from
the all-too-familiar quandary. Gunew explains that autobiographical work – like digital
storytelling – is read by the dominant culture as an offering from the 'native informant'.
This is an offering from what Chow refers to as a 'secret (or defiled) ethnic . . . group'
(cited in Gunew 2005, p. 369). As such, the ethnic informant is confined to a past storytelling: 'repetitively trapped in offering uniquely "personal" elements at the same time
that they contribute to the general profile (stereotypes) of their group or community.
Thus, difference becomes wholly commodified as both recognizable and repetitious'.
While this argument is put forward by Chow, Gunew works carefully to show that, despite the many traps present, ethnic subjects are capable of eluding confinement to abjection by blurring 'those very boundaries that are part of both stereotyping and abjection
in Chow's depictions of this schematic' (ibid.).

Gunew focuses on Chow's argument that theoretical writing by ethnic authors tends
to retreat to the temporality of personal, past experiences, despite theory being, for
Chow, the opposite: 'declarative, future-oriented, rational and abstract' (p. 135). Gunew
illustrates that a 'going back to the future' in the spirit of Lyotard does allow for the creation of theory. The going back is mediated by abjection but it allows for a critique of
the abjection at the same time as it references the personal, or autobiographic. In that
manner the Other is able to turn the mirror back towards the dominant gaze so that, as
Michael Taussig has suggested, the West is reflected via the perspective and dexterity of
its others (1996, cited in Gunew 2005, p. 376). In short, it returns to the past to reshape
the future.

Digital storytelling that is based on this backwards-forwards looping offers an alternative pathway for work on cultural difference and provides an alternative model for a
critical everyday multiculturalism. Gilroy (2006) describes this kind of approach as postmodernism in action. The approach is postmodern in its ability to go back and redress
at the same time that it insists on the retranslation of cultural difference, so that, as
Bhabha (1996, p. 199) articulates, 'the process of being subjected to, or the subject of,
a particular historicity of system of cultural difference and discrimination has to be, as
they say, "recounted" or reconstituted as a historical sign in a continua of transformation'. A kinetic form of postmodernism allows understandings of cultural diversity to
be propelled by a recognition of the limits we are embedded within when we attempt to
recreate the world, rather than being revealed 'in the composition of identity from "the
fragmentary remains of odd cultures and religions"' (Gilroy 2006, p. 80). Instead of
making cultural diversity the revolution (to return to Sivanathan's claim), cultural diversity is revolutionised.

I have been building the argument that in order to create productive possibilities for the
ethnic subject, new methodologies of imagining alternative bodies and performances are
required – and an alternative model of everyday multiculturalism is, too. Theoretically
this task might seem reasonable, but concerns might be raised about its practical enact-
ment. The type of vacillatory critique required is, however, more familiar to us than it
initially appears. The contemporary moment, or 'postmodern predicament', as Gilroy

describes it, might be complicated, but it also provides an opportunity for new kinds of connection. Mass migration, diasporic communities, seasonal travel, tourism and global communication networks have created situations whereby it is necessary to move frequently between past and present, self and Other, so as to reorder and make sense of the multiplicity of our encounters (see Urry 2005; Gilroy 2006, p. 75).

Indeed, when examining the digital archive that Curious Works is creating, it appears that the organisation is *already* enacting this type of critical everyday multiculturalism. Sivanathan (2014a) recognises that the digital represents a rupture, allowing different ideas to be shared and new alliances to be forged across space and time. The use of this rupture as a way to redefine belonging as an ongoing endeavour subtly surfaces in its archive, even within digital stories typical of the genre. The promotional digital story for *The Stories Project*, for example, begins typically: the faces of 'multicultural' youth (read: non-white passing) are zoomed in on and a voice-over explains why the digital storytelling programme is important. The 'camera is a window of imagination', we are told, but the use of the face and eyes seems standard and thus pre-empts a *particular kind of* imagination and foreclosure.

The short film edits together a series of clips from a range of digital works it has created, before returning us to the faces. However, this time, the faces make small glances to the side of the screen after speaking, glances that become more obvious towards the film's closing. Something is happening beyond the frame; the subject is looking elsewhere, to the edges. The 'happy migrant' is distracted by other things, and now, so is the viewer. Where are they looking? Is it towards the future?

Khaled vs. Khaled and the unsatisfied future-to-come

The short film *Khaled vs. Khaled* (*KvK*, 2014), made for the *Meet+Eat* project by Curious Works, provides a useful example of the alternative model of migrant digital storytelling I am attempting to map out. The *Meet+Eat* project initiates meetings between two individuals or groups of individuals, each of whom prepares a meal to share at the meeting. The Curious Works film crew spends time with each person/group in the lead up to the meetings, so that the final films include interview-style snippets and footage of the participants preparing meals, sharing food and conversing. In *KvK*, a mature Lebanese-Australian male, Khaled Sabsabi, has dinner with young Lebanese-Australian male, Khaled Miriam. Sabsabi is a new media artist and talks about his role as an interventionist, or somebody who begins a conversation through his art. He is also a community worker, involved in many Lebanese-Australian organisations. In the set-up to the meal, Sabsabi explains that he met Miriam at one of the community work groups he was involved with several years ago. Sabsabi became Miriam's mentor.

Within the first minute, we get a sense that the two characters are approaching this arranged meal very differently. Miriam tells us that he is going to invite his Aunty over to help him prepare the meal for Sabsabi. A frame with the words 'Aunty Fatima Knows Best' then appears. We are taken to Aunty Fatima's kitchen – where 'Aunty Fatima' is actually Miriam in disguise. Miriam embellishes the stereotype of Muslim women in Australia: 'Aunty Fatima' cooks a 'traditional' Lebanese meal using Campbell's

Figure 11.1 (L-R) Screenshots from Curious Works' short film *Khaled vs. Khaled* (2014): the first three show 'Aunty Fatima' cooking for Sabsabi (the written text on the box mid-left reads: 'Halal Powder'); the mood is contrastingly serious in the remaining shots showing Sabsabi preparing his traditional Lebanese dish and then sharing it with Miriam. Courtesy of the author.

beef stock and an Uncle Toby's kebab. The kebab is cut using a sword-sized 'knife'. Meanwhile, Sabsabi is shown preparing his meal with sincerity: 'This meal reminds me of my Mother', he tells us (Figure 11.1).

When Miriam arrives, Sabsabi kisses him twice on each cheek. Miriam plays on this gesture and starts performing the kissing ritual again, exaggerating the greeting until Sabsabi withdraws and scolds Miriam under his breath. The two men talk over food, in a mostly convivial way. Nonetheless, the tension between the two is apparent, and it becomes clear that the ways the individuals have approached this meal is indicative of the ways the two approach their Lebanese Australian identity. Sabsabi stresses the importance of respect for older migrants and attempts to reach out to Miriam by telling him, 'I haven't had it [this particular dish] for a while, I thought it would be nice to share it with you.' Miriam laughs – he 'cannot believe' Sabsabi has prepared such a traditional meal. Miriam expresses his annoyance at certain aspects of Lebanese culture in Australia; Sabsabi defends these aspects. They both share a connection to their Muslim faith, but otherwise, they have conflicting ideas about how to connect with their Lebanese heritage. This conflict further highlights how precarious the interface of cultural 'connection' is. Sabsabi is shown to be unsettled by Miriam's interventions, even though Sabsabi himself provocatively intervenes in the conversation about Lebanese Australia.[2]

What makes *KvK* particularly significant is Sivanathan's comments about the encounter prior to its release. At a *Spectres of Evaluation* (2014) Q&A session I serendipitously attended, a member of the audience asked Sivanathan if clashes ever occur between Curious Works and its youth participants. Sivanathan (2014b) referred to the film *Khaled vs. Khaled*, describing his personal concern about the way the younger male (Miriam) turned the meal-sharing into a spoof by dressing up as a stereotypical Muslim woman ('Aunty Fatima'). He felt Miriam would look back on the collaboration with disappointment, perhaps even feel ashamed that he disrespected the older participant's (Sabsabi) values. In the spirit of Curious Works, in the spirit of allowing participants to explore and test cultural boundaries, the film production was allowed to go ahead, and the film is now available online. By stepping back and allowing the collaboration to 'play out', Curious Works enabled the interaction to develop in the moment of encounter, and the result is arguably more productive because of it.

Understanding community as community-at-distance, or community-in-provision, is relevant for all levels of cultural work and analysis – both personal and public. As Khan (2011, p. 60, 158) illustrates, community is designed to create belonging, but the act of defining 'community' necessitates infinite exclusions and often overlooks *who* it is that community is constructed for. Khan wants to maintain an active interest in the instability of community and work on the construction of community at a distance (p. 59). She is inspired here by Gerard Delanty (2003) who argues that community might still be a useful concept if defined as 'an open ended system of communication about belonging' (cited in Khan 2011, p. 60). Community as a provisional space might mean the community is constituted differently tomorrow. If considered in this way, community and, in this case, cultural diversity are 'at less risk of lapsing into the sorts of consensual and morally prescriptive frameworks we have observed' (Khan 2011, p. 60).

Working through cultural difference in this way is not revolutionary,[3] as Curious Works hopes. However, it does create its own type of translation while avoiding the reinstatement of whiteness so frequently seen in community-based art projects about cultural diversity. This translation is one in which the subject actively operates within (rather than outside of) the productive space of hybridity. In contrast to most of the digital stories researched for this book, the digital stories by Curious Works do not create a particular multicultural subject; the 'I' of the multicultural subject is displaced, and it

2. Sabsabi's new media installations create conversations about cultural connection and disconnection within Lebanese Australia, frequently providing a tension between traditional and contemporary iterations of this community.
3. A point reaffirmed by Gilroy (2006, p. 80).

becomes difficult to demarcate the ethnic Australian body. The vacillatory experience of cultural diversity shines through. Thus, the role of Curious Works in creating these cultural encounters is not to find common aims or attributes across cultures, but to cut and edit a story that reformats normative notions of identity and historical memories, at first undoing the subject and then allowing for a redoing that creates what Bhabha (1996) calls the 'continua of identification'.

In a multicultural studies context, the work enabled by Curious Works here is reflective of what Bhabha (1996), Gilroy (2006) and Hall (2002b), respectively, term unsatisfied multiculturalism, ordinary cosmopolitanism and vernacular cosmopolitanism. Each of these terms has their particular characteristics, but common to all of them is the idea that identity and community never become fully defined: 'not because it is mimetically in/non-adequate, but because "unsatisfaction" is a sign of the movement or relocation of revision of the "universal" or the general, such that it is producing a process of "unanticipated transformation" of what is local and what is global' (Bhabha 1996, p. 202). As a structure that organises both everyday life and institutional policies, multiculturalism requires our reflective distance and an unsatisfied attention. An unsatisfied multiculturalism is not an ethical failure or the deferral of 'facing up' to material implications of the present. It is, on the contrary, the activation of an ethical relationship to the Other. It allows us to do justice to the cultural violences of colonialism that occurred in the past, but that reverberate in the present moment of post-colonialism. It allows for this because in order to embark on an ' "unanticipated transformation" of what is local and what is global' (ibid.), we must go back, albeit with a different lens. The field of everyday multiculturalism has emerged because of continued frustration with a multiculturalism that doesn't seem to move, or moves only to discursively repeat proverbial patterns of whiteness. Although eager to move forward the same patterns will emerge if we do not ask of culturally diverse societies such as Australia: what has been missed? What requires reinterpretation?

Conclusion

When cultural organisations like Curious Works focus on a particular future, whether one of redundancy or the saturation/normalisation of cultural difference, the problem remains that a utopian future gets re-envisioned, one that tries to morph 'universality' into a unitary, singular meaning for all. A better strategy thus might be to think about producing work that pushes the normative boundaries that exist in the current moment; but, later, performing work that pushes the normative boundaries of *that* moment. In other words, to think about its goals not as linear – and moving from revolutionary to redundant – but as circular and evolving with each orbit.

Parallels can be drawn between this type of multicultural work and the type of democracy that Butler conceptualises. Samuel A. Chambers and Terrell Carver describe Butler's 'democracy' as the active incitement of troubling politics. For Butler (2000, p. 268), this emphasis requires a 'commitment to a conception of democracy which is futural, which remains unconstrained by teleology, and which is not commensurate with any of its "realizations" requires a different demand, one which defers realization permanently. Paradoxically [. . .] democracy is secured precisely through its resistance to realization. [. . .] Whatever goals are achieved [. . .] democracy itself remains unachieved' (cited in Chambers and Carver 2008, p. 97). What Butler is describing is a democracy-at-distance, an unsatisfied democracy. In other words, she argues that we can only maintain a democratic life if we never realise 'democracy', if democracy always remains a 'future-to-come' (Chambers and Carver 2008, p. 97). What needs to be stressed, and what Grossberg (2010b) helps to illustrate, is that this futurity cannot collapse into a particular future or utopia. He writes:

> One understands that reality is making itself and it will continue to, and that therefore there is a contingency about the world that opens up possibilities. Not in the utopian way that leads to misunderstandings and accusations like you are a gradualist or something because you want to take it step by step to get 'there'. I don't really want to get *there*. I just want to take that one step, and hope that that one step makes the world a bit better, and then we'll figure out what that context is and take another step. (pp. 318–19)

The present conjuncture of cultural life needs to be mapped before we can take our next step, and this map must address the fissures and ghosts of colonialism that surface in everyday Australia but are ignored or 'disappeared' repeatedly. When we do take that next step, we map that conjuncture and proceed once again.

Such an approach allows us to carry out cultural work amid the precarious momentum of performativity – that space where 'something' is always on its way but will never fully arrive. Performativity is not linear, it moves cyclically and, with affect, inwards and outwards across a network of relations. Accordingly, community-based work can endeavour to create and pass on knowledge but with an understanding that this knowledge can, and should, come back in some way for reinterpretation. In this manner, nothing becomes redundant in the strict sense of the word; we can – and must – continue working, adding, re-producing. Bhabha (1996, p. 202) explains:

> The process and indeed the performance of translation, the desire to make a dialect: to vernacularize is to 'dialectize' as a process; it is not simply *to be* in a dialogic relation with the native or the domestic, but it is to be on the border, *in between*, introducing the global-cosmopolitan 'action at a distance' into the very grounds – now displaced – of the domestic. (Emphases in the original)

In other words, not to fully exist in 'cultural diversity', or to have achieved the desired outcome (i.e. the catch-cries for 'cultural tolerance', 'celebration of difference', etc.), but to be in-between outcomes, just before, on the borders.

CONCLUSION: REMEDIATING MULTICULTURALISM

> We have to think about the possibility of living in a vibrating reality.
>
> – Hage (2017b)

In this book I have attempted to reimagine twenty-first century conceptualisations of multiculturalism. Although I focused on Australian multiculturalism, the analysis was always situated within the broader framework of multicultural and ethnic studies, specifically within the context of Western liberal multiculturalism. I argued that more attention needs to be paid to the ways in which normative whiteness continues to perpetuate the construction of Othered bodies in Australia and other Anglo settler colonies, even in supposedly everyday or community-oriented contexts.

It is clear that while multiculturalism has been an important aspect of the Australian narrative for over 50 years, it has always been plagued by issues of white managerialism. More recently, it has become the subject of public and scholarly criticism, accused of being empty, irrelevant or even 'dead'. It is also clear that contemporary multiculturalism has reached a conceptual crossroads – conflicted by a long-standing binary that has re-established itself in relation to the particularities of postmodern life. Like ethnic and cultural studies more broadly, multiculturalism is now charged with negotiating the effects of rapid globalisation, namely, increased mobility, interconnectedness and identity fragmentation; and the various reactionary responses to these effects which have mostly taken the forms of tightened border security, concentrated political uprisings and increased nationalism. By the turn of the century, the term 'cultural diversity' had largely overtaken multiculturalism, deployed by multiculturalism as an AoS so as to render race historical and 'invisible'. Multiculturalism as a topic is as alive and necessary as ever, but currently operates as a mode of crisis – a crisis of contradiction.

There are two main approaches to this crisis. The first reclaims the positive aspects of multiculturalism, avidly petitioning for the asset of cultural diversity in contemporary society. This strategy has been highly influenced by the popular – and important – critiques that diasporic artists of the 1980s and 1990s enabled, as well as the broader work on identity recognition and liberalism. The second approach, broadly defined as critical multiculturalism, has focused on the complex and contradictory elements of multicultural life and mapped new forms of cultural interactions. Some strands of critical multiculturalism have recently employed Balibar's (1991) concept of neo-racism to argue that contemporary racism is based on cultural rather than biological differences.

I have argued that although racism contorts across time and space, biological notions of whiteness continue to haunt new migrant communities in Anglo-settler colonies. Currently, Australia promotes itself as open and welcoming to cultural diversity; however, violence at the level of subjectivity and the body continues to occur in everyday life on the basis of cultural difference. Frequently, this violence collapses cultural difference into long-standing biological notions of whiteness. Thus, culturally diverse communities are constructed in relation to new, postmodern forms of knowledge translations, but these constructs harbour normative concepts of race, first mapped onto the Australian imaginary by white colonial invasion and via the biopolitics of race and science. Further, even though cultural diversity seems to have overtaken multiculturalism in popular rhetoric, multiculturalism discourse continues to influence both private and public aspirations of Australianness.

To temper this paradoxical predicament, and indeed, to try to use the paradox productively, I adopted a critical approach to everyday multiculturalism. Everyday multiculturalism represents a new scholarly direction that aims to deal with what is recognised as a gap between the managerial notions of multiculturalism and the lived experiences of cultural difference. The field has been driven by Australian scholars who, motivated by the development of Islamophobia in the early part of the century, have tried to 'fill in' the so-called gap. Their work draws on analyses by Ang, Essed, Hage and Stratton, among others that pioneered everyday aspects of racialisation. I joined this inquiry by exploring the ways in which everyday multiculturalism manifests itself as a corporeal accomplishment in Australia and comparable nation-states. I argued that the contemporary focus on cultural diversity is a reformulation of what Hage critiqued as a 'cosmo-multiculturalism' in *White Nation*. The use of a Foucauldian framework of power helped to illustrate that cultural diversity projects, often seen in community-arts contexts, are implicated discernibly in the reproduction of racialised bodies.

I used the digital storytelling genre as a prism through which to develop a critical methodology for everyday multiculturalism. Digital storytelling is a relatively new form of media that frequently engages cultural diversity. The principles and methodological approaches of the genre have many similarities to everyday multiculturalism, mainly, the sharing of marginalised stories that exist in the everyday, and, as such, the attempt to fill in a 'gap' between ordinary experience and dominant (and institutionalised) perceptions. A review of digital storytelling scholarship revealed a lack of critical analysis of the genre. Most of the literature begins with assumed positive aspects of digital storytelling as an inherent component of the genre rather than something to be critically investigated. This characteristic has some resonance with certain derivatives of everyday multiculturalism that at times risk reinstating a binary approach to multiculturalism even though acknowledging the phenomenon's complexity.

Everyday multiculturalism could easily be conceptualised as an oppositional critique of institutional or theoretical multiculturalism, thereby overlooking (and reinstating) structural deployments of whiteness. The methodological framework for analysing digital storytelling and everyday multiculturalism needs to remain aware of what Hall and Grossberg refer to as 'the background' or conjuncture. Namely, to ask: what work is done by the term 'everyday' in these cases?

A new framework for analysing migrant digital storytelling

I offered in this book a framework for analysing digital story case studies that draws on three theoretical optics. The first optic was used to identify the broader relations of power that operate at a public level to ensure the disciplining of the personal. This tier, which might be read as a macro level of analysis, combined Foucault's work on biopolitics and disciplinary power to highlight how liberal multiculturalism operates as an AoS. Apparatuses of security target the population as a whole, exercising certain programmes, policies and measurements that group the public into a single, self-managing body. At the same time, these apparatuses are dependent on Foucault's earlier conception of disciplinary power – willing the individual to discipline itself in ways that complement the national multiculturalism discourse.

Due to the public/private entanglement of the multicultural body, the use of Butler's theory of performativity became the second optic for analysing everyday multiculturalism in this book. I argued that, as highly constructed representations of the multicultural experience, typical migrant digital stories operate as a stage in which certain scripts of ethnicity are animated. These scripts are frequently linked to national aspirations of a white Australia and become embodied as a 'performative accomplishment' (Butler 1997b).

Finally, the analytical framework included affect theory, in particular, Grossberg's concept of affective economies. Utilising the work of Ahmed, Nayak and Thrift, this inclusion of affect allowed the case study analysis to evince the political performativities that are administered via non-discursive forces and, in Ahmed's term, 'sticky feelings'. The case study analysis moved across these three theoretical levels to deconstruct the conjuncture of lived multiculturalism in the contemporary, mediated moment.

Application of the framework to individual and collaborative migrant digital stories revealed common patterns. In individual stories, these included three distinct narrative sections, a linear movement from past to present/bad to good, the condensing of convoluted experiences into a palatable trajectory and a summation of the whole experience of a once-in-a-lifetime migration. Fatma Coskun's *New Life, New Country* (2007) and Sam Haddad's *Loving Lebanon and Australia* (2007) exemplified this typical migrant digital story. The protagonists were interpellated as 'ethnic' in relation to an implied white audience, and they carefully animated a successful, assimilatory multicultural narrative that supported the AoS of multiculturalism.

This type of digital storytelling contrasted with Big hART's *Junk Theory*, representative of what was defined as collaborative digital storytelling. *JT* involved the collaboration of several community members over an 18-month period, resulting in one long digital story that merged all participants' 'voices'. The performativity of whiteness manifested in slightly different ways in *JT*. The multiplicity of participants, the location of the project and departure from the StoryCenter's Seven Steps methodology provoked a more abstract digital story that gave everyday multiculturalism an intricate texture. However, it was also shown that though the project produced instances of counter-normativity, the framework often resulted in what Poynting et al. (2004) refer to as the collapse of diffe-rence into a white imaginary. The fact that cultural difference is perpetually positioned as an aspect of Australian society needing to be fixed does little to rectify this problem.

The digital stories tended to be structured according to a move from a sad and dif-ficult past to a happy and successful future. Various affective economies circulated in the stories to promote a sense of ethnic worth and to orient the migrants towards the multicultural promise or Australian 'good life'. In accordance with the digital story's goal of creating intimacy between the subject and the consumer of multiculturalism, these tactics attempted to draw in the viewer to the 'human' behind the culturally diverse face. Common aesthetics were used to outline the body, the face in particular, so that the face became a synecdoche for the body – part for whole but implying a fetishist anxiety. The digital stories are thus in danger of replicating binary forms of thinking, which demar-cate the white body from the ethnic or non-white body.

This binary is frequently cited and hard to avoid; however, the actual complexities involved in everyday multicultural life provide possibilities for derailing the normative trajectory of liberal multiculturalism and the accompanying white versus ethnic binary. These possibilities were exhibited by atypical stories, namely, Raymond Nashar's *el ajnabi* (2007), Adam Nudelman's *The Shoemaker* (2007), Carla Pascoe's *The Spaces In Between* (2007) and Ximena Silberman's *Second Life* (2007), all of which resisted the pressure emerging from the multiculturalism AoS and the disciplinary power exercised within the digital storytelling genre. These stories presented ambivalent multicultural subjects who harnessed the mobile and vacillatory aspects of cultural diversity in order to remap the public Australian archive. Opportunities for corporeal rearticulation were consequently revealed.

In the final section of the book I argued that combining aspects of individual and collaborative digital storytelling could exploit these opportunities or performative glitches. Using the Newman Film Group's *The Chronicles of Liam's Hair* (*COLH*, 2010), I demonstrated how an estranged and unsatisfactory multiculturalism can produce cul-tural work that is both reparative and reconstitutive. *COLH* appeared typical of the genre, but in fact it cleverly exposed everyday inclusions and exclusions, testing the boundaries of 'community' and interrogating the terms of Australian multiculturalism and 'cultural diversity'.

Sam and diasporic intimacy

In the final chapter, I began to point to what I see as a productive convergence between diasporic intimacy, performativity and critical cosmopolitanism. I attempted to illustrate how this convergence, this particular conjuncture as Grossberg might call it, creates an excess that begins to displace the ongoing forms of identity frameworks that ultimately end up cornering all of us in our critiques. I began this book by suggesting that I wanted to remain astute to how all critiques, including my own, can become cornered. As it happens, I had an experience in the weeks of editing this manuscript that incidentally

Figure C.1 Portrait of Sam Haddad.

displaced my critique, displaced my book and ultimately displaced the critical frameworks I myself have fallen prey to at times over the past eleven chapters.

I was at my home in Melbourne/Naarm, Australia, applying my makeup. Being both a millennial (read: having a short attention span) and a woman (read: trained to do too many things at once), I paused the application process at one point to check my email on my phone. The night before, I had sent an email to some of the authors of the digital stories I use in this book to seek copyright permission for use of their images and or/ quotations. I was not expecting responses so soon, and took a sharp inhale when I saw the name Salem Haddad at the top of my new emails list.

I opened the email, reading it quickly and with my breath held. Salem, or Sam, the author of *LLAA*, was happy for me to include images from his story in this book and had returned all necessary paperwork. Exhale. But there was another request attached to his consent: 'Please see attached consent signed and dated', he wrote, 'and also a picture I like you to use if you can with the others.' I opened the attached picture: an ordinary and somewhat predictable portrait of Sam, who was wearing a suit and holding a glass of champagne up to whomever was behind the camera, as if to say 'cheers'. He was beaming.

Looking at the photograph, I was jolted by the fact that he had aged. I had become familiar with Sam, this 'face that speaks', but the email with his personal request reminded me that my familiarity with him, my reading of his face, sits within a particular moment, a particular framing, a particular giving and receiving. Time moves on, and he is a different 'Sam' from the 'Sam' in the digital story. My feeling of familiarity thus sat alongside a strange feeling of disconnect.

I was also struck by how joyful and proud he looked in the photo. I suspected he was presently feeling proud that someone from university had taken interest in his story. In the email, he asked to be advised when the book was released, noting he would like a copy, 'even if' he had to purchase it. I began crying.

I immediately shared a video story with my Instagram 'close friends' about this sudden wave of emotions I was experiencing (I am not only a millennial woman, I am also a digital humanities scholar – social media is a continuum of my everyday life). I told them 'something about it [this email] has undone me'.

I then started pacing around my house trying to compose myself. I needed to finish putting my makeup on and it was obviously counter-productive to do that while crying. Plus, I was trying to figure out why this email had made me so emotional. It was not a sadness per se that I was experiencing, though sadness certainly existed among what was a tangled knot of many feelings. And then it occurred to me: what I was experiencing was a diasporic pang that had, in Boym's phrase, snuck in through my back door.

I was doing my makeup when I read the email, and doing my makeup is pretty ordinary. The photograph came via an email with paperwork, which is also pretty ordinary. In short, the encounter with Sam took place in the realm of the everyday, an example of everyday multiculturalism. But the encounter was not *simply* everyday. There was so much more going on here.

Certainly, there was something deeply personal (beyond my bathroom setting) about viewing this portrait of happy Sam in his nice suit at an official gathering. I felt an immediate, albeit inarticulate affinity with him in this picture. It reminded me that the subjects of my research, the so-called characters of the digital stories, were also people living their lives, sending emails that landed in my inbox. Part of me felt a flutter of fear – what if he does not like what I have written about his story? What if I disappoint him? But my complicated sense of attachment to the man in this photo was not simply because of my research on his story, but because in this picture he reminded me of members of my own migrant family, of my father, in particular. So, I was also projecting my own fraught familial history and relationships onto this man. The projection meant, as a consequence, that I was aware, above and beyond my years of ethnography, what it meant for an elderly non-Anglo-Celtic migrant to be standing in front of a camera in a suit smiling, to feel accomplished. I had an intimate sense of the enormity of life experiences that had occurred behind that photo in order for it to be taken in the first place, in order for it to come to mean something so special to Sam that he hoped it would be used in my book.

Perhaps this is one of the simple reasons I struggle with the notion of everyday multi-culturalism – I know that the people who form the narrative of multiculturalism have often 'made it', 'against all odds'. But this accounts mostly for the 'lucky ones', and even then I am unsure exactly how lucky they are. The unlucky ones are *still trying to* 'make it', still hoping to be allowed to fully arrive and belong. In other words, perhaps it is because I know that in order to feel even fleetingly accomplished or comfortable in a multicultural nation, or indeed, to simply feel a sense of survival, multicultural bodies have been on a tumultuous journey that is not ordinary at all. On the contrary, the journey is complex and extraordinary and probably has not ended.

What became clear is that the sense of being 'undone' by Sam's email was not something that 'just was', it did not 'just happen', though of course it is tempting to prescribe it that kind of potency. It certainly felt outside the realm of institutions and structures. But, this sense of being 'undone' is, I think, diasporic intimacy in action, and is meaningful and powerful only in relation to the normative structures that work on us day after day, that frame us and contain us. Diasporic intimacy is an erupted affect, a spillage that carries an unexpected freedom, a momentary release from those structures of organisation.

In the days following the unexpected emotional response to Sam's email, I realised, more carefully, that the 'everyday' that everyday multiculturalism scholars are likely trying to pin down and exacerbate is not so much 'the everyday' but 'the excess.'

Excess in everyday multiculturalism

In the final chapter, I examined digital stories produced by Curious Works to illustrate the excess that exists in any translation and consider the possibilities for this excess. I argued that digital storytelling can provide a new avenue for imagining these possibilities. However, in order to do so, the genre needs to cease trying to shift cultural diversity from a position of under-representation to one of representation, and instead focus on an enduring (re)presentation of identity. In other words, it ought to seek to maintain a persistent examination of how representations of 'culture', in all their varieties, are produced and organised. The digital story *Khaled vs. Khaled* illustrated the ability of Curious Works to provide spaces for encounters that might surprise, go wayward, even agitate, and I argued that this capacity is actually its biggest asset and the one that should remain its focus.

In this way, digital storytelling, and everyday multiculturalism more broadly, can both attend to past and present experiences of cultural difference, while also ensuring this attention does not hurry forward into a predetermined and ultimately suffocating narrative predicated on racialisation. Common understandings of identity, implicitly tied to racism, can be deconstructed, but not in an empty or insincere way, as many postmodern approaches are accused of being. Approaching cultural work in this manner will better track and narrate the diasporic intimacies and aesthetics of contemporary Australia and other nations associated with liberal multiculturalism. It will not erase the work of normative categories; however, it will utilise the performative loop in an interrogative and resistant manner so that these norms can be perpetually refashioned. Importantly, the reperformance shifts the boundaries of materiality for the ethnic subject, doing more than attempting to 'harmonize the local and general, the poetic and the political as an abstract identity' (Bhabha 1996, p. 198).

Digital interventions have an important function to play in redressing the fictive but forceful white imaginaries of British settler colonies such as Australia. We must continue the endeavour of rewriting the margins into the centre, of collecting and reinterpreting migrant narratives. However, there is a clear and well-documented violence enabled by the conventional archive that always excludes in order to include, and too often produces a normative nationalist imaginary of everyday multicultural life within which the white body is reaffirmed as authoritative. This is shown to be the case even when well-meaning intentions motivate work on cultural diversity.

Thus, in order for digital storytelling to do productive work on cultural difference in these contexts, the work must occur at a distance, deliberately detached from the common tropes of the digital storytelling genre and the broader discourse of multiculturalism it is embedded in. Doing so can harness the precariousness of performative identities, the diasporic intimacies that sneak in through our back doors when we are applying makeup, to create active archives of estrangement. The stories, people and ideals collected are always inverted, displaced and reassessed so that the multicultural country becomes an ongoing process, rather than a final destination. Only then can multiculturalism enable the human to be undone and redone in new, more inclusive ways. Only then can multiculturalism be worthy of our constant pursuit. In fact, it is only *as* constant, critical pursuit that multiculturalism can be worthwhile.

REFERENCES

Abbott, T. 2013. 'Canberra Press Conference remarks'. Retrieved 14 October 2014. http://australianpolitics.com/2013/08/04/abbott-responds-to-election-announcement.html.

ACMI (Australian Centre for the Moving Image). 2013. 'About us'. Retrieved 8 October. https://www.acmi.net.au/about-us/about-acmi/.

Ahmed, S. 2000. *Strange encounters: Embodied others in post-coloniality*. London: Routledge.

———. 2004. *The cultural politics of emotion*. Edinburgh, UK: Edinburgh University Press.

———. 2010a. 'Happy objects'. In *The affect theory reader*, edited by M. Gregg and G. J. Seigworth, 29–51. Durham, NC: Duke University Press.

———. 2010b. *The promise of happiness*. Durham, NC: Duke University Press.

———. 2012a. 'Whiteness and the general will: Diversity work as willful work'. *philoSOPHIA*, vol. 2, no. 1: 1–20.

———. 2012b. *On being included: Racism and diversity in institutional life*. Durham, NC: Duke University Press.

———. 2013. 'Not without ambivalence: An interview with Sara Ahmed on postcolonial intimacies with P. Antwi, S. Brophy, H. Strauss and Y.-D. Troeung'. *Interventions: International Journal of Postcolonial Studies*, vol. 15, no. 1: 110–26.

———. 2014. 'Wilful subjects: Responsibility, fragility, history'. Keynote paper presented to AWGS Biennial International Conference, University of Melbourne, 23–25 June.

———. 2015. 'Melancholic universalism'. *feministkilljoys*. Retrieved 24 April 2019. https://feministkilljoys.com/2015/12/15/melancholic-universalism/.

Alexandra, D. 2008. 'Digital storytelling as transformative practice: Critical analysis and creative expression in the representation of migration in Ireland'. *Journal of Media Practice*, vol. 9, no. 2: 101–12.

Althusser, L. (1970) 2006. 'Ideology and ideological state apparatuses (notes towards an investigation)'. In *The anthropology of the state: A reader*, edited by A. Sharma and A. Gupta, 86–111. Malden, MA: Blackwell.

Ama and Chan's Kitchen Rescue Episode 1: Fluffy White Rice. 2012. Short online film by A. Lao, E. Nkrumah and E. Winkler, in association with Curious Works and Matta Media, 25 November 2012. Retrieved 9 March 2014. http://www.curiousworks.com.au/stories/ama-chan-s-kitchen-rescue-episode-1-fluffy-white-rice/.

Ang, I. 1996. 'The curse of the smile: Ambivalence and the "Asian" woman in Australian multiculturalism'. *Feminist Review*, vol. 52, no. 1: 36–49.

———. 1999. 'Racial/spatial anxiety: "Asia" in the psycho-geography of Australian whiteness'. In *The future of Australian multiculturalism: Reflections on the twentieth anniversary of Jean Martin's 'The Migrant Presence'*, edited by G. Hage and R. Couch, 189–204. Sydney: Research Institute for Humanities and Social Sciences, University of Sydney.

———. 2001. *On not speaking Chinese: Living between Asia and the West*. London: Routledge.

———. 2003. 'Cultural translation in a globalised world'. In *Complex entanglements: Arts, globalisation and cultural difference*, edited by N. Papastergiadis, 30–41. London: Rivers Oram.

———. 2011. 'Ethnicities and our precarious future'. *Ethnicities*, vol. 11, no. 1: 27–31.

Ang, I., J. Brand, G. Noble and D. Wilding. 2002. *Living diversity: Australia's multicultural future*. Artarmon, NSW: Special Broadcasting Service Corporation.

Ang, I., G. Hawkins and L. Dabboussey. 2008. *The SBS story: The challenge of cultural diversity.* Sydney: UNSW Press.

Ang, I., E. Lally, K. Anderson, P. Mar and M. Kelly. 2011. 'Introduction: What is the art of engagement?' In *The art of engagement: Culture, collaboration, innovation,* edited by E. Lally, I. Ang and K. Anderson, 1–13. Crawley, Western Australia: UWA Publishing.

Ang, I., and B. St Louis. 2005. 'Guest editorial: The predicament of difference'. *Ethnicities,* vol. 5, no. 3: 291–304.

Ang, I., and J. Stratton. 1998. 'Multiculturalism in crisis: The new politics of race and national identity in Australia'. *Topia: Canadian Journal of Cultural Studies,* no. 2, Spring: 22–41.

Antwi, P., S. Brophy, H. Strauss and Y.-D. Troeung. 2013. 'Postcolonial intimacies: Gatherings, disruptions, departures'. *Interventions: International Journal of Postcolonial Studies,* vol. 15, no. 1: 1–9.

Appignanesi, R., ed. 2010a. *Beyond cultural diversity: The case for creativity: A Third Text report.* London: Third Text.

———. 2010b. 'Introduction: "Whose culture?" Exposing the myth of cultural diversity'. In *Beyond cultural diversity: The case for creativity: A Third Text report,* edited by R. Appignanesi, 5–15. London: Third Text.

Araeen, R. 2003. 'Come what may: Beyond the emperor's new clothes'. In *Complex entanglements: Art, globalisation and cultural difference,* edited by N. Papastergiadis, 135–55. London: Rivers Oram.

———. 2010a. 'Cultural diversity, creativity and modernism'. In *Beyond cultural diversity: The case for creativity: A Third Text report,* edited by R. Appignanesi, 17–34. London: Third Text.

———. 2010b. 'Ethnic minorities, multiculturalism and celebration of the postcolonial other'. In *Beyond cultural diversity: The case for creativity: A Third Text report,* edited by R. Appignanesi, 37–59. London: Third Text.

Armitage, A. 1995. *Comparing the policy of Aboriginal assimilation – Australia, Canada and New Zealand.* Vancouver: UBC Press.

Ashcroft, B., G. Griffiths and H. Tiffin. 1998. *Key concepts in post-colonial studies.* London: Routledge.

Aung Thin, M. 2013. 'Skin, intimacy and authenticity'. *Interventions: International Journal of Postcolonial Studies,* vol. 15, no. 1: 67–77. doi: 10.1080/1369801X.2013.771004.

Back, L., and S. Sinha. 2016. 'Multicultural conviviality in the midst of racism's ruins'. *Journal of Intercultural Studies,* vol. 37, no. 5: 517–32.

Balabsubramanium, D. 2012. Interview with Daniella Trimboli, Melbourne, 5 July.

Balibar, É. 1991. 'Is there a neo-racism?' In *Race, nation, class: Ambiguous identities,* edited by É. Balibar and I. Wallerstein, translated by C. Turner, 17–28. London: Verso. Retrieved 10 April 2015, University of Melbourne e-book database.

Balibar, É., and I. Wallerstein. 1991. *Race, nation, class: Ambiguous identities.* London: Verso.

Bannerji, H. 2000. *The dark side of the nation: Essays on multiculturalism, nationalism and gender.* Toronto: Canadian Scholars' Press and Women's Press.

Bell, V. 2007. *Culture and performance: The challenge of ethics, politics and feminist theory.* Oxford: Berg.

Beng-Huat, C. 2005. 'When difference becomes an instrument of social regulation'. *Ethnicities,* vol. 5, no. 3: 418–21. doi: 10.1177/1468796805000500310.

Berlant, L. 1998. 'Intimacy: A special issue'. *Critical Inquiry,* vol. 24, no. 2: 281–88.

———. 2008. *The female complaint: The unfinished business of sentimentality in American culture.* Durham, NC: Duke University Press.

———. 2011. *Cruel optimism.* Durham, NC: Duke University Press.

Berliner, L. S. 2018. *Producing queer youth: The paradox of digital media empowerment.* New York: Routledge.

Bhabha, H. 1994. *The location of culture.* London: Routledge.

———. 1996. 'Unsatisfied: Notes on vernacular cosmopolitanism'. In *Text and narration: Cross-disciplinary essays on cultural and national identities,* edited by L. García-Moreno and P. C. Pfeiffer, 191–207. Columbia, SC: Camden House.

Big hART. 2007. *Junk Theory final report.* Prepared by Michelle Kotevski, Sydney, NSW.

———. 2011. Retrieved 11 May. http://bighart.org/.

Bishop, C. 2006. 'The social turn: Collaboration and its discontents'. *Artforum International*, vol. 44, no. 6: 178–83.

———. 2012. *Artificial hells: Participatory art and the politics of spectatorship*. London: Verso.

Bjørgen, A. M. 2010. 'Boundary crossing and learning identities – digital storytelling in primary schools'. *Seminar.Net: Media, Technology and Life-Long Learning*, vol. 6: 161–78.

Blanchot, M., and S. Hanson. 1987. 'Everyday speech'. *Yale French Studies*, no. 73: 12–20.

Blonski, A. 1992. *Arts for a Multicultural Council 1973–1991: An account of Australia Council policies*. Redfern, NSW: Australia Council.

Blum-Ross, A. 2015. 'Filmmakers/educators/facilitators? Understanding the role of adult inter-mediaries in youth media production in the UK and the USA'. *Journal of Children and Media*, vol. 9, no. 3: 308–24. doi: 10.1080/17482798.2015.1058280.

Borghuis, P., C. de Graaf and J. Hermes. 2010. 'Digital storytelling in sex education: Avoiding the pitfalls of building a "haram" website'. *Seminar.Net: Media, Technology and Life-Long Learning*, no. 6: 234–47.

Bowen, C. 2011. *The genius of Australian multiculturalism*. Speech given on 16 February, Sydney.

Boym, S. 1998. 'On diasporic intimacy: Ilya Kabakov's installations and immigrant homes'. *Critical Inquiry*, vol. 24, no. 2, Intimacy (Winter 1998): 498–524.

Bromley, R. 2010. 'Storying community: Re-imagining regional identities through public cultural activity'. *European Journal of Cultural Studies*, vol. 13, no. 1: 9–25.

Bruguera, T. 2014. *Spectres of Evaluation: Rethinking: Art/Community/Value Conference*. Video interview with Marnie Bardham. Footscray, Victoria, 6–7 February.

Bruzzi, S. 2006. *New documentary*, 2nd edn. London: Routledge.

Burgess, J. 2006. 'Hearing ordinary voices: Cultural studies, vernacular creativity and digital story-telling'. *Continuum: Journal of Media and Cultural Studies*, vol. 20, no. 2: 201–14.

Buskirk, M. 2003. *The contingent object of contemporary art*. Cambridge, MA: MIT Press.

Butcher, M., and A. Harris. 2010. 'Pedestrian crossings: Young people and everyday multicultur-alism'. *Journal of Intercultural Studies*, vol. 31, no. 5: 449–53.

Butler, J. 1993. *Bodies that matter: On the discursive limits of 'sex'*. New York: Routledge.

———. 1997a. *The psychic life of power: Theories in subjection*. Stanford, CA: Stanford University Press.

———. 1997b. 'Performative acts and gender constitution: An essay in phenomenology and feminist theory'. In *Writing the body: Female embodiment and feminist theory*, edited by K. Conboy, N. Medina and S. Stanbury, 401–17. New York: Columbia University Press.

———. 2004. *Undoing gender*. New York: Routledge.

———. 2006. *Precarious life: The powers of mourning and violence*. London: Verso.

———. 2008. '"An account of oneself"'. In *Judith Butler in conversation: Analyzing the texts and talk of everyday life*, edited by B. Davies, 19–38. New York: Routledge.

———. 2009. *Frames of war: When is life grievable?* London: Verso.

———. 2015. *Notes towards a performative theory of assembly*. Cambridge, MA: Harvard University Press.

Castells, M. 2001. *The internet galaxy: Reflections on the internet, business, and society*. New York: Oxford University Press.

Castles, S. 1992. 'Australian multiculturalism: Social policy and identity in a changing society'. In *Nations of immigrants: Australia, the United States and international migration*, edited by G. P. Freeman and J. Jupp, 184–201. Melbourne: Oxford University Press.

Castles, S., M. Kalantzis, B. Cope and M. Morrissey. 1988. *Mistaken identity: Multiculturalism and the demise of nationalism in Australia*. Sydney: Pluto.

CDS (Center for Digital Storytelling). 2012. 'About us'. Retrieved 15 April. http://storycenter. org/about-us/.

The Celebrity Apprentice Australia. 2011. Television program, Nine Network Australia, Fremantle, WA.

Chambers, S. A., and T. Carver. 2008. *Judith Butler and political theory: Troubling politics*. London: Routledge.

Chow, R. 2014. *Not like a native speaker: On languaging as a postcolonial experience*. New York: Columbia University Press.

The Chronicles of Liam's Hair. 2010. The Newman Film Group, in association with Curious Works. Retrieved 9 March 2014. http://www.curiousworks.com.au/stories/the-chronicles-of-liams-hair/.

Clough, P. T. 2007. 'Introduction'. In *The affective turn: Theorizing the social*, edited by P. T. Clough, 1–33. Durham, NC: Duke University Press.

Cooper, D. 2004. *Challenging diversity: Rethinking equality and the value of difference*. Cambridge: Cambridge University Press.

Copeland, S., and C. Miskelly. 2010. 'Making time for storytelling: The challenges of community building and activism in a rural locale'. *Seminar.Net: Media, Technology and Life-Long Learning*, vol. 6, no. 2: 192–207.

Cotton, C. 2009. *The photograph as contemporary art*, 2nd edn. New York: Thames and Hudson.

Culture Victoria. 2013. 'State film centre'. Retrieved 8 October. http://www.cv.vic.gov.au/stories/creative-life/state-film-centre/.

Curious Works. 2013. 'Community circles (aka strengths and struggles)'. Retrieved 20 October. http://toolkit.curiousworks.com.au/content/community-circles-aka-strengths-struggles-reflection-community.

Cvetkovich, A. 2003. *An archive of feelings: Trauma, sexuality, and lesbian public cultures*. Durham, NC: Duke University Press.

———. 2007. 'Public feelings'. *South Atlantic Quarterly*, vol. 106, no. 3 (Summer): 459–68. doi: 10.1215/00382876-2007-004.

Dancing with the Stars. 2004. Television program, Channel 7, Melbourne.

Davis, D. 2011. 'Intergenerational digital storytelling: A sustainable community initiative with inner-city residents'. *Visual Communication*, vol. 10, no. 4: 527–40.

Deo, S. 2017. *The agonist*, UQP Poetry Series. St Lucia: University of Queensland Press.

Derrida, J. 1979. 'Living on. Borderlines'. In *Deconstruction and Criticism*, translated by J. Hulbert, 75–176. New York: Continuum.

Dharwadker, V. 2015. 'Emotion in motion: The *Nāṭaśāstra*, Darwin, and affect theory'. *PMLA*, vol. 130, no. 5: 1381–404.

Diversity Arts Australia. 2019. *Shifting the balance: Cultural diversity within the Australian arts, screen and creative sectors*. Diversity Arts Australia with BYP Group and Western Sydney University, with funding from the Australian Commission for UNESCO, Paramatta, NSW. Retrieved 27 August. http://diversityarts.org.au/app/uploads/Shifting-the-Balance-DARTS-small.pdf.

do Prado, P. 2011. *Almas Gemelas/Twin Souls*, exhibited at Sensorial Loop: Tamworth's Textile Triennial 2011–13, touring exhibition, Australia.

———. 2012a. *Mellorado*, solo exhibition at Gallery Smith, North Melbourne, Victoria.

———. 2012b. Interview with Daniella Trimboli, Melbourne, 22 March.

Dreher, T. 2009. 'Listening across difference: Media and multiculturalism beyond the politics of voice'. *Continuum: Journal of Media and Cultural Studies*, vol. 23, no. 4: 445–58.

———. 2012. 'A partial promise of voice: Digital storytelling and the limits of listening'. *Media International Australia*, no. 142: 157–66.

Dunford, M., and T. Jenkins, eds. 2017. *Digital storytelling: Form and content*. United Kingdom: Palgrave Macmillan.

Dunn, K. M. 2006. 'Performing Australian nationalisms at Cronulla'. In *Lines in the sand: The Cronulla riots, multiculturalism and national belonging*, edited by G. Noble, 76–94. Sydney: Institute of Criminology Press.

Dyer, R. 1997. *White: Essays on race and culture*. London: Routledge.

el ajnabi. 2007. Digital story, R. Nashar, in association with Australian Centre for the Moving Image. Retrieved 11 July 2013. http://www.cv.vic.gov.au/stories/immigrants-and-emigrants/second-generation/el-ajnabi/.

Essed, P. 1991. *Understanding everyday racism: An interdisciplinary theory*. Newbury Park: Sage.

Fanon, F. (1952) 2008. *Black skin, white masks*. Translated by R. Philcox. New York: Grove.

Feeling multicultural: Decolonizing affect theory colloquium. 2006. Centre for Women's and Gender Studies, University of British Columbia, Vancouver, 25–27 June.

Feld, S. 1998. 'They repeatedly lick their own things'. *Critical Inquiry*, vol. 24, no. 2: 445–72. doi: 10.2307/1344174.

Felman, S. 2002. *The scandal of the speaking body: Don Juan with J.L. Austin, or seduction in two languages*. Stanford, CA: Stanford University Press.

Fisher, J. 2010. 'Cultural diversity and institutional policy'. In *Beyond cultural diversity: The case for creativity: a Third Text report*, edited by R. Appignanesi, 61–91. London: Third Text.

Ford, M. 2009. *In your face: A case study in post multicultural Australia*. Darwin: Charles Darwin University Press.

Foster, L., and D. Stockley. 1984. *Multiculturalism: The changing Australian paradigm*. Clevedon, UK: Multilingual Matters.

Fotiadi, E. 2011. *The game of participation in art and the public sphere*. Maastricht: Shaker.

Foucault, M. 1977. *Discipline and punish: The birth of the prison*. Translated by A. Sheridan. New York: Vintage Books.

———. 1978. *The history of sexuality, volume one: An introduction*. Translated by R. Hurley. London: Penguin Books.

———. 1982. 'The subject and power'. *Critical Inquiry*, vol. 8, no. 4 (Summer): 777–95. doi: http://www.jstor.org/stable/1343197.

———. 1988. 'Technologies of the self'. In *Technologies of the self*, edited by L. H. Martin, H. Gutman and P. H. Hutton, 16–49. Amherst: University of Massachusetts Press.

———. 2003. *Society must be defended*. Translated by D. Macey. New York: Picador.

Four corners. 2006. Television program, ABC1, Sydney, 13 March.

Frankenberg, R. 1993. *White women, race matters: The social construction of whiteness*. Minneapolis: University of Minnesota Press.

Fraser, N. 1989. 'Foucault on modern power: Empirical insights and normative confusions'. In *Unruly practices: Power, discourse, and gender in contemporary social theory*, edited by N. Fraser, 17–34. Minneapolis: University of Minnesota Press.

———. 1997. *Justice interruptus: Critical reflections on the 'postsocialist' condition*. New York: Routledge.

Fries-Gaither, J. 2010. 'Digital storytelling supports writing across content areas'. *Ohio Journal of English Language Arts*, vol. 50, no. 1: 9–13.

Frisina, A. 2010. ' "Young Muslims", everyday tactics and strategies: Resisting Islamophobia, negotiating Italianness, becoming citizens'. *Journal of Intercultural Studies*, vol. 31, no. 5: 557–72.

Gelder, K., and J. Jacobs. 1995. 'Uncanny'. *Cultural Geographies*, vol. 2, no. 2: 171–85. doi: 10.1177/147447409500200204.

Gilroy, P. 1987. *There ain't no black in the union jack: The cultural politics of race and nation*. London: Unwin Hyman.

———. 1990. 'The end of anti-racism'. *Journal of Ethnic and Migration Studies*, vol. 17, no. 1: 71–83. doi: 10.1080/1369183x.1990.9976222.

———. 2000. *Against race: Imagining political culture beyond the color line*. Cambridge, MA: Belknap Press of Harvard University Press.

———. 2005. *Postcolonial melancholia*. New York: Columbia University Press.

———. 2006. *After empire: Melancholia or convivial culture*. New York: Routledge University Press.

Goonewardena, K. 2008. 'Marxism and everyday life: On Henri Lefebvre, Guy Debord, and some others'. In *Space, Difference, Everyday Life: Reading Henri Lefebvre*, edited by K. Goonewardena, S. Kipfer, R. Milgrom and C. Schmid, 117–33. New York: Routledge.

Gow, G. 2005. 'Rubbing shoulders in the global city – refugees, citizenship and multicultural alliances in Fairfield, Sydney'. *Ethnicities*, vol. 5, no. 3: 386–405. doi: 10.1177/1468796805054962.

Grewcock, M. 2014. 'Back to the future: Australian border policing under Labor, 2007–2013'. *State Crime Journal*, vol. 3, no. 1 (Spring): 102–25. Retrieved 4 June. http://www.jstor.org/stable/10.13169/statecrime.3.1.0102.

Grossberg, L. 1987. 'The in-difference of television'. *Screen*, vol. 28, no. 2: 28–45.

———. 1997. *Dancing in spite of myself: Essays on popular culture.* Durham, NC: Duke University Press.

———. 2010a. *Cultural studies in the future tense.* Durham, NC: Duke University Press.

———. 2010b. 'Affect's future: Rediscovering the virtual in the actual'. Interviewed by G. J. Seigworth and M. Gregg in *Affect theory reader*, edited by G. J. Seigworth and M. Gregg, 309–38. Durham, NC: Duke University Press.

———. 2015. *We all want to change the world: The paradox of the U.S. Left: A polemic*, Creative Commons Non-Commercial. ISBN: 9781 910448 496 (e-pub).

Grossman, A., and À. O'Brien. 2011. '"Voice", listening and social justice: A multimediated engagement with new immigrant communities and publics in Ireland'. *Crossings: Journal of Migration and Culture*, vol. 2, no. 1: 39–58. doi: 10.1386/cjmc.2.39_1.

Grostal, C., and G. Harrison. 1994. 'Community arts and its relation to multicultural arts'. In *Culture, difference and the arts*, edited by S. Gunew and F. Rizvi, 147–64. St Leonards, NSW: Allen and Unwin.

Gunew, S. 1997. 'Postcolonialism and multiculturalism: Between race and ethnicity'. *Yearbook of English Studies*, no. 27: 22–39.

———. 1998. 'Reinventing selves'. In *Foreign dialogues: Memories, translations, conversations*, edited by M. Zournazi. Annandale: Pluto.

———. 2003. 'The home of language: A pedagogy of the stammer'. In *Uprootings/regroundings: Questions of home and migration*, edited by S. Ahmed, C. Castañeda, A.-M. Fortier and M. Sheller, 41–58. Oxford: Berg.

———. 2004. *Haunted nations: The colonial dimensions of multiculturalisms.* London: Routledge.

———. 2005. 'Between auto/biography and theory: Can "ethnic abjects" write theory?' *Comparative Literature Studies*, vol. 42, no. 4: 363–78.

———. 2009. 'Subaltern empathy: Beyond European categories in affect theory'. *Concentric: Literary and Cultural Studies*, vol. 35, no. 1: 11–30.

———. 2012. 'Multiculturalism'. In *The Wiley-Blackwell Encyclopedia of Globalization, Vol III: 1-No*, edited by G. Ritzer, 1450–53. Malden, MA: Blackwell.

———. 2017. *Post-multicultural writers as neo-cosmopolitan mediators.* London: Anthem.

———. 2018. 'Museums of identity and other identity thefts'. Keynote paper presented to *Who shot the albatross? Gate-keeping in Australian Culture* conference, University of Adelaide, Adelaide, 26 April.

Gunew, S., and J. Mahyuddin. 1988. *Beyond the echo: Multicultural women's writing.* St Lucia: University of Queensland Press.

Gunew, S., and F. Rizvi, eds. 1994. *Culture, difference and the arts.* St Leonards, NSW: Allen and Unwin.

Hage, G. 1998. *White nation: Fantasies of white supremacy in a multicultural society.* Sydney: Pluto.

———. 2002a. 'The differential intensities of social reality'. In *Arab-Australians today: Citizenship and belonging*, edited by G. Hage, 173–91. Carlton South, Melbourne: Melbourne University Press.

———. 2002b. 'Citizenship and honourability: Belonging to Australia today'. In *Arab-Australians today: Citizenship and belonging*, edited by G. Hage, 1–15. Carlton South, Melbourne: Melbourne University Press.

———. 2009. 'Waiting out the crisis: On stuckedness and governmentality' [online manuscript version], 1–9. Retrieved 6 July 2014. https://www.academia.edu/1990512/Waiting_out_the_crisis_on_stuckedness_and_governmentality.

———. 2010. 'The affective politics of racial mis-interpellation'. *Theory, Culture and Society*, vol. 27, no. 7–8: 112–29. doi: 10.1177/0263276410383713.

———. 2014a. 'Continuity and change in Australian racism'. *Journal of Intercultural Studies*, vol. 35, no. 3: 232–37. doi: 10.1080/07256868.2014.899948.

————. 2014b. 'What is a critical anthropology of diaspora?'. Paper presented to Faculty of Arts, University of Melbourne, 2 April.

————. 2017a. *Is racism an environmental threat?* Cambridge, UK: Polity.

————. 2017b. 'Closing remarks'. *Aesthetic anxiety or performative subjectivity: National narratives encountering migrant architecture in Australia.* Alfred Deakin Institute for Citizenship and Globalisation Symposium, Deakin University Geelong Waterfront Campus, Geelong, 16–17 November.

Hall, S. 2000. 'Conclusion: The multi-cultural question'. In *Un/settled multiculturalisms: Diasporas, entanglements, 'transruptions'*, edited by B. Hesse, 209–41. London: Zed Books.

————. 2002a. 'Whose heritage? Un-settling "The Heritage", re-imagining the post-nation'. In *The Third Text Reader*, edited by R. Araeen, S. Cubitt and Z. Sardar, 72–84. London: Continuum.

————. 2002b. 'Political belonging in a world of multiple identities'. In *Conceiving cosmopolitanism: Theory, context, and practice*, edited by S. Vertovec and R. Cohen, 25–31. Oxford: Oxford University Press.

————. 2003. 'Créolité and creolization'. In *Documenta II_Platform 3*, 29–41. Ostfildern-Ruit, Germany: Hatje Cantz.

Hancox, D. 2012. 'The process of remembering with the forgotten Australians: Digital storytelling and marginalized groups'. *Human Technology*, vol. 8, no. 1: 65–76.

Handler Miller, C. 2004. *Digital storytelling: A creator's guide to interactive entertainment.* Massachusetts: Elsevier.

Harris, A. 2010. 'Young people, everyday civic life and the limits of social cohesion'. *Journal of Intercultural Studies*, vol. 31, no. 5: 573–89.

Hartley, J., and K. McWilliam. 2009. 'Computational power meets human contact'. In *Story circle: Digital storytelling around the world*, edited by J. Hartley and K. McWilliam, 3–15. Oxford: Wiley-Blackwell.

Hawkins, G. 1993. *From Nimbin to Mardi Gras: Constructing community arts.* St Leonards, NSW: Allen and Unwin.

Hewitt, T. 2016. 'Rethinking encounter: Intercultural interactions between parents in Australia's culturally diverse primary schools'. *Australian Geographer*, vol. 47, no. 3: 355–70. doi: 10.1080/00049182.2016.1187177.

Higgins, J. W. 2011. 'Peace-building through listening, digital storytelling, and community media in Cyprus'. *Global Media Journal: Mediterranean Edition*, vol. 6, no. 1: 1–13.

Ho, C. 2011. 'Respecting the presence of others: School micropublics and everyday multiculturalism'. *Journal of Intercultural Studies*, vol. 32, no. 6: 603–19. doi: 10.1080/07256868.2011.618106.

Holland, P. 1991. 'Introduction: History, memory and the family album'. In *Family snaps: The meaning of domestic photography*, edited by J. Spence and P. Holland, 1–14. London: Virago.

Horsley, C. 2014. 'Public displays of affection – or how I stopped worrying and learned to love the consent process'. Paper presented to *Spectres of evaluation: Rethinking: Art/community/value conference*. Footscray, Victoria, 6–7 February.

Hug, T. 2012. 'Storytelling – EDU: Educational - digital – unlimited?' *Seminar.Net: Media, Technology and Life-Long Learning*, no. 8: 16–26.

Huttenback, R. A. 1972–73. 'No strangers within the gates: Attitudes and policies towards the non-white residents of the British Empire of settlement'. *Journal of Imperial and Commonwealth History*, vol. 1: 271–302.

Huyssen, A. 2007. 'Geographies of modernism in a globalizing world'. *New German Critique* 100, vol. 34, no. 1 (Winter): 189–207. doi: 10.1215/0094033X-2006-023.

Idriss, S. 2016. 'Racialisation in the creative industries and the Arab-Australian multicultural artist'. *Journal of Intercultural Studies*, vol. 37, no. 4: 406–20.

Ithal Damat = Imported Groom. 2007. Digital story, H. Duman, in association with Australian Centre for Moving Image. Retrieved 17 July 2013. http://www.acmi.net.au/dst_ithal_damat.htm.

Ivison, D. 2010. 'Introduction: Multiculturalism as a public ideal'. In *The Ashgate research companion to multiculturalism*, edited by D. Inison, 1–16. Farnham, UK: Ashgate.

Jakubowicz, A. 1994. 'Ethnic leadership, ethno-nationalist politics and the making of multicultural Australia'. *People and Place*, vol. 2, no. 3: 20–28.

———. 1998. 'Is Australia a racist society? Reflections on globalisation, multiculturalism and Pauline Hanson'. *Migration Action*, vol. 20, no. 2: 31–37.

———. 2011. 'Empires of the sun: Towards a post-multicultural Australian politics'. *Cosmopolitan Civil Societies Journal*, vol. 3, no. 1: 65–85.

Jakubowicz, A., and C. Ho, eds. 2013. *'For those who've come across the seas. . .': Australian multicultural theory, policy and practice*. North Melbourne, Victoria: Australian Scholarly Publishing.

Jamissen, G., and G. Skou. 2010. 'Poetic reflection through digital storytelling – a methodology to foster professional health worker identity in students'. *Seminar.Net: Media, Technology and Life-Long Learning*, vol. 6, no. 2: 177–91. Retrieved 28 November 2013. http://seminar.net/images/stories/vol6-issue2/Jamissen_prcent_26Skou-Poeticreflectionthroughdigitalstorytelling.pdf.

Jenkins, H. 2006. *Convergence culture: Where old and new media collide*. New York: New York University Press.

Jupp, J. 1984. *Ethnic politics in Australia*. Sydney: Allen and Unwin.

———. 2007a. *From white Australia to Woomera*, 2nd edn. Port Melbourne: Cambridge University Press.

———. 2007b. 'The quest for harmony'. In *Social cohesion in Australia*, edited by J. Jupp and J. Nieuwenhuysen, 9–20. New York: Cambridge University Press.

Kaaire, B. H. 2012. 'The self and the institution'. *NORDICOM Review*, vol. 33, no. 2: 17–26.

Khaled vs. Khaled. 2014. Short film, Curious Works, *Meet+Eat* project, 16 June 2014. Retrieved 20 June 2014. http://curiousworks.com.au/stories/khaled-vs-khaled-meet-eat-episode-5/.

Khan, R. 2011. 'Reconstructing community-based arts: Cultural value and the neoliberal citizen'. PhD thesis, School of Culture and Communication, University of Melbourne, Melbourne.

———. 2015. *Art in community: The provisional citizen*. London: Palgrave.

Khorana, S. 2014. 'From "de-wogged" migrants to "rabble rousers": Mapping the Indian diaspora in Australia'. *Journal of Intercultural Studies*, vol. 35, no. 3: 250–64. doi: 10.1080/07256868.2014.899950.

Kim, C. 2014. 'The smell of communities to come: Jeremy Lin and post-racial desire'. *Journal of Intercultural Studies*, vol. 35, no. 3: 310–27. doi: 10.1080/07256868.2014.899954.

Klaebe, H. G. 2006. 'Sharing stories: Problems and potentials of oral history and digital storytelling and the writer/producer's role in constructing a public place'. Master's, Queensland University of Technology, Brisbane.

Klaebe, H. G., M. Foth, J. E. Burgess and M. Bilandzic. 2007. 'Digital storytelling and history lines: Community engagement in a master-planned development'. *13th International Conference on Virtual Systems and Multimedia (VSMM'07)*, Brisbane.

Knijnik, J. 2018. 'Imagining a multicultural community in an everyday football carnival: Chants, identity and social resistance on Western Sydney terraces'. *International Review for the Sociology of Sport*, vol. 53, no. 4: 471–89.

Koleth, E. 2010. 'Multiculturalism: A review of Australian policy statements and recent debates in Australia and overseas'. Research paper, no. 6, 2010–11, Social Policy Section, Department of Parliamentary Services, Canberra.

Kotevski, M. 2012. Interview with Daniella Trimboli, Carriage Works, Sydney, 2 August.

Kwon, M. 2002. *One place after another: Site-specific art and locational identity*. Cambridge, MA: MIT Press.

Kymlicka, W. 2007. *Multicultural odysseys: Navigating the new international politics of diversity*. Oxford: Oxford University Press.

———. 2010. 'The rise and fall of multiculturalism? New debates on inclusion and accommodation in diverse societies'. In *The multicultural backlash: European discourses, policies and practices*, edited by S. Vertovec and S. Wessendorf, 32–49. Routledge, ProQuest Central ebook.

———. 2012. *Multiculturalism: Success, failure, and the future*. Washington, DC: Migration Policy Institute.

Lambek, M., and P. Antze. 1996. 'Introduction: Forecasting memory'. In *Tense past: Cultural essays in trauma and memory*, edited by P. Antze and M. Lambek, xi–xxxviii. New York: Routledge.

Lambert, J. 2006. *Digital storytelling: Capturing lives, creating community*, 2nd edn. Berkeley: Digital Diner.

———. 2009. *Digital storytelling: Capturing lives, creating community*, 3rd edn. Berkeley: Digital Diner.

———. 2013. *Digital storytelling: Capturing lives, creating community*, 4th edn. New York: Routledge.

Lee-Shoy, T., and T. Dreher. 2009. 'Creating listening spaces for intergenerational communication – Tiffany Lee-Shoy in conversation with Tanja Dreher'. *Continuum: Journal of Media and Cultural Studies*, vol. 23, no. 4: 573–77.

Lefebvre, H. (1947) 1991. *Critique of Everyday Life*. Translated by J. Moore. London: Verso.

Levey, G. B. 2008. *Political theory and Australian multiculturalism*. Oxford: Berghahn Books.

———. 2010. 'Liberal multiculturalism'. In *The Ashgate research companion to multiculturalism*, edited by D. Inison, 19–37. Farnham, UK: Ashgate.

Levinas, E. 1985. *Ethics and infinity: Conversations with Philippe Nemo*. Trans;ated by R. A. Cohen. Pittsburgh, PA: Duquesne University Press.

Literat, I., N. Kliger-Vilenchik, M. Brough and A. Blum-Ross. 2018. 'Analyzing youth digital participation: Aims, actors, contexts and intensities'. *Information Society*, vol. 34, no. 4: 261–73. doi: 10.1080/01972243.2018.1463333.

Lopez, M. 2000. *The origins of multiculturalism in Australian politics 1945–1975*. Carlton South, Melbourne: Melbourne University Press.

Loving Lebanon and Australia. 2007. Digital story, Sam Haddad, in association with Australian Centre for the Moving Image. Retrieved 29 December 2012. http://www.acmi.net.au/dst_loving_lebanon_australia.htm.

Lovvorn, J. F. 2011. 'Theorizing digital storytelling: From narrative practice to racial counterstory'. In *Narrative acts: Rhetoric, race and identity, knowledge*, edited by D. Journet, B. A. Boehm and C. E. Britt, 97–112. New York: Hampton.

Lowe, L. 2005. 'Insufficient difference'. *Ethnicities*, vol. 5, no. 3: 409–14. doi: 10.1177/146879680500500308.

Marotta, V. P. 2008. 'The hybrid self and the ambivalence of boundaries'. *Social Identities*, vol. 14, no. 3: 295–312. doi: 10.1080/13504630802088052.

Matias, C. E., and T. J. Grosland. 2016. 'Digital storytelling as racial justice: Digital hopes for deconstructing whiteness in teacher education'. *Journal of Teacher Education*, vol. 67, no. 2: 152–64.

Meadows, D. 2001. 'Polyphoto'. Photobus. Retrieved 21 January 2019. https://www.photobus.co.uk.

Mercer, K. 1999. 'Ethnicity and internationality: New British art and diaspora-based blackness'. *Third Text*, vol. 13, no. 49: 51–62. doi: 10.1080/09528829908576822.

Merleau-Ponty, M. (1962) 1986 *Phenomenology of perception*. Translated by C. Smith. London: Routledge and Kegan Paul.

Miller, N. K., and J. Tougaw. 2002. 'Introduction: Extremities'. In *Extremities: Trauma, testimony, and community*, edited by N. K. Miller and J. Tougaw, 1–21. Urbana: University of Chicago Press.

Mishra, V. 2012. *What was multiculturalism?: A critical retrospective*. Melbourne: Melbourne University Press.

Modood, T. 2005. *Multicultural politics: Racism, ethnicity, and Muslims in Britain*. Minneapolis: University of Minnesota Press.

———. 2007. *Multiculturalism: A civic idea*. Cambridge, UK: Polity.

Moewaka Barnes, H., T. R. Gunn, A. Moewaka Barnes, E. Muriwai, M. Wetherel and T. McCreanor. 2017. 'Feeling and spirit: Developing an indigenous wairua approach to research'. *Qualitative Research*, vol. 17, no. 3: 313–25. doi: https://doi.org/10.1177/1468794117696031.

Möntmann, N., ed. 2009. *Public: Art, Culture, Ideas*. Special issue: 'New Communities', Spring, issue 39.

Moreton-Robinson, A. 2000. *Talkin' up to the white woman: Indigenous women and white feminism*. St Lucia: University of Queensland Press.

Morrison, T. 1992. *Playing in the dark: Whiteness and the literary imagination*. Cambridge, MA: Harvard University Press.

Nakamura, L. 2002. *Cybertypes: Race, ethnicity, and identity on the internet*. New York: Routledge.

———. 2007. *Digitizing race: Visual cultures of the internet*. Minneapolis: University of Minnesota Press.

Navarro, V. 2012. 'Nonfictional performance from portrait films to the internet'. *Cinema Journal*, vol. 51, no. 3: 136–41.

Nayak, A. 2017. 'Purging the nation: Race, conviviality and embodied encounters in the lives of British Bangladeshi Muslim young women'. *Transactions*, vol. 42: 289–302. doi: 10.1111/tran.12168.

New Life, New Country. 2007. Digital story, F. Coskun, in association with Australian Centre for the Moving Image. Retrieved 29 December 2012. http://www.cv.vic.gov.au/stories/immigrants-and-emigrants/60s-70s-waves/new-life-new-country/.

Ngo, H. 2019. '"Get over it?" Racialised temporalities and bodily orientations in time'. *Journal of Intercultural Studies*, vol. 40, no. 2: 239–53. doi: 10.1080/07256868.2019.1577231.

Nhdlovu, F. 2014. 'A decolonial critique of diaspora identity theories and the notion of superdiversity'. *Diaspora Studies*, vol. 9, no. 1: 28–40.

Nichols, B. 2008. 'Documentary reenactment and the fantasmatic subject'. *Critical Inquiry*, vol. 35, no. 1: 72–89. doi: 10.1086/595629.

Nicolacopoulos, T., and G. Vassilacopoulos. 2010. 'Racism, foreigner communities and the onto-pathology of white Australian subjectivity'. In *Whitening race: Essays in social and cultural criticism*, edited by A. Moreton-Robinson, 32–47. Canberra: Aboriginal Studies Press.

———. 2011. 'Australian multiculturalism: Beyond management models'. In *Managing ethnic diversity: Meanings and practices from an international perspective*, edited by R. Hasmath, 141–62. Surrey, UK: Ashgate.

Nilsson, M. 2010. 'Developing voice in digital storytelling through creativity, narrative and multimodality'. *Seminar.Net: Media, Technology and Life-Long Learning*, no. 6: 148–60.

Noble, G. 2005. 'The discomfort of strangers: Racism, incivility and ontological security in a relaxed and comfortable nation'. *Journal of Intercultural Studies*, vol. 26, no. 1–2: 107–20. doi: 10.1080/07256860500074128.

———. 2009. 'Everyday cosmopolitanism and the labour of intercultural community'. In *Everyday multiculturalism*, edited by A. Wise and S. Velayutham, 46–65. Hampshire: Palgrave Macmillan.

———. 2011. '"Bumping into alterity": Transacting cultural complexities'. *Continuum: Journal of Media and Cultural Studies*, vol. 25, no. 6: 827–40.

Noble, G., and S. Poynting. 2010. 'White lines: The intercultural politics of everyday movement in social spaces'. *Journal of Intercultural Studies*, vol. 31, no. 5: 489–505.

Nudelman, A. 2012. Interview with Daniella Trimboli, Melbourne, 25 July.

O'Connor, P. 2010. 'Accepting prejudice and valuing freedom: Young Muslims and everyday multiculturalism in Hong Kong'. *Journal of Intercultural Studies*, vol. 31, no. 5: 525–39.

OJ on Broadway. 2010. Short film, M. Blijabu and C. Taylor, in association with Curious Works. Retrieved 9 March 2014. https://www.youtube.com/watch?v=F67OgCJVCXc.

Olson, J. 2004. *The abolition of white democracy*. Minneapolis: University of Minnesota Press.

Papacharissi, Z. A. 2010. *A private sphere: Democracy in a digital age*. Cambridge, UK: Polity.

Papastergiadis, N. 1995. 'Restless hybrids'. *Third Text*, vol. 9, no. 32: 9–18. doi: 10.1080/09528829508576560.

———. 1997. 'Tracing hybridity in theory'. In *Debating cultural hybridity: Multi-cultural identities and the politics of anti-racism*, edited by P. Werbner and T. Modood, 257–79. London: Zed Books.

———. 1999. 'Turbulence'. *Meanjin*, vol. 58, no. 3: 96–105.

———. 2000. *The turbulence of migration: Globalization, deterritorialization and hybridity*. Cambridge, UK: Polity.

————. 2005. 'Hybridity and ambivalence: Places and flows in contemporary art and culture'. *Theory, Culture and Society*, vol. 22, no. 4: 39–64. doi: 10.1177/0263276405054990.

————. 2006. *Spatial aesthetics: Art, place and the everyday*. London: Rivers Oram.

————. 2012a. *Cosmopolitanism and culture*. Cambridge, UK: Polity.

————. 2012b. 'MoNow forum: What is the role of art in the 21st century?', Panel speech, National Gallery of Victoria Studio, Melbourne, 19 April.

Papastergidais, N., and D. Trimboli . 2019. 'From global turbulences to spaces of conviviality: The potentialities of art in mobile worlds'. In *Handbook of art and global migration: Theories, practices, and challenges*, edited by B. Dogramaci and B. Mersmann, 38–53. Berlin: De Gruyter.

Papastergiadis, N., A. Yue, R. Khan and D. Wyatt. 2015. 'Multiculturalism and governance: Evaluating arts policies and engaging cultural citizenship: 4 year project report'. Australian Research Council, University of Melbourne, Melbourne.

Pardy, M. 2011. 'Hate and otherness – exploring emotion through a race riot'. *Emotion, Space and Society*, vol. 4, no. 1: 51–60. doi: http://dx.doi.org/10.1016/j.emospa.2010.12.001.

Pardy, M., and J. C. H. Lee. 2011. 'Using buzzwords of belonging: Everyday multiculturalism and social capital in Australia'. *Journal of Australian Studies*, vol. 35, no. 3: 297–316. doi: 10.1080/14443058.2011.591412.

Phillips, S. K., ed. 2001. *Everyday diversity: Australian multiculturalism and reconciliation in practice*. Altona, Victoria: Common Ground.

Podkalicka, A., and C. Campbell. 2010. 'Understanding digital storytelling: Individual "voice" and community-building in youth media programs'. *Seminar.Net: Media, Technology and Life-Long Learning*, vol. 6, no. 2: 208–18.

Poletti, A. 2011. 'Coaxing an intimate public: Life narrative in digital storytelling'. *Continuum: Journal of Media and Cultural Studies*, vol. 25, no. 1: 73–83.

Povinelli, E. 1998. 'The State of shame: Australian multiculturalism and the crisis of Indigenous citizenship'. *Critical Inquiry*, vol. 24, no. 2, Intimacy (Winter): 575–610. doi: http://www.jstor.org/stable/1344180.

————. 2002. *The cunning of recognition: Indigenous alterities and the making of Australian multiculturalism*. Durham, NC: Duke University Press.

Poynting, S., G. Noble, P. Tabar and J. Collins. 2004. *Bin Laden in the suburbs: Criminalising the Arab Other*. Sydney: Sydney Institute of Criminology.

Pratsinakis, M., P. Hatziprokopiou, L. Labrianidis and N. Vogiatzis. 2017. 'Living together in multi-ethnic cities: People of migrant background, their interethnic friendships and the neighbourhood'. *Urban Studies*, vol. 54, no. 1: 102–18. doi: 10.1177/0042098015615756.

Price, C. A. 1974. *The great white walls are built: Restrictive immigration to North America and Australasia 1836–1888*. Australian Institute of International Affairs in association with Australian National University Press, Canberra.

Probyn, E. 2005. *Blush: Faces of shame*. Minneapolis: University of Minnesota Press.

————. 2010. 'Writing shame'. In *The affect theory reader*, edited by M. Gregg and G. J. Seigworth, 71–90. Durham, NC: Duke University Press.

Quijada, A., and J. Collins. 2009. 'Traditional and youth media education: Collaborating and capitalizing on digital storytelling'. *Youth Media Reporter*, no. 3: 165–67.

Radford, D. 2016. 'Everyday otherness – intercultural refugee encounters and everyday multiculturalism in a South Australian rural town'. *Journal of Ethnic and Migration Studies*, vol. 42, no. 13: 2128–45. http://dx.doi.org/10.1080/1369183X.2016.1179107.

Raimist, R., C. Doerr-Stevens and W. Jacobs. 2010. 'The pedagogy of digital storytelling in the college classroom'. *Seminar.Net: Media, Technology and Life-Long Learning*, no. 6: 280–85.

Ram, K. 2005. 'Phantom limbs: South Indian dance and immigrant reifications of the female body'. *Journal of Intercultural Studies*, vol. 26, no. 1–2: 121–37. doi: 10.1080/07256860500074342.

Rankin, S. 2007. Interview on *Big hART: Junk Theory*, film, Big hART Productions, Sydney.

Rankin, S., and J. Bakes. 1996. *Big hART: A big idea: Book 1*. Commonwealth Department of Employment, Education, Training and Youth Affairs (Youth Bureau), Canberra. Retrieved 29 May 2014. http://bighart.glarus.streetlinemedia.com/wp-content/uploads/2014/07/Book-1-A-BIG-Idea-1.pdf.

Rathzel, N. 2010. 'The injuries of the margins and the restorative power of the political: How young people with migrant backgrounds create their capacity to act'. *Journal of Intercultural Studies*, vol. 31, no. 5: 541–55.

Reclaim Australia. 2015. 'Reclaim Australia: Australia Wide: Will you be a part of history?' Retrieved 10 April 2015. http://www.reclaim-australia.com/.

Reed, A., and A. Hill. 2010. ' "Don't keep it to yourself!": Digital storytelling with South African youth'. *Seminar.Net: Media, Technology and Life-Long Learning*, vol. 6, no. 2: 268–79.

Robin, B. 2006. 'The educational uses of digital storytelling'. *Technology and Teacher Education Annual*, no. 1: 709.

Robinson, A. M. 2011. 'More than a marketing strategy: Multiculturalism and meaningful life'. In *Managing ethnic diversity: Meanings and practices from an international perspective*, edited by R. Hasmath, 29–46. Surrey, UK: Ashgate.

Rodríguez, K. 2010. 'Digital storytelling in study abroad: Toward a counter-catalogic experience'. *Seminar.Net: Media, Technology and Life-Long Learning*, no. 6: 219–33.

Rolón-Dow, R. 2011. 'Race(ing) stories: Digital storytelling as a tool for critical race scholarship'. *Race, Ethnicity and Education*, vol. 14, no. 2: 159–73.

Said, E. (1978) 1992. 'Orientalism'. In *A critical and cultural reader*, edited by A. Easthope and K. McGowan, 59–65. Sydney: Allen and Unwin.

Sartre, J.-P. 1948. *Anti-Semite and the Jew*. Translated by G. Becker. New York: Schocken Books.

Scott Nixon, A. 2009. 'Mediating social thought through digital storytelling'. *Pedagogies*, vol. 4, no. 1: 63–76.

Second Life. 2007. Digital story, X. Silberman. Retrieved 11 July 2013. http://www.cv.vic.gov.au/stories/immigrants-and-emigrants/digital-stories-of-immigration/second-life/.

Seeto, A. 2011. 'Transcultural radical'. *Artlink: Contemporary art of Australia and the Asia-Pacific*, vol. 31, no. 1: 28–31.

Seigworth, G. J., and M. Gregg. 2010. 'An inventory of shimmers'. In *Affect theory reader*, edited by G. J. Seigworth and M. Gregg, 1–25. Durham, NC: Duke University Press.

Semi, G., E. Colombo, I. Camozzi and A. Frisina. 2009. 'Practices of difference: Analysing multiculturalism in everyday life'. In *Everyday multiculturalism*, edited by A. Wise and S. Velayutham, 66–84. Hampshire: Palgrave Macmillan.

Shan, H., and P. Walter. 2015. 'Growing everyday multiculturalism: Practice-based learning of Chinese immigrants through community gardens in Canada'. *Adult Education Quarterly*, vol. 65, no. 1: 19–34. doi: 10.1177/0741713614549231.

Sherman, D., and I. Rogoff, eds. 1994. *Museum culture: Histories, discourses, spectacle*. Minneapolis: University of Minnesota Press.

The Shoemaker. 2007. Digital story, A. Nudelman, in association with Australian Centre for the Moving Image. Retrieved 19 July 2012. http://www.cv.vic.gov.au/stories/immigrants-and-emigrants/second-generation/the-shoemaker/.

Simondson, H. 2012a. Interview with Daniella Trimboli via Skype, 16 November.

———. 2012b. Interview, *About digital storytelling*, online. Retrieved 11 November. http://www.acmi.net.au/dst_about.htm.

Sivanathan, S. 2014a. Panel interview with Marnie Bardham, *Spectres of Evaluation: Rethinking: Art/Community/Value Conference 6–7 Feb*, Footscray, Victoria, 7 February.

———. 2014b. Film screening Q and A, *Spectres of Evaluation: Rethinking: Art/Community/Value Conference 6–7 Feb*, Footscray, Victoria, 6 February.

Skouge, J. R., and R. Rao. 2009. 'Digital storytelling in teacher education: Creating transformations through narrative', *Educational Perspectives*, vol. 42, no. 1–2: 54–60.

Smaill, B. 2010. *The documentary: Politics, emotion, culture.* Hampshire: Palgrave Macmillan.

The Spaces In Between. 2007. Digital story, C. Pascoe, in association with Australian Centre for the Moving Image. Retrieved 11 July 2013. http://www.cv.vic.gov.au/stories/immigrants-and-emigrants/second-generation/the-spaces-in-between/.

Spinks, T. 2001. Cited in Thrift, N. 2004. 'Intensities of feeling: Towards a spatial politics of affect'. *Geografisika Annaler*, vol. 86B, no. 1: 64.

Spivak, G. 2012. *An aesthetic education in the era of globalization.* Cambridge, MA: Harvard University Press.

The Stories Project. 2010–12. Digital story project, Curious Works. Retrieved 9 March 2014. http://thestoriesproject.com.au/.

Stratton, J. 1998. *Race daze: Australia in identity crisis.* Sydney: Pluto.

———. 1999. 'Multiculturalism and the whitening machine, or how Australians become white'. In *The future of Australian multiculturalism: Reflections on the twentieth anniversary of Jean Martin's 'The Migrant Presence'*, edited by G. Hage and R. Couch. Sydney: University of Sydney.

———. 2009. 'Preserving white hegemony: Skilled migration, "Asians" and middle-class assimilation'. *borderlands e-journal*, vol. 8, no. 3: 1–28.

———. 2011. 'Non-citizens in the exclusionary state: Citizenship, mitigated exclusion, and the Cronulla riots'. *Continuum: Journal of Media and Cultural Studies*, vol. 25, no. 3 (June): 299–316.

Stratton, J., and I. Ang. 1994. 'Multicultural imagined communities: Cultural difference and national identity in Australia and the USA'. *Continuum: Journal of Media and Cultural Studies*, vol. 8, no. 2: 124–58. doi: 10.1080/10304319409365672.

Tabar, P., G. Noble and S. Poynting. 2010. *On being Lebanese in Australia: Identity, racism and the ethnic field.* Beirut: Lebanese American University Press.

Taylor, A. 2006. 'Australian bodies, Australian sands'. In *Lines in the sand: The Cronulla riots, multiculturalism and national belonging*, edited by G. Noble, 111–26. Sydney: Institute of Criminology Press.

Taylor, C. 1994. 'The politics of recognition'. In *Multiculturalism: Examining the politics of recognition*, edited by A. Gutmann, 25–73. Princeton: Princeton University Press.

Thrift, N. 2004. 'Intensities of feeling: Towards a spatial politics of affect'. *Geografisika Annaler*, vol. 86B, no. 1: 57–78.

Tolia-Kelly, D. 2006. 'Affect – an ethnographic encounter? Exploring the "universality" imperative of emotional/affectual geographics'. *Area*, no. 38: 213–17.

Tomkins, S. 1995. 'Modifications in the theory – 1978'. In *Exploring affect: The selected writings of Silvan S. Tomkins*, edited E. Virginia Demos. Cambridge: Cambridge University Press.

Trimboli, D. 2019. 'Rereading diaspora: Reverberating voices and diasporic listening in Italo-Australian digital storytelling'. *Journal of Citizenship and Globalisation Studies*, vol. 2, no.1: 49–62. doi: https://doi.org/10.2478/jcgs-2018-0006.

Turner, G. 2008. 'The cosmopolitan city and its Other: The ethnicizing of the Australian suburb'. *Inter-Asia Cultural Studies*, vol. 9, no. 4: 568–82. doi: 10.1080/14649370802386487.

Urry, J. 2005. *Global complexity.* Cambridge, UK: Polity.

Vertovec, S. 1996. 'Multiculturalism, culturalism, and public incorporation'. *Ethnic and Racial Studies*, vol. 19, no. 1: 49–69.

Vertovec, S., and S. Wessendorf. 2010. 'Assessing the backlash against multiculturalism in Europe'. In *The multiculturalism backlash: European discourses, politics and practices*, edited by S. Vertovec and S. Wessendorf, 1–31. Routledge, ProQuest Central ebook.

Villawood Mums. 2010. Digital story, G. Gonzalez and S. Jari, in association with Curious Works. Retrieved 9 March 2014. http://thestoriesproject.com.au/archives/villawood-mums/.

Vivienne, S. 2011. 'Trans digital storytelling: Everyday activism, mutable identity and the problem of visibility'. *Gay and Lesbian Issues and Psychology Review*, vol. 7, no. 1: 43–54.

Vivienne, S., and J. Burgess. 2013. 'The remediation of the personal photograph and the politics of self-representation in digital storytelling'. *Journal of Material Culture*, vol. 18, no. 3: 279–98.

Warren, J. T. 2003. *Performing purity: Whiteness, pedagogy, and the reconstitution of power.* New York: Peter Lang.

Watkins, J., and A. Russo. 2009. 'Beyond individual expression: Working with cultural institutions'. In *Story circle: Digital storytelling around the world*, edited by J. Hartley and K. McWilliam, 269–78. Oxford: Wiley-Blackwell.

Wexlar Love, E., D. Flanders Cushing, M. Sullivan and J. Brexa. 2011. 'Digital storytelling within a service-learning partnership: Technology as product and process for university students and culturally and linguistically diverse high school youth'. In *Higher education, emerging technologies, and community partnerships: Concepts, models, and practices*, edited by M. A. Bowden and R. G. Carpenter, 88–105. Hershey, PA: Information Science Reference.

What Is Meaningful Life? 2013. Digital story, Theresa, in association with PEI Association for Newcomers to Canada as part of the Canadian Museum of Immigration at Pier 21's Digital Storytelling program. Retrieved 21 January 2019. https://pier21.ca/digital-storytelling/charlottetown-theresa.

Where Are You From? 2012–13. Digital story, Berjoska, in association with Canadian Museum of Immigration at Pier 21's digital storytelling project. Retrieved 21 January 2019. https://pier21.ca/digital-storytelling/halifax-berjoska.

Where Do I Belong? 2007. Digital story, R. el-Khoury, in association with Australian Centre for the Moving Image. Retrieved 11 July 2013. http://www.cv.vic.gov.au/stories/immigrants-and-emigrants/second-generation/where-do-i-belong/.

White, S. K. 1999. 'As the world turns: Ontology and politics in Judith Butler'. *Polity*, vol. 32, no. 2: 155–77.

Wise, A. 2009. 'Everyday multiculturalism: Transversal crossings and working class cosmopolitans'. In *Everyday multiculturalism*, edited by A. Wise and S. Velayutham, 21–45. Hampshire: Palgrave Macmillan.

———. 2016. 'Convivial labour and the "joking relationship": Humour and everyday multi-culturalism at work'. *Journal of Intercultural Studies*, vol. 37, no. 5: 481–500. doi: 10.1080/07256868.2016.1211628.

Wise, A., and S. Velayutham. 2009a. 'Introduction: Multiculturalism and everyday life'. In *Everyday multiculturalism*, edited by A. Wise and S. Velayutham, 1–17. Hampshire: Palgrave Macmillan.

———, eds. 2009b. *Everyday multiculturalism*. Hampshire: Palgrave Macmillan.

———. 2019. 'Humour at work: Conviviality through language play in Singapore's multicultural workplaces'. *Ethnic and Racial Studies*. doi: 10.1080/01419870.2019.1588341.

Wong, G. 2016. 'Coping through leisure, leisure through coping: A critical ethnography of Filipino foreign domestic workers' day-off leisure experiences in Gulong Gulong, Singapore'. Thesis, School of Humanities and Social Sciences, Nanyang Technological University, Singapore. Retrieved 10 October 2019. https://repository.ntu.edu.sg/handle/10356/69247.

Yeni Hayat = New Life. 2007. Digital story, K. Besiroglu, in association with Australian Centre for Moving Image. Retrieved 17 July 2013. http://www.cv.vic.gov.au/stories/digital-stories-of-immigration/4960/yeni-hayat-=-new-life/.

Yue, A., and D. Wyatt. 2014. 'New communities, new racisms: A critical introduction'. *Journal of Intercultural Studies*, vol. 35, no. 3: 223–31. doi: 10.1080/07256868.2014.899947.

Zoettl, P. A. 2013. 'Images of culture: Participatory video, identity and empowerment'. *International Journal of Cultural Studies*, vol. 16, no. 2: 209–24.

INDEX

www.ingramcontent.com/pod-product-compliance
Lightning Source LLC
Chambersburg PA
CBHW022355280326
41935CB00007B/191